"Keeping children always confined to houses, buildings, cars, and heavy clothing will eventually cut them off from what life is all about. You take away all possibility for them to really feel the intensity of life . . . By encapsulating our children, we cut them off from feeling anything real, and we teach them to resist the forces of nature . . . If you are going to the beach, the woods, the swamps, or the wilderness, really get into it, roll in it, and get rid of all protection that will separate you from fully appreciating where you are. Become alive, not removed and insulated, and teach your children to do the same."

—Tom Brown, Jr.

*Berkley Books by Tom Brown, Jr.*

THE TRACKER
(as told to William Jon Watkins)

THE SEARCH
(with William Owen)

TOM BROWN'S FIELD GUIDE TO WILDERNESS SURVIVAL
(with Brandt Morgan)

TOM BROWN'S FIELD GUIDE TO NATURE
OBSERVATION AND TRACKING
(with Brandt Morgan)

TOM BROWN'S FIELD GUIDE TO CITY
AND SUBURBAN SURVIVAL
(with Brandt Morgan)

TOM BROWN'S GUIDE TO LIVING WITH THE EARTH
(with Brandt Morgan)

TOM BROWN'S GUIDE TO WILD EDIBLE
AND MEDICINAL PLANTS

TOM BROWN'S GUIDE TO THE FORGOTTEN WILDERNESS

TOM BROWN'S GUIDE TO NATURE
AND SURVIVAL FOR CHILDREN
(with Judy Brown)

THE VISION

THE QUEST

THE JOURNEY

GRANDFATHER

AWAKENING SPIRITS

THE WAY OF THE SCOUT

THE SCIENCE AND ART OF TRACKING

CASE FILES OF THE TRACKER

## ABOUT THE AUTHOR

At the age of eight, Tom Brown, Jr., began to learn tracking and hunting from Stalking Wolf, a displaced Apache Indian. Today Brown is an experienced woodsman whose extraordinary skill has saved many lives, including his own. He manages and teaches one of the largest wilderness and survival schools in the U.S. and has instructed many law enforcement agencies and rescue teams.

# TOM BROWN'S FIELD GUIDE TO NATURE AND SURVIVAL FOR CHILDREN

Tom Brown, Jr., with Judy Brown

Illustrated by Heather Bolyn
and Trip Becker

**B**

BERKLEY BOOKS, NEW YORK

**THE BERKLEY PUBLISHING GROUP**
**Published by the Penguin Group**
**Penguin Group (USA) Inc.**
**375 Hudson Street, New York, New York 10014, USA**
Penguin Group (Canada), 90 Eglinton Avenue East, Suite 700, Toronto, Ontario M4P 2Y3, Canada
(a division of Pearson Penguin Canada Inc.)
Penguin Books Ltd., 80 Strand, London WC2R 0RL, England
Penguin Group Ireland, 25 St. Stephen's Green, Dublin 2, Ireland (a division of Penguin Books Ltd.)
Penguin Group (Australia), 250 Camberwell Road, Camberwell, Victoria 3124, Australia
(a division of Pearson Australia Group Pty. Ltd.)
Penguin Books India Pvt. Ltd., 11 Community Centre, Panchsheel Park, New Delhi—110 017, India
Penguin Group (NZ), 67 Apollo Drive, Rosedale, North Shore 0632, New Zealand
(a division of Pearson New Zealand Ltd.)
Penguin Books (South Africa) (Pty.) Ltd., 24 Sturdee Avenue, Rosebank, Johannesburg 2196,
South Africa

Penguin Books Ltd., Registered Offices: 80 Strand, London WC2R 0RL, England

This Field Guide is intended to introduce children, under appropriate adult supervision, to an understanding of nature and to basic survival skills. Children should not be left unsupervised in wilderness situations.

The Publisher and Author disclaim any liability for injury that may result from following the techniques and instructions described in the Field Guide, which could be dangerous in certain situations. In addition, some of the techniques and instructions may be inappropriate for adults and children suffering from certain physical conditions or handicaps.

The publisher does not have any control over and does not assume any responsibility for author or third-party websites or their content.

TOM BROWN'S FIELD GUIDE TO NATURE AND SURVIVAL FOR CHILDREN

A Berkley Book / published by arrangement with the author

PRINTING HISTORY
Berkley trade paperback edition / March 1989

ISBN: 978-0-425-11106-2

PRINTED IN THE UNITED STATES OF AMERICA

Dedicated to my sons, Paul and Tommy; and my daughter, Kelly, who first taught me how to teach children . . .

and special thanks to my son Tommy, the resident critic and technical adviser of this book; Lisa Rochelle, for her tireless work in editing and her love; Wanda Terhaar, for her technical advice and her love of working with the children of the Tracker Children's Classes; to Frank Rochelle, for doing much of the legwork; to Frank and Karen Sherwood, and Karl (Bear) Povisils, for their constant support. Most of all, thanks to my wife, Judy, for writing this book with me.

# CONTENTS

# INTRODUCTION

As I look at society, schools, and the children of today, I see an extreme need. Most of what is taught to our children is lopsided, feeding only the logical mind, while doing nothing for children's awareness, creativity, relationship to nature and life, or for cultivating spiritual needs. Most children lose their identities through the school years and become, over time, enslaved to outside "shoulds" and social goals. They seem to lose the yearnings of their hearts and are stripped of true awareness, adventure, excitement, and the rapture of living fully. Children also lose their connection to the earth and creation as their feet are removed from the soil and transplanted into a world of electronics, concrete, and plastic.

Our children are bombarded with computers, magazines, electronic games, and television. In some cases TV has replaced true experience to such an extent that children sometimes don't know if they really even lived an event, or saw it on TV. Many children would rather *watch* a nature film than go out into the wilderness. Experience today is limited to a civilized and structured life-style, wilderness carved into a series of safe trails and areas, so that children walk through nature rather than in it.

I feel that we can no longer rely on our schools or society to teach our children the most important things in life. School is oriented toward success in society, providing children the skills they will need to get through practical life. But as parents, we must teach our children the deeper things in life: how to find peace, love, joy, and purpose within themselves. We must lead them back to the earth, back to pure awareness, to adventure, and to the awesome rapture of living. We must cultivate their sense of oneness with creation, an experience of themselves as not separate from nature and the cosmos, but an integral part of the whole. And we must inspire our children to think and live through their hearts, to be guided by the deeper yearnings of life.

This book does not instruct about all these areas—only the closeness to and oneness with the earth. But through this book children—and parents—can find the pathway to everything else, all aspects of life. This book is not the only place one might begin—many fine books have been written on this same subject—nor is it an end, but you, as parents, while you and your children learn, love, and grow together, will reach realms beyond this book. I sincerely hope that through this book, you can save the inner life of your children, and thus, in turn, save what is left of the earth. Children are the future, and without children rooted to the earth, there can be no future.

## HOW TO USE THIS BOOK

I suggest that parents and teachers read this book first and become proficient in the skills mentioned. Then the book can be used as a field guide. Some of the techniques and skills are best learned together; others are best mastered by adults first, so that parents or teachers can answer questions from their own experiences. Children learn best by example.

The book is divided into two parts. The first part offers and illustrates techniques for building children's awareness. It is not a nature guide, but more a guide to the senses. I suggest that you also acquire a good nature identification guide for the field. This book's second part deals with survival, and survival skills are here broken down in order of descending importance. Most of the skills are easily learned, even by younger children. Also included are a number of games and experiences to illustrate each skill.

**Note:** We suggest that parents and teachers might want to use *Tom Brown's Field Guide to Wilderness Survival* as a backup reference. This book, however, has been written to stand alone, and does not depend on any other backup guides.

This book has been one of my most difficult to write. Each child is different, and each child's affinity with nature is different; thus it is difficult to generalize. Typically older children, those longer and more firmly entrenched in the system, are harder to teach, but with patience, rapid success can still be achieved. Most of my experience comes from raising my own children and running several children's classes. Much comes from parents who have come through my schools, many of them concerned about their children's complacency about the earth and life.

However, the greatest input has come from my wife, Judy, who has coauthored this book.

Now, I do not hold a Ph.D. in Education, nor am I a child psychologist. What I am is both a careful observer, and an observer with a vision. I believe that our children are not receiving a total education and that without such, a child can only become half a person. It is my ambition, my vision, to get children back in touch with themselves, with creation and with life, in a real and viable way. What is needed is a well-rounded education, producing complete children, and that is the responsibility of the parents.

## COYOTE TEACHING

Grandfather never answered any of our questions the way most people would answer a question. He would either point us in the direction of the answer, or ask us a series of questions, all designed to make us think. A "coyote teacher" makes every learning experience exciting, something we desperately want to know. He planned each lesson like a chess game or jigsaw puzzle, where one teaching led to another. But he never forced any teaching on us; instead, he maneuvered the situation so we had to know, had to go on. I firmly believe that if our schools approached education in this way, we would have fewer dropouts, and children would reach higher academic levels. I believe that even the driest subjects can be made exciting, but it all depends on the vision of the teacher, and subsequently, the system.

A good example of Grandfather's "coyote teaching" was when we were following him back to camp one afternoon. We had only known Grandfather for a short time, but we deeply admired his skills, and especially his awareness. He seemed to sense things beyond the physical capabilities of the senses, knowing things that were happening all around, and at long distances. We never walked alongside him, but far behind, not only out of respect, but because from that distance we could carefully watch his actions as he traveled through the wilderness. We in turn could duplicate his actions and thus see things that we would have normally overlooked.

As we followed him that day, we noticed that he walked slowly, watching the ground carefully. We did the same, taking turns watching him and watching the ground, wondering what he saw, written, almost invisibly, on the dusty surface. Suddenly he turned around and said to us, "Don't disturb him." We had no idea what he was talking about, but we were sure we had missed something. In desperation we scanned the ground but could find nothing out of the ordinary. We searched the immediate landscape, finding nothing but the scurry of a few mice. The harder we looked, the more frustrated we got, and the less we saw. It was then Rick looked up into the tree above us and saw, just a few feet from our heads, a great horned owl.

Certainly we were amazed to see such a beautiful and elusive bird so close, but even more startling was how Grandfather had known the owl was in the tree without looking up. We ran to him and, in utter amazement, asked, "How did you know the owl was in the tree? You never looked up!" He smiled and replied, "Go ask the mice." We expected just that sort of answer, but it was the same with everything. "How do we build a shelter?" we would ask. He would answer "Ask the squirrels." We would ask "How does a bow-drill fire work?" and he would answer "Rub your hands together." Or we would ask "How can we track foxes better?" and he would reply "Track mice." He made each teaching special, exciting, and something we desperately needed to know. And as always, the lessons would go far deeper than just the superficial, reaching to all realms of our lives.

When Grandfather said "Go ask the mice," we lay on our bellies for months, watching mice, in all sorts of weather. Not only did we learn what mice did when owls were around, but we also learned what mice did when everything else was around. Yet the teachings went far deeper. We learned that nothing could move in nature without affecting everything else. When an animal moved, he or she sent out concentric rings that touched other animals. Thus we learned to read these rings, and through them, tell of the far-off movements of other animals. We learned that everything is interconnected and part of the whole. Through the mice, we learned that there is no separation of the self, no inner or outer dimension. Our tracks move within the realm of creation, and creation moves within our tracks. We finally understood what Grandfather meant by "oneness with all things."

All parents would do well to develop a sense of teaching in this way—instead of spoon-feeding answers to children, having them answer their own questions by thinking through patterns of the whole in nature. Each teaching can be made in this way exciting and enjoyable like a mystery just aching to be solved.

# PART ONE

# AWARENESS

# INTRODUCTION

When I first laid out the class description for my school, I set forth all I wanted to teach people, all the skills and techniques necessary to round people out and teach them to live as one with the Earth. At the top of the list was "awareness," and I had stated in the school brochure that I "consider it the most important skill." At the time, I gave no thought about how to teach that skill, what techniques to use, or how to convey years of Grandfather's teachings through any type of lesson.

Awareness was very important to Grandfather, and something he taught us every day. In fact, it was the essence of most of what he taught about earth skills and living in nature. To him, awareness was the key to good tracking, good survival, and the doorway to the realms of the spirit. His teachings in awareness were more like experiments than simple sets of defined skills and techniques. Most awareness and observation lessons were taught by example, the lessons spanning a little more than ten years. Awareness became my most important physical skill and each and every day over the years I would work on becoming more aware, more attuned to creation.

Facing my first standard class, I had no idea how I could successfully instill awareness in students with whom I would spend only one week, yet I knew it had to be taught. My inability to teach awareness only became apparent, suddenly, as I faced the last few days with the class. The students and I had covered tracking, stalking, fox walking, survival skills, and one day they asked when I was going to teach them awareness. I was shocked when I realized that I had no idea where to start, not to mention how to teach awareness; there seemed to be no real concrete skills or techniques. I subsequently put them off and went on to other topics; however, I struggled that whole night to work out some sort of plan, some kind of technique to share with the class. I continued to avoid the issue day after day, until finally the last day of class approached, with me no closer to answers for my questions. In desperation, I dragged the class into the woods and pointed out everything I saw or heard, overwhelming them with what they had not seen all week. They went away happy, not realizing they had learned nothing. All they had learned was what they hadn't seen, and I had made a circus out of myself.

For the next two weeks I thought long and hard about what to teach the upcoming class, my second standard session. By the time that the class had begun, I had no more of an answer to my predicament than I had had for the last class. By mid-week, I was thoroughly upset, realizing I could not teach awareness, fearing my students would go home with only memories of what *I* saw, rather than any real awareness skills. On the second to the last day of that class, on the way up to the barn, the answers finally hit me, and hit me hard. They had actually been there all the time, but I had been too close to see them.

On my way to the barn, I passed Judy and little Tom, sitting by the pond. Little Tom was still quite young, not yet eight months old, but what he taught me that day I will never forget. He was lying next to the pond, petting the water, his hand stroking the surface as if it were a living animal, and the water seemed to respond. He let out squeals of utter delight and on his face, I saw such fascination. It was then I flashed back to watching Grandfather doing the same thing in the same way. I realized then and there that I could never *teach* people awareness, because people are among the most aware animals on earth naturally. Awareness is a gift from the creator, an inborn instinct, and our birthright.

I can't teach people to be aware, but I can teach them to spot the walls, the obstacles to their awareness. I can teach them what society and school do to rob them of their birthright, and why the senses become dulled, then finally atrophy. When I went back to the barn, I finally taught awareness. I didn't present it as a skill, but rather sought to convey techniques that would revitalize the students' natural awareness. When the class ended, I was sure in my heart that people had learned. They had learned what not to do, not what to do. They were well on their way to regaining the gifts stolen from them by society and modern life.

Part One of this book deals with awareness in the same manner. It draws attention to the barriers to awareness and teaches us how to guide our children through them. It identifies the reasons children's senses become dull and eventually deteriorate and shows how to restore children's appreciation of the grander things in life. Young children are naturally aware but soon lose their awareness through entrenchment in society and modern life. Show children the pitfalls and you give them the gift of life.

# 1

# SOCIETY
# OF ROBOTS

Awareness is not learned; it is a gift from the creator. Children are among the most aware creatures on earth, but soon, because of the modern rush of society and our education system, this inborn awareness becomes dulled and soon begins to atrophy. After just a few years of formal education, most of children's natural awareness has already taken a backseat, and they begin to live like robots, devoid of real awareness. Concentrating on TV, magazines, and flashy forms of entertainment, and even books, does little, if anything, to build upon children's natural gift of awareness, but can instead retard growth.

We, as parents and teachers, can realize the flaws of modern living, and begin to teach children how to augment their natural awareness. Modern society and education are skewed toward the logical, rational mind, but do little to acknowledge or encourage artistic ability, creativity, awareness, or sensitivity to the spiritual side of life. If we become aware of how this attitude can affect our children, and the ramifications of this potential loss of their acute awareness, then we can take steps to foster what society does not nurture. We have an obligation to balance out the lacks in children's education and to teach what society or school doesn't. As I learned with my students, and from my son, I cannot teach you how to *teach* your children to be aware; your children are naturally very aware. Instead, what I can do is teach you what society, sometimes in a very subtle way, does to your children to remove their innate awareness. If I can draw your attention to what dulls or obliterates awareness, then you can take the steps to make sure your children do not fall prey to those negative influences. It is then up to you, as parents or teachers, to augment your children's education and to prevent them from falling into the unconsciousness of modern living.

# WHAT HAPPENS TO OUR CHILDREN

## Society of Robots

One of the first lessons that society and school teach our children is routine. Even before some children enter school, they are already established in some sort of routine. As children enter school, their lives become linked to a clock. Everything becomes regimented: a time to work, a time to eat, and a time to play, whether the children feel like it or not. There is little real time for children to be uninhibited and free. The clock, the regimen, and the endless routine preclude any spontaneity. Unfortunately, with the way society and most schools are now set up, there is no alternative to this routine. Society seems to think that children are better controlled if they are treated like cattle.

This routine is further intensified as we force children to adhere to the beaten path. Pressures of society, school, and parents, force children to live and work for the future. The spontaneity of living fully in the moment is taken away and the children must concern themselves with doing well in school, finishing high school, going on to college, finding an excellent job, getting married, having a family, and working until they die. All efforts seem to focus on this path, and the path gets so worn and so deep, it soon becomes a rut. The ruts are so pervasive and oppressive that the children cannot even see over their sides; there are just goals at the end of a long tunnel, and nothing else.

Excitement, adventure, and children who follow their hearts are rare. All too early in life, children begin to feel what Thoreau called "quiet desperation." They sense there must be more to life, but they do not know how or where to find it, nor can they stray from the ruts of school and society. As children grow older, they not only lose a sense of self, but lose a sense of adventure. Midway through school, many children are lost with no real alternatives in life. To dull the pain or boredom, many seek the oblivion of alcohol, the false escape of drugs, the adventure of vandalism, and sometimes the freedom of suicide.

We as parents and teachers must realize the deadening effects that such routine can have on our children's lives, spirits, and senses. Certainly there is no real alternative now to school or the demands of society, but we can take steps to minimize and override the effects that these ruts have on our children. To free children from the ruts is to preserve their spirit. Teach children to build a passion for living each moment fully, for seeking adventures, and for following their hearts.

Minimize and strip the power away from the ruts of society and school, and once the power is removed, children will flourish.

Parents and teachers should develop within themselves a sense of spontaneity and adventure. Remember that teachings are best given by example. The ruts of modern education and social demands may still be there, but when children are not in school, they do not have to be enslaved to routine. Abandon the clock when school and work end, do things on the spur of the moment, and seek adventure, even in the little things. What should be foremost on parents' minds is living from the heart, not the wallet or the mind. Your example will greatly influence your children. If you are caught in your own rut, then so will your children be, but if you break free, then you give your children freedom.

### Society Removes Awareness

Let us face the fact that children do not need awareness to function in modern society or school. How much awareness—and I'm not talking about simply concentration—does it take to read a book, listen to teachers, watch television, listen to a stereo, or conduct most everyday affairs. In ancient times, when we were a hunter/gatherer society, sensory awareness was important to keep us alive, but in modern society, sensory awareness is hardly necessary. Education and society build children's minds and logic but do nothing for children's senses, or awareness. Existence in this society is in a clustered environment of bold artificial stimuli, where it is no longer necessary to be keenly aware. Thus children's natural awareness is no longer used, and may in turn wither and die.

As children grow older, we begin to see the effects of the dulled senses. They seek wilder forms of entertainment such as amusement parks and wild rides, listen to music at deafening levels, or stare blankly at TV and video games. They no longer hear the whisper of wind in the grasses, the music of insect wings, or the sights, feel, and fragrances of quiet nature. All experience seems to be gleaned not from reality and life, but from a TV set. Deadened sensory awareness is equivalent in effect to exposure to a sensory deprivation tank: behavior becomes bizarre, and for relief, children seek to blast their senses.

As parents, we must realize that society and school do not aim to stimulate children's senses, and we must begin to teach what is not taught. We must take the initiative to enhance children's sensory awareness, building on their natural gifts. Children's environments should be filled with all manner of natural sensory stimuli. As parents and teachers we should seek to develop a form of natural education that would heighten the senses. We should take children into nature frequently so the senses are fed, nurtured, and become keen. We should set an example, by pointing out subtle sounds, sights, smells, tastes, and feelings. Only through our careful attention and nurturing will children ever hope to reach their full sensory potential. Keen sensory awareness is one of the most important skills children can have in life, and it is sensory awareness that makes life full and rich.

### Encapsulation

We also tend to remove our children from the elemental forces of nature and life. We keep our children in controlled environments such as houses and buildings, where temperatures are set at 68°F and the humidity is artificially adjusted. They are cut off from outdoor reality. We take our children *through* the environment in automobiles, which are in themselves contained, controlled environments. We overdress our children in an attempt to fight nature, teach them to wear heavy clothing, heavy shoes, and otherwise try to keep them warm, dry, comfortable and essentially untouched. We tell our children to stay out of the dirt, to stay dry. Thus we remove them from the reality and the intensity of life.

I find these lessons of safety, security, and comfort to be, in their extremes, only euphemisms for death. Keeping children always confined to houses, buildings, cars, and heavy clothing will eventually cut them off from what life is all about. You take away all possibility for them to really feel the intensity of life. Think of all the most vivid memories you have in life, and I'll bet that at those times you were neither safe, secure, nor comfortable. Then, why would you want to cut your children off from those same potential memories by teaching them a lust for deadening comfort? In essence, by encapsulating our children, we cut them off from feeling anything real, and we teach them to resist the forces of nature.

For a prime example of cutting yourself off from the natural forces, watch people at the beach. They first set down a blanket, then prop up an umbrella and possibly a beach chair, then pop on a hat and sunglasses. Further cutting themselves off from the beach, they blast radios, so that all natural sounds are eliminated. They might as well be atop a building in New York City, for all they will experience of the beach surroundings. They are away from the sand, out of the sun, and deafened by the radio. To those people, getting splashed with water or sand has the same effect as if someone had spit on them. In fact, if you as adults, just sat or lay in the sand, you would be considered strange, but do just that, and your children will follow your example. If you are going to the beach, the woods, the swamps, or the wilderness, really get into it, roll in it, and get rid of all protection that will separate you from fully appreciating where you are. Become alive, not removed and insulated, and teach your children to do the same.

Most of all, teach your children not to resist nature or nature's forces. To resist nature is to fight nature, and if we fight nature, we can never win. In my first book, *The Tracker*, in the chapter called "Cold Training," I described what happens when we fight nature. Rick and I were at the Medicine Cabin one night preparing for our walk home through a snowstorm. Just before we left the warmth of the Medicine Cabin, Grandfather asked us to give him our clothes. Without questioning, we stripped to our shorts and gave Grandfather all of our clothing, wondering what he wanted with our clothes. As he turned toward the door to leave, he looked back at us and said "Now go home, and you will never feel the cold again." With that he left, leaving us to our astonishment and fear.

We were in a state of shock, not knowing what we were going to do. In my mind, we would surely freeze to death before we ever reached the halfway point, and the fear kept me huddled close to the fireplace. We postponed leaving until we were almost out of firewood, and then, without a word to each other, we slipped out the door and into the cold night. The winds seemed to bite through our flesh, and the snow stung our skin. We began to run wildly, chased by fear and the cold, biting storm. We ran for miles, the wind tearing at our flesh. Every muscle in my body ached with tightness from fighting the chill. We were so wrapped up in the fear of the cold and resisting it that we were completely unaware that we were sweating profusely from running.

Certainly Grandfather in his wisdom knew the storm would not hurt us. It only seemed cold, for it was well above freezing and he knew we would run all the way home. There was no way two young bucks would freeze to death in that mild storm. But to us the storm was very real, very cold, and very frightening. When we finally saw the lights of Rick's house, however, something miraculous happened—we realized we were no longer cold. We stopped running, now that we were almost to safety, and began to play. The winds felt refreshing and the snows soft. It was not the act of traveling in the cold weather and the building up of endurance that took away the cold. It was simply that we had stopped resisting the environment. When we gave in to the cold, we no longer were cold.

Obviously, if it had been a violent storm, both Rick and I could have died. But facing the cold was not the lesson Grandfather wanted to teach. He wanted us to learn that we should not resist the forces of nature, since to resist is a losing battle. The only way I can explain it is to have you go outside in the rain without a shirt. At first the raindrops will feel like thousands of icy needles piercing the skin, but at the point where you stop resisting, the rain will feel like a refreshing shower. If you go to the ocean and stand firm against the pounding waves, then you will be smashed to shore like a piece of broken driftwood. But if you relax and give in to the force of the waves, you will be washed to shore gently, like the most delicate shell.

So teach your children not to resist the forces of nature, to stop fighting and fearing the elements, but rather to come to enjoy their energy. Certainly that does not mean that you should put your children's lives in danger by subjecting them to the fierce elements without clothing, but do allow them to savor the reality of nature's forces and not to resist them. It is the resistance, and subsequent muscle tension, that tends to make an experience painful. Once children learn to tolerate a little supposed discomfort, they will find the situation not really uncomfortable at all, but rather, invigorating. In this way children can learn to feel the full intensity of living.

### Keep Your Children's Feet on the Earth

One of the greatest hindrances to children's experience of nature is that today our children's feet are removed from the earth, both literally and figuratively. Society in general has lost its connection to the earth, and hence has no conscious sensitivity to its mothering power. Once the connection is lost, people lose respect for the land, the trees, and the animals. That is why we can so easily destroy the land, by dumping our waste, or by randomly and thoughtlessly building against the earth's natural contours. I often wonder how many of our children, when reaching for a loaf of bread see a wheat field, or taking an apple from a shelf, see a tree, or when eating a hamburger, know that an animal had to die to give them its flesh. I wonder how many know that if it weren't for the earth, no life as we know it could exist.

I remember vividly the first time my stepson, Paul, witnessed a steer being slaughtered. I had only known Paul a few months when he accompanied me to the house of a local farmer. I had told Paul that I was going to get a steer hide to make some moccasins for his sister and him. Excited at both the prospect of helping me and getting a present, he decided to go with me. I guess he remembered that the last time I had picked up a hide, he got to play with the animals on the farm. That time, however, the hide was neatly wrapped, ready to be picked up.

We arrived at the farm a little early, and the farmer was running late. As we drove around behind the barn, we were confronted by a gruesome sight. There on a cross beam hung the freshly slaughtered steer, with a streaming gut pile beneath it, and the farmer's hands, arms, and apron splattered with blood. As I got out of the truck, I called back to Paul to come with me so that we could help the farmer skin the steer. As I walked on I noticed that he hadn't moved but was staring straight ahead at the hanging animal. His face was pale and eyes wide with terror. I went back to the truck and asked him what was wrong. He asked, in utter horror, "What are they doing?" Though I probably shouldn't have been, I was startled by his question and replied, "Butchering a steer." With an amazed voice he asked, "Why?" My first response was anger as I took in his terror and disgust. When I asked him where he thought "those little packages of hamburger meat come from," he simply said, in fear and amazement, "Noooo," and got sick to his stomach.

It was several days before he could talk about the incident, but when he did, it amazed me. I asked him if they ever taught him in school where beef came from. He answered, "Yes, from cattle." I then asked him how he thought it got from the cattle to the hamburger, and he said that he had never thought about it before. This whole incident scared me terribly, for my son had never understood where meat, or for that matter, food comes from. Logically, yes, but realistically no. It was then I realized there must be countless other children who do not understand food and killing for food. Without that understanding, they certainly could not understand the connection between themselves, the food, and the earth.

I firmly believe this kind of limited education is at the seat of the destruction of the earth. Once people are connected to the earth, each piece of land matters, and is important. Then there is no random, thoughtless destruction. Only by starting here, I believe, can the Earth be saved. We, as parents and teachers, must take the time to reconnect our children to the earth in a real way, not just with words and pictures and descriptions, but by providing them with real experience. We must show them wheat fields, apple trees, farms, and slaughterhouses, and we must teach them the connection of all life forms to the earth. They must understand that, no matter how far removed they are from the earth, they are still connected in a real way. Schools and society do not teach any such real and tangible communion.

## False Gods of the Flesh

In my mind there are only four things people seek in life—peace, love, joy, and a higher purpose—and these can only be found within ourselves. Yet we, school and society, teach our children to find these things in externals. We drive our children along the rutted pathways of life, making them chase elusive goals of the future in a blind and mindless rush. We tell them to go to school, graduate high school, go to college, find a good job, get married, raise a family, send the kids to school, retire, and die. Clichéd advice to plan for the future, save for the future, work for the future are the battle cries of modern societies. Yet when these goals are obtained, there is always something missing. These goals never produce happiness. And so the searching continues with bigger cars, bigger houses, bigger titles, and more money. Yet the results are always the same—so many people of all ages, lost and searching for peace outside of themselves.

This type of rush toward shallow, future goals, teaches children to live in the future and not in the now. We must guide our children inside themselves, and teach them to find that lasting peace, boundless joy, love, and a profound purpose in life. They must certainly work toward something, but that must not be the main driving force in life. They must learn to slow down and to live each moment fully. We must teach them to savor every moment, and to follow goals directed by their hearts, not their minds or their wallets. They must learn to live by their intuition, not the dictates of external "shoulds" and social demands. If we can teach children to follow their hearts and enjoy every moment, then we have given them a gift as great as life itself.

There are many other ways that children, as well as adults, cut themselves off from being aware. There are erroneous ways of thinking and interpreting the senses that have been learned from society and school, and oftentimes from parents. Lack of awareness many times results not from children's inability, but negative programming or conditioning, which distorts children's perceptions and their sense of wonder. I do not know exactly how this negative conditioning creeps into children's consciousness and takes hold, but I do know what it is and how best to prevent it from becoming children's only reality.

## THE "SAME OLD" TRAP

I once watched Grandfather gazing at a distant bush, thoroughly engrossed in some movement. He stood for the better part of an hour, silent and still, eyes glued to that bush. I could tell by the way that bush moved it was some sort of bird. And by the way Grandfather was paying attention, it must have been some exotic, exciting bird, I thought. I slowly stalked toward Grandfather, desperate to see what had so captivated his attention. As I drew close, I could see the movements of the lower branches and the bird, but I could not make out what kind of bird it was. Grandfather remained silent, his gaze still affixed to the bush and the unknown bird.

Just as I was about to ask him what type of bird he was watching, a common robin flew from the brush. Robins were as common as pine trees, so I continued to stare at the bush, but there was no longer any movement. I asked Grandfather what he was looking at and, smiling, he replied, "A robin." "But, Grandfather," I attested, "it's just a common robin. What's so interesting about a robin?" His smile broke to a frown of displeasure and he muttered, "Just a robin!" With that he took a stick and drew a picture of a bird on the ground and, handing me the stick, he ordered, "Show me where all the black marks on a robin are located." He then asked me what colors the robins' feet were, the color of each feather, and exactly how they build their nests.

Needless to say, I was humiliated. I had no answers; I didn't even have the vaguest idea how many black marks the bird had. I looked at Grandfather sadly and admitted, "I just don't know." "Then," he instructed, "it's not *just* a robin. No two robins are ever the same," he continued; "each is as different as you and I, and we can never exhaust the possibilities of learning something new each time we observe a robin. That is also true of everything else in life, every experience, every situation, every bird, tree, rock, water, and leaf, for we can never know enough about anything. Finally," he continued, "you do not even begin to know an animal until you touch it, and feel its spirit. Then and only then can you ever begin to know."

I see so many children, and adults alike, caught up in the "same old" trap. Because they have seen something once, because they know the name, because they have encountered something several times, they think they know that entity, when in reality, as Grandfather showed me with the robin, they don't really *know* anything. Falling into that "same old" trap makes it impossible to learn anything new, or even to do anything new. Teach children that because they grow and learn each day, because each day is new, nothing in life is ever the *same old* anything.

### Don't Think a Feeling

Along the same lines as the "same old" trap is another pitfall. We should teach our children not to think a feeling but to live it fresh and new every time it occurs. Many times, because we have done something once, or even several times, we allow that experience to totally prejudice our thinking: Mountain streams are always cold; mud always stinks; swamps always have mosquitoes—are just the type of thinking that precludes any new experience, or any new feeling.

To illustrate this type of prejudiced thinking and feeling, I refer to a class I once had in the upper Rockies. Not only did thinking a feeling affect the outcome of the experience, but it affected the entire class, each and every student. We had been out foraging the entire day, cold and rain-laden winds had pummeled us repeatedly, and now that we were on our way back to camp, the going was slow and people were cold. As we got closer to camp, nightfall had overtaken us and temperatures were nearing the freezing point. It was then I commented that we would have to cross a mountain stream to get back to camp; otherwise we would have to go several miles out of our way.

Once I had told one student, it wasn't long before everyone knew, and the group began to complain. People began to argue with me, saying that the stream would make everyone colder than they already were, and even though camp was only a few hundred yards away, they were afraid they would suffer from hypothermia. I turned a deaf ear, and ignored the complaints. I could feel the intensity of the students' concern and I could hear conversations drifting around concerning the frigid waters yet to come. Some students began to visibly shiver at the thought of the cold water.

Suddenly, in the dark, the stream loomed out of the darkness. Without a word, I slipped in and immersed myself to the neck. One by one the students entered, screaming, shivering, and complaining—until they realized that what they were crossing was a hot spring. Upon questioning them, I learned most were at least up to their knees before they realized it was indeed a hot spring and not cold water. Most of them, in fact, ignored the presence of the steam and the smell of sulfur. Everything but the cold of the water had been removed from their minds, and subsequently, their senses.

I often wonder how much preconceived thoughts and feelings play a prejudicial part in our experience. I wonder if, in fact, people ever experience things purely, without prejudicial thoughts. I've seen children so often choose not to do something because of past experience, or do something, only to have the same feelings time and time again. As parents and teachers, we can guide children to new and fresh experience each time they go out into wilderness. We can look deeper than just the superficial feeling and search out new and fresh ways of experiencing the "same old" things. We can teach them to seek adventure and excitement, even in the commonplace, for there is no commonplace for those who enter an experience purely.

## Mediocrity or Intensity

To be safe, secure, and comfortable is, I feel, just another way to signify death. People who teach this life-style and children who live it are not really living at all. Our most vivid memories are of times we were not all that safe, secure, and definitely not comfortable. We place a great emphasis on these states, granting them too much power over our lives. The result is that our children live lives of mediocrity, avoiding the real rapture of life.

Teach children to live on the edge, and to seek adventure, excitement, and intensity in living. I am not suggesting that children put their lives in danger, or take unnecessary risks. All I am saying is that children should be able to run wild in the rain, get wet, get dirty. Teach children to have fun and not to give discomfort too much power.

Encourage children to literally and physically immerse themselves in nature and the elements. So what if they get a little uncomfortable; at least they'll know they are alive living life with intensity, and not suffocating, restricted by the quest for comfort.

## Take Away the Power of Names

Our society and schools seem to rest too much faith in the power of names and labels. We are, I think, wrongly led to believe that if we know the name of something, we know that entity. The quest seems to be only in learning the name of something; when the name is learned, the quest to know apparently stops. Naming tends to remove the mystery, and when the mystery is gone, there is no further searching.

What's in a name? White Oak, *Quercus alba*: does the name tell us of the five foods and five medications that come from the tree? Does the name tell us the color of the flames when burned, the scent of the smoke, the color the smoke gives to our buckskins, or the unique taste it gives to our cooked foods? Does the name tell of the dyes and glues that can be gleaned from the acorns and inner bark, or does it tell what animals feed upon it or find shelter in its branches? Of course not, yet most people are content knowing only the name.

I was once walking with a group of children through a section of woods near their school. Questions came, frequent and fast: what kind of tree is this? what is this plant? what made this hole? or what kind of bird is that? were just a few. It was when the same question had been asked and answered several times that I realized the children were not really listening. I also realized they only cared about the name and not about the spirit of the animal. It was then I changed my answers and began to lead the children into a greater understanding of the woods. Keep in mind that the children did not change, but my method of answering did.

One little boy came up to me with a spotted wood snail on the back of his hand and asked its name. Without answering his question, I asked, "Where are its eyes?" He began to look at the snail closer, searching for its eyes, while another few children joined him in his search. I then asked, "How does it eat? What colors are found on its shell? Where are its legs? Where does it live?" And so many other questions. By the time I was done, all the children of the group had gathered around, and we had spent more than an hour figuring out that snail. The snail also led us to explore its habitat, and more avenues opened by the questions were explored. Each time a child asked the name of something, I asked another question. For the remainder of the walk we stayed in one small area, but the children knew more about the forest than they ever had.

After that experience, I could clearly see why Grandfather always said, "Know the spirit before you know the name." Grandfather recognized the human penchant for life-listing, where names become substitutes for real and intimate knowing, as a dead end. He led us away from placing a misguided importance on names toward the joys of searching for deeper answers. That is what we must teach our children to do: to abandon the labels and names, and to begin to *know*, intimately. This can be easily accomplished by redirecting our answers into questions, guiding children to look deeper than names. Only after animals or plants are intimately known should names be given, for naming deceptively removes the mystery.

### Wandering

We shackle our children with many rules that carry over into their life in nature. When children take a walk, we unconsciously shackle them with the confines of time and destination. Unfortunately time and destination block true and spontaneous awareness. I believe we should teach our children to wander in nature, without time or destination. When we give them destination, the destination becomes the goal, and foremost in their minds. When we give them a time, that time causes them to rush by, never sensing anything fully. I feel that children should follow their hearts rather than a clock or a place.

I was told by a group of students that they were going out to find some deer and they would be back to camp before sundown. They had been gone for several hours but upon returning, they told me they had seen no deer. In fact, I found out they had seen nothing. I spent the last remaining minutes before dark guiding them back along their route to find deer. Along the way I showed them several rare wildflowers, numerous reptiles, and a wealth of animals, ranging from foxes to shrews. Finally, just at dusk, a small herd of deer entered the field. All the students were amazed at what they had missed. It was then I explained what time and destination had done, and how it had stood in the way of pure awareness. *Hike* became a dirty word, and *wander* became a way of life. If children really want to see and experience nature to the fullest, then teach them to wander.

### The Sit

By far the best way to experience nature is not to travel long distances or to visit exotic places, but to simply sit. Nature seems to love people who sit patiently and quietly, and it is then, and only then, that creation will put on a grand show. Most of my best experiences with the animal world have been during the times I have been sitting, patiently waiting.

It was then, in the stillness, externally and internally, that the animals would come around. In fact, I can see and experience more sitting for an hour than most people can hiking all day.

One night I couldn't sleep, so I decided to go up to the Appalachian Trail and watch the sunrise. My wife, Judy, thought I was crazy because at that time of year the trail was heavily used by backpackers. Disregarding her reservation I decided to go anyway, making my way up the trail and sitting under an old oak tree. The tree was located several yards away from a major crossroad, and a usually busy area, but it was early and the backpackers were not out yet. As I settled in, the sky began to grow light, and animal activity began to increase all around me. Birds landed on my head, chipmunks scurried across my legs, and deer passed along a run just a few inches from where I sat. The whole forest was active, and I sat unobserved, part of the whole life process.

Suddenly the whole woods went into a frenzy of animals running for cover. Squirrels chattered from high limbs, chipmunks dove down holes, and birds let out alarm cries. Within moments, the area that was once a peaceful blend of animal activity was now deserted. I knew it was a sure sign backpackers had entered the trails. I knew also that to continue sitting would be somewhat futile, for most animals had now vacated the area, so I returned to the trail.

After a short walk, I encountered the origin of the disturbance. Three backpackers stumbled up the trail toward me, talking, shuffling, heads bowed toward the ground. They almost ran me down before they realized I was standing there. We got into a conversation and they told me that they had left their camp just before dawn, hoping to reach the second camp, twenty miles away, before nightfall. It was then I asked, "Did you see any animals?" One of them answered thoughtfully, "Naw, just a few birds." It was obvious their quest for time and destination overshadowed all they could have seen. In fact, I would venture to say they saw nothing more that day than "just a few birds." Teach your children to sit, patiently watching nature unfold before them.

# GRANDFATHER AND THE FISHERMAN:

## *The Wisdom of Choice*

One of the stories I like telling the best is of Grandfather and the fisherman. The story was a very powerful teaching in my life and illustrates beautifully that awareness has to be a conscious choice. Living fully a life of rapture has to be a conscious, never-ending effort. The alternatives are a living death, and I believe that the story is worth retelling here, even reading aloud, to children, as an illustration of this point.

Sometimes we must look at old things anew, changing our perspective and vision, and abandon the old ruts of thinking and experiencing. Grandfather was my greatest teacher; he taught me lessons on every level. In every part of his life, I found so many lessons, many without words, reaching far beyond the physical realms. One day Grandfather taught me a powerful lesson by just being himself, going about his life as he always did. I don't suspect even he knew what a profound effect his actions had on my life. Sometimes teachers come when you least expect them, bearing precious gifts of knowledge that somehow tie everything together. These gifts can even sometimes come through failure or negativity, though there are no failures, or negatives, only teachings. So it was with me and an old fisherman. Unbeknownst to him, he became, also, one of my greatest teachers. In my life, these two events connect to each other and stand out above so many others. I call this story "The Wisdom of Grandfather and the Fisherman."

The story of Grandfather and the fisherman is the story of two separate worlds, a contrast of separate realities. The representation of one world has shown me the essence of the other, and they both have shown me how to live, one in very positive terms and the other in negative. Little did I know that the differences between each could be fused into my consciousness as one harmonious teaching. But that is the natural order of things, if one knows how to learn without prejudice and with purity, since it is only from this vantage point that associations and similarities arise unhampered, and connections emerge where there could be none before. Within the natural order a balancing of opposites occurs, one world complements the other and produces a picture sharper for its depth than if each element is viewed separately. The teachings set forth in the following tale occurred at separate times, many years apart, but taken together, they illustrate for me the essence of living as taught jointly by two very different people.

I was sitting on an old cedar stump, watching the dawn advance across the swamp. The morning was thick with mist, especially near the stream that cut through the boggy cedar swamp. The trunks of the huge old cedar trees faded from sight as they reached to the pale skies, plunging through the dense sheet of mist that clung to their upper crowns. The cedar forest appeared as a mystical temple, something of vision or dream rather than reality. Its beauty was breathtaking; reverence for this place saturated my soul. Shafts of angled sunlight cut through the lower forest with a hazy yellow-orange light that cast shadows into strange shapes and mists into flowing apparitions. Dew clung to every leaf and furrowed trunk, dripping here and there, mingling with the symphony of awaking birds and the gentle surging flow of the stream. I felt as if I sat on the edge of some primordial forest at the dawn of creation.

I was deep in prayer, consciously and unconsciously, losing myself in meditation and in the deeper recesses of the misty shadows. I know of no one who could have sat in this place, at the edge of misty sun and shadowy forest, who would not have been in prayer, at peace with creation and flooded with unspeakable awe. This kind of morning always tears away all cares and duties, all fleshy wants, and bares the soul to the elements, to be washed and purified. The thrashings of the mind evaporate like the mists of dawn, and true thoughts come into ever-sharpening focus. Adding their own mystique to this magical morning, deer drift in and out of the mists, disappearing momentarily behind brush or fusing their color with that of distant trees. Everywhere animals move, their motion blending with the flow of forest.

Another flow entered this morning. Grandfather drifted slowly down the trail to the stream. I was excited to see him because he had been away in another part of the forest. I wanted to go to him but the intrigue of sitting there watching him held me in place. I am almost certain that he knew I was there, for there was little he missed in the woods and I am sure nuances and disturbances easily gave away my location. Whether he knew I was there or not, however, he showed no interest, and continued walking slowly toward the stream. He stood for a long time, gazing at the water. He glanced up and down the stream, leisurely yet methodically, as if searching for something. His eyes rested on the cathedral of cedars for a longing moment, and I caught the glisten of a tear on his cheek. To me, he appeared as if he was about to enter a temple, about to see God.

As I sat and watched, my mind took a strange turn, changing reality and shedding consciousness of the self. All analysis ceased and I began to look at Grandfather as if I were watching some stranger. It was a nebulous feeling, a thinking with no perimeters or consciousness of time or place. Watching him was like watching a surrealistic dance or play, with unnamed characters and dreamlike landscapes. The whole relationship between Grandfather and me seemed of a different time, a distant reality not of this place. I was fascinated and intrigued by his actions. I saw each move as if I had never seen it before.

Though I had known Grandfather for over eight years, his movements overwhelmed me now. Sometimes one gets so close to something or someone that one can only see it in parts, unconnected to the whole. Sometimes, too, one gets so familiar with something that it becomes commonplace; the awe that can and should be derived from the everyday fades from view. That is essentially what I had done to Grandfather, turned the power of his everyday teachings into a faded commonplace event.

As I sat there, Grandfather approached close to the water's edge and stood with his arms raised in an attitude of worship. Looking up- and downstream as if searching, he paused at every glistening riff and misty hollow with his gaze. I could clearly see the streams of tears on his cheeks glistening in the sun and the contented smile on his face. He knelt down solemnly and touched the water, ever so gently, watching his own concentric rings ripple and mix with those of the water striders. He began to stroke the water as if it were a living being, looking deep into its color, to the mosaic of sand and pebbles at the bottom. He drew his face close to smell the water. Then he took a light sip. He sat back with the water in his mouth and swished it back and forth. His actions would have put the most experienced wine tasters to shame. Reaching deeper into the water with cupped hands, he raised the water to the creator in thanksgiving. Then and only then did he drink. Standing erect, once again, he dropped his blanket, his sole garment, and entered the water. I could see his entire body trembling with excitement, and the smile on his face, as he lay back in the water, was one of total rapture.

Rapture is something I rarely see in the modern world; it exists as a word, not an emotion. Society does not seem to know what rapture is, far less what it feels like. To society, water is something to guzzle, put here for its use or misuse, and never given a second thought. To Grandfather, water was earth mother's blood, a precious gift of life for all things living and growing, not just for humans.

My mind raced back over the events of what I'd seen, searching for meaning. I should not have been shocked at all, for Grandfather had done nothing new. He always approached the water that way—solemnly, in reverence, like a child. Even though he had swum in thousands of different waters, stood at the foot of the most magnificent waterfalls, and drunk the purest waters of the earth, all his life he still entered water this way. No, it should not have shocked me, for this was the way he was with everything—the whole of creation. That day I had backed away, broadened my perspective, and seen for the first time what had always been there.

Grandfather savored everything in life as he savored the water, fully and with all his senses, to a state of utter rapture. He would walk through the forests, fondling leaves, touching flowers, hugging trees, and lifting loam in cupped hands to smell. He would observe even the most common things for long periods of time, extracting every nuance from them. Life was always new and fresh to him, an adventure packed with excitement. He was a child, endlessly curious, always at play, always searching, tasting, touching, smelling, hearing, and seeing the world and life to its fullest. To him, every entity of earth was an object of worship, his life a constant prayer of thanksgiving, and his quest always for rapture. In watching him live that day, I learned how to live, and why. But then there was the fisherman, who taught me how not to live.

Many years after Grandfather's physical death, I was seated on another beach, awaiting the sunrise. The ocean was still black, the waves accented by the pale glow of first dawn. The silhouettes of gulls appeared at the edge of the darkness. Lonely cries of gulls, the soft wind moving the sand in a gentle hissing, and the light clap of waves created a soothing music for the soul. Prayers seemed to reach to the skies, penetrating the scant cloud cover, now etched in the liquid gold of dawn. The beach was deserted except for a lone fisherman who sat on a beach chair a dozen yards from me. He was gray and weathered, his skin showed overexposure to the sun and surf, and his clothes were of styles long forgotten. He stared intently at the tip of his rod, watching it bob and shift with the rise and fall of wave and wind. He seemed to concentrate solely on that rod tip, looking away only to his watch, probably out of habit.

In time, I moved closer to him, the sun now fully breaking the horizon. It had grown warm. Gull voices increased, and the old fisherman and I slipped into a light conversation. We talked of fishing and tides, weather and fishing beaches, but mostly about him. He said that he had been fishing these beaches for over thirty years and since his retirement a few years ago, he'd bought a house near the beach. Now he fished every day without fail. The only time he said he didn't was when the beaches were crowded, on cold winter days, or when storms made it impossible. Our conversation soon trailed off. I went back to my sunrise and he to his rod tip.

As my thoughts drifted with the tides, I unconsciously picked up a handful of beach sand and began studying its texture and color. I smelled it awhile, then held it up to the sunlight, watching it sparkle and change color. I've always loved beach sand and how it changes its size, color, shape, and texture with each new beach. I guess I was so caught up in what I was doing that I didn't notice the fisherman staring at me. He must have thought I was holding some sort of shell when he asked, "What you got there?" Taken aback somewhat at his question, I answered matter-of-factly, "Beach sand!" "It's all the same, white and gray; sticks to everything," he responded. I wouldn't have paid this statement even a second thought except that it had been uttered mockingly. "White and gray?" I asked. "Old man, please, pick up some beach sand and look." He grumbled something and went back to watching his pole.

I got up and had walked a few steps away when some feeding terns caught my eye and I sat back down to watch. While I was watching them hovering and diving near the edge of the jetty I happened to glance back at the fisherman. In his weathered hand he held a handful of beach sand, stirring it around with his finger, and holding it close to his face. I heard him talking, half out loud and half to himself. "My

God," he exclaimed, his voice bitter and breaking, "My God, I never realized." As I left the area I glanced back at the old man to wave good-bye but he wasn't watching me. In his outstretched hands he held a bluefish to the sun. I could see the colors glistening in the sun and I could see the tears on the old man's cheeks. His hands trembled. Dropping the fish, he hunched over, sobbing silently to himself. I wanted to go to him, but I knew there was nothing I could do.

The horror, I thought. Here was a man who had spent the better part of his lifetime fishing these beaches but who did not know what beach sand looked like. Here was an old man, who in the twilight of his life had seen a bluefish for the first time. A fish he loved so much to catch but never really knew. The words of Marcus Aurelius thundered in my brain. "It is not dying that a man should fear, but a man should fear never having lived at all." This is what had brought the old fisherman to tears: realizing at this late time in life all the things he had missed, all the things he would never see, all the wasted time; time that has been spent, never to be made up; the horror of it all, the absolute senseless waste of life, the living dead. I learned from that old man more than he could ever know. I learned not to waste my life, living to die, but rather live a life of rapture and wonderment.

I never saw that old man again, though I have been back to that beach many times. He will always be with me, however, and I think of him often. I carry him in my heart as one of my greatest teachers, and I wonder how many more people are out there just like him, people who will never really see a sunrise or sunset, who will never know the sands or the sparkle of bluefish. How many will never know how to savor water, touch, really touch someone they love, or know the rapture of life? I wonder how many people are rushing through life blindly, never really sensing what living is all about. Every day, several times, I ask myself, Am I being Grandfather or am I being the fisherman? The choice is always up to me. Everyone has to make that choice, sooner or later; hopefully, not so late in life as the fisherman.

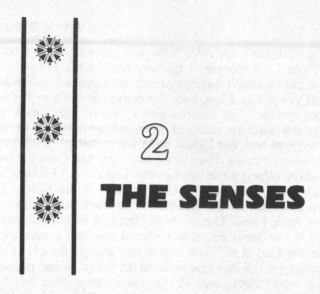

# 2

# THE SENSES

As I stated in the last chapter, through society and school our children's senses become dulled and eventually atrophy. We make certain mistakes and pick up certain bad habits, which hinder our ability to sense clearly and observe keenly. There are many techniques that will help exercise, and ultimately sharpen, children's senses. With practice, children can regain the acuity of sensory awareness that they once had, and reverse the damage caused by poorly used senses and acquired bad habits. Breaking bad habits and changing the way children have learned to use their senses will have immediate and positive results in all aspects of their lives.

## RELAXATION

Grandfather called relaxation the "sacred silence." To him, it was the most important aspect of awareness, and it was practiced on an everyday basis, much like a physical workout. Relaxation means that both the internal and external self are at peace, open, much like a quiet pond or an unexposed sheet of photographic paper, ready to receive the impressions of the natural world. The human senses and mind can be likened to a pond: when quiet, it reflects the natural surroundings perfectly, yet when that pond is disturbed, when its surface is trembling and excited, the reflected image becomes distorted and obscured. The human spirit, also, when stirred up, distorts the images of nature. If the mind is tense, all functions are impaired and perceptions obscured, and the ability to observe keenly is hampered. But when the mind is at peace, we function better, learn better, and are keenly aware. This quieting, this relaxation, society calls meditation.

Grandfather taught us to meditate, to reach the "sacred silence" more by practice and example, rather than by rote teaching. Grandfather knew it would be difficult to teach any child to meditate since children are naturally active—and because Rick and I especially had a difficult time sitting still. Thus, he worked the "sacred silence" into other lessons, so that the act of meditation became an accessory to the main lesson. We learned meditation and relaxation while quietly waiting for animals, where we were required to sit still for long periods of time. We spent hours working with our hands, doing detailed bead or quill work, carving, or making intricate paintings. We learned to relax by watching tracks and tracking, all of which caused us to slow down, and to find that deep inner peace.

It has been shown especially through biofeedback, and in the philosophical and theological teachings of many cultures, that meditation is a vital tool on any spiritual path and a means toward enlightenment. The more relaxed one becomes the more heightened one's learning ability, and hence the more heightened and keen one's sensory awareness.

Generally it can be difficult to teach children meditation; however, because its results can be so beneficial to learning and awareness it is well worth parents' effort to try. Fortunately there are many ways to circumvent the difficulties of teaching meditation to children, since we can reach the same results through many informal techniques. What is important is not the method, but the result. Children often find the sedentary nature of classic meditation exercises difficult to execute, so we might also do well to teach a kind of meditation that is dynamic and moving.

When you teach children to meditate, it usually must be done under the guise of some other activity. This way the children will concentrate on learning a new lesson, never guessing that you are teaching them to slow down and be at peace. The results will be the same as if the child had learned meditation through one of the classic disciplines. It is important to remember here that we must try to teach children this meditation so it can be used unconsciously and on a daily basis. What good will this wisdom be if the child cannot use it easily?

According to Dr. Herbert Benson in his book *The Relaxation Response*, there are four elements needed for good meditation. First is a comfortable position and second is relaxation. Keep in mind that people can be relaxed and comfortable when walking, hiking, swimming, or working with their hands. The third element necessary is a passive attitude. The fourth is a point of concentration, meaning that the mind must be focused and concentrating on *something*, such as a skill, a flower, or nature itself. The passive attitude comes into play at the point when any stray thought or distraction breaks that concentration; we must never force a stray thought out of the mind, but gently—passively—allow it to pass. The act of "trying" is in and of itself contrary to an effective meditative attitude.

When teaching children to meditate, we must include all these elements so the meditation will happen naturally. One way to teach children to meditate is to use a skill that requires one to concentrate and work with the hands. Beadworking, quill working, pottery, basket making, painting, carving, sewing, and playing an instrument, all produce many of the elements needed for a good meditation. It is best, if possible, to have the children perform these skills in an outdoor, natural setting. Sitting quietly, observing animals, is also a good form of meditation. Children concentrate on the animal and relax, thus fulfilling all the elements of a good meditation. Later in the chapter I will discuss how to move this basic meditation to a dynamic, moving meditation, which makes possible fox walking and wide-angle vision.

When we teach children to slow down, relax, and be at peace in nature, we give them the ability to sense purely. They begin to see, hear, and experience things they would normally pass by. I believe the frenzy of this fast-paced society is the cause of people's, and children's, inability to slow down. We, as parents, must recognize what the pace of society does to our children and take the proper steps to reverse it, and thus reverse the tension felt in modern living. Meditation is of the utmost importance for fully observing nature, and for effective living.

## TOTAL SENSORY AWARENESS

We must treat our senses as we optimally do our bodies and minds. Many of us do some sort of daily physical workout—like weight lifting, running, aerobics, and sports—or we read books and play games to feed our minds. But we should also learn to exercise our senses every day, and we should teach our children to do the same. Teach children to reach out with their senses. Encourage them to watch the landscape carefully, paying attention to colors, textures, shapes, shadows, and movement. Help them to slow down so they learn to really taste foods they eat, and to pay attention to scents and where those smells come from. Have them listen carefully to the various songs of nature, and let them touch, feel everything they can. By teaching children to exercise their senses, you sharpen those senses, make them more vivid and inexorably effect a reversal of the dulling routines of society.

# SENSORY EXERCISES

## Sight

To exercise the sight, have children pick out color, texture, shape, shadow, and movement on a landscape. Have them search the landscape for the less subtle colors and textures. Have them study details carefully. Teach them to look deeply at flowers, leaf shapes, grains of sand, and feathers. Have them observe closely the pattern of insects, spider webs, and other intricate things. Have them push their sight from the near to the far, and have them scan the landscape in ever-widening semicircles, from their feet to the horizon. Have them draw to describe an entity exactly. At times, have the children use magnifying glasses to scan the forest floor, to see pebbles or little plants.

## Hearing

To help children develop their sense of hearing, teach them to listen to the purity of sounds. Don't tell them what to concentrate on or give wordy descriptions. Have them listen near and far, and urge them to pinpoint as best they can the exact position of what they hear. Have them listen to the wind in the trees, the shrubs, and the grasses, and pick out the variations in the tone of each. Have them listen to the music of insect wings, the gurgling of water, and the trembling sounds of brush vibrating in the breezes. Have them trace sounds to their sources. A good practice is to have children listen to the symphony of nature as a whole, then separate each part, until they know the origin and instrument of each sound.

Teach children to focus their hearing by cupping their hands around their ears, making a shape like a deer's ear. By doing this, children can hear in one direction and pick up sounds that would normally escape them. Another good practice is to blindfold the child; this removes the preponderance of attention on sight and brings hearing into a sharper focus. Blindfolding will enchance all the other senses, making them more acute.

## Touch

Teach children to expand the sense of touch. Touch involves the entire body. Have children lie on the ground and *feel* the earth, the wind in their hair, the sun on their faces, and the clothing on the body. Have them really feel the atmosphere, the cool and warm places, and the damp and dry places. Have the child *touch* everything, the rough bark of trees, the earth, flowers, feathers, tracks, water, insects, and plants of all types. Again, by blindfolding children, you will enhance their sense of touch and hence their ability to concentrate. Most important, though, is to have children pay close attention to whatever they are touching and feeling.

### Taste and Smell

These two senses go hand in hand, for they are dependent upon each other. Teach children to taste their food fully, to relish it, much like a wine taster savors a fine wine. Have them taste the water in this same way and see if they will know the difference between bottled water, potable stream water, well water, and tap water. Brew some exotic teas made from wild edible plants and teach them nature's flavors. Taste everything including the air of the various natural areas.

Ask children to sample nature's bouquet of aromas; separate the scents, tracing each to its source. See if they can smell the difference between woods by the smells they give off when burning, tell a wild-flower, or the source of drinking water by scent alone. Teach them to pay attention to the odors that would normally escape them. Have them smell the ground at various locations and see if they can tell the difference in each area. Have them smell animal dens, runs, and trails to see if they can detect the smell of that animal in the landscape. Have them smell what is ordinarily not smelled, like leaves, the bark of trees, oncoming storms, or rocks. The more you can get children to slow down and pay attention to the taste and smell of things, the sharper they will be in picking out the various scents of the landscape.

### Varied Vision

We are a very sight-oriented society, and wherever the sight goes, so follow the other senses. For instance, as you read this book, all your senses are concentrated on the book and the area around the book. Noises in the room, smells, and feelings are filtered out, and only those items and stimuli immediately around this book are sensed. Now, if you look up and out the window, all your senses will follow your sight, reaching out the window, and all sensation of the room will eventually disappear. While we are paying such close attention to one given thing, we are sacrificing our experience of the whole.

In school, we were taught to pay rapt attention, but Grandfather taught us to pay intermittent attention. Grandfather knew that if rapt attention was paid to anything, not only would we blot out everything that was happening around us, but in concentrating so hard, we would eventually negate the very thing on which we were focused; concentra-tion would itself become the focus. Thus, we must teach children to vary their vision—to pay intermittent attention—to keep their eyes and senses moving, but always coming back to rest on the primary subject. The consequence of doing otherwise can best be illustrated by something that happened to me when I was very young.

Rick and I were watching tracks near one of our favorite swamps. The tracks were intriguing because it was one of those days when the ground was constantly in change, sometimes frozen, and at other times thawing. After several hours of watching tracks, Grandfather stopped by to see how we were coming along. Once we had expounded on what the tracks themselves had done, Grandfather commented, "The deer took notice, the owls didn't care, the fox watched for a while, but the raccoon ran away." It was then we realized we had spent so much time looking at the tracks, that we failed to see, as Grandfather had, all the things going on around us.

When we take children into nature, we should encourage them to look at more than just the trail ahead. We also should be moving our eyes, so that we can draw their attention to things that they would otherwise miss. Keep their senses active, keep them moving, and keep showing them exciting things so that they will want to keep their eyes moving. We have to reverse the bad habit of rapt attention given to our children by school, television, video games, computers, and the like. And rid your vocabulary of demands like: "Look at me when I talk to you." or "Stop looking out the window and pay attention." I truly believe that a child who masters the ability to pay intermittent attention will learn better and understand more.

### Wide-Angle Vision

Children are taught to tunnel their vision, until tunnel vision becomes an insidious habit. By the time children get into second grade, this way of seeing is the only approach they will use. Children are taught to tunnel their vision by reading books, watching a teacher, staring at a television or video screen. Unfortunately tunneling vision also tunnels the senses, for where the sight goes, so go the senses. When children, and adults, look at something to the exclusion of everything else, their vision is totally concentrated on that one item; everything else is blotted out. Tunnel vision is exceptionally poor vision for travel in nature, and for much of life in general. It limits not only night vision, but more important, minimizes the ability of the eye to pick up movement. This tunnel vision also limits the senses, and limits perception of the overall landscape to one small area.

Wide-angle, or full peripheral, vision, is a better way of observing nature. By taking in the full picture, the sight becomes very sensitive to movement, and thus animals, birds, and insects can more easily be

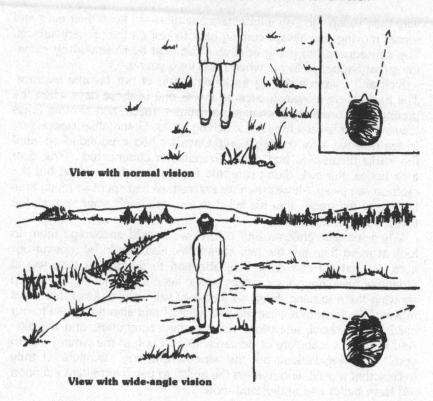

**View with normal vision**

**View with wide-angle vision**

detected. Also, since wide-angle vision opens up more of the eye, increasing its sensitivity to lower levels of light, it will vastly improve children's ability to see at night. With the expansion of the vision comes an expansion of the senses. The dimensions of the natural world are broadened, and more is experienced. Wide-angle vision also tends to be very relaxing, both physically and mentally, which in a way produces its own unique form of meditation.

Children, and adults, use tunnel vision about ninety-nine percent of the time. Instead we should aim to use tunnel vision and wide-angle vision each about 50 percent of the time. Grandfather wanted us to use wide-angle vision most of the time, resorting to tunnel vision only when it was necessary to concentrate on only one thing. Teaching children to use wide-angle vision takes some time, even though it is the natural way of seeing, for they must break a bad habit, and bad habits are hard to break. Teaching this skill will take a lot of work and awareness on the part of parents, for parents must constantly reinforce the wide-angle vision habit.

To begin teaching wide-angle vision to children, have them look out into a landscape as they normally would. Then have them widen their vision, pretending the whole scene is a picture hanging on the wall. Have them observe the landscape in its entirety, pushing the frame as far out as they can. Automatically children will start picking up movement and begin to sense things on a broader level. These dividends do not need to be taught but are a natural result of wide-angle vision. To further enhance wide-angle vision, have children stand with their arms stretched out from their sides at right angles to the body and move their fingers. Have them look ahead, attempting to expand their vision until their moving fingers come into view. This is a tremendous way to teach children to go to their full peripheral visual limits.

There is a great method for teaching children to use wide-angle vision when they are walking. Children seem to enjoy it immensely and, through it, learn quickly. After you are sure the children have mastered the first two exercises in learning wide-angle vision, then you can play the stone game. Pick up a handful of small white stones and have the children walk down a trail a few yards in front of you. Every so often throw a stone wide to the children's left, or right, or high over their heads. As soon as the children see the stone, they should point to it, and call out. The object of the game is to point out the stone just as it breaks the frame of peripheral vision. Keep doing this for quite some time, decreasing the frequency of throws. Thus, your children will hold the wide-angle vision longer without the interruption of the stones, and it will soon become a habit.

## AUTOMATIC VISION

There is a problem that occurs with all people, called automatic vision. Once a landscape is viewed for the first time, the mind *automatically* keys in on prominent features. Subsequently each time that landscape is viewed, the vision automatically comes back to rest on those familiar, prominent features. Thus, the areas between those familiar features are obscured, or not seen at all, and much is missed. The more familiar children become with a particular landscape, the more they will look only at the prominent features, and the more the area between will remain unseen. That is why, when one enters upon a strange place for the first time, one usually sees more animals but with each successive trip, one sees fewer and fewer.

The important point here is to teach children to always be "tourists," looking at even the most familiar landscapes as if each time were the first time they were ever there. Have children view the landscape differently—vary the angle of vision; take a different path, constantly picking out new things they have never seen before. One game that teaches children to look at a landscape in a new way is for you to hide something on that landscape. The children should then try to find that object, which will force them, through the guise of the game, to look at the landscape differently.

Another approach is to explain to children the drawbacks of automatic vision. Have them pick out the objects they usually look at and then make a conscious effort to look between them. See if you can't make a game of finding new things among the old and obvious things. Generally older children will take to this method easily.

Another good way to teach older children to look in little-seen areas is to play a form of hide-and-seek. Have one child hide alongside a trail, especially in the less-seen places, and as the other children walk along, have them try to find the hiding person, without leaving the trail. If you are running a summer camp, you can tell the children that at any time you may be hiding along the trails, and they should be vigilantly trying to find you. Rick and I used to play this game over and over again, only the person hiding was usually armed with a handful of thick mud, ready for the other to pass by.

Again, we must teach children to treat the senses as they do their bodies and minds—they must be exercised daily. Since it is no longer necessary to be keenly aware in everyday life in this society, the senses soon become dulled. All children's activities hardly use the senses to the fullest, and consequently many bad habits are picked up along the way. Remember, the best way for children to reverse the process of dulling the senses is to exercise them, continuously and religiously. Clear, sharp senses will not only be an asset in the woods, but will serve children well in all life endeavors as well.

# 3
# MOVING IN NATURE

Learning how to move in nature is very important if children want to fully observe. There are proper techniques of moving and these techniques are much like learning dance or such oriental art forms as t'ai chi. These techniques should be used whenever children enter the woods, but will preferably be used on an everyday basis, so they become unconscious acts. What children will have to do is rid themselves of the bad method of modern walking . . . and that will take some doing. The proper way of moving in nature requires quieting the walk, doing less damage to the landscape and body, being more flowing, less dangerous, and very comfortable.

The first thing children must be taught to do upon entering nature is to slow down, way down. Generally children should slow their walk to about a quarter of the speed of their normal walk. No one can experience all the grandeur of nature when rushing, and society certainly teaches children to rush. Not only does the pace have to be slowed, but so does the mind. This can be accomplished easily by first having the children go through some of the relaxation exercises mentioned in the previous chapter. If the mind is racing, it will skip over so many sights, and unfortunately, as with walking, modern society demands that children think fast. But speed is a bad habit that must be broken.

## THE FOX WALK

Children, and adults of today, walk the wrong way. As a tracker, I have studied walks for much of my life and I know there is no possible way for modern humans to walk correctly. Grandfather's walk was so silent,

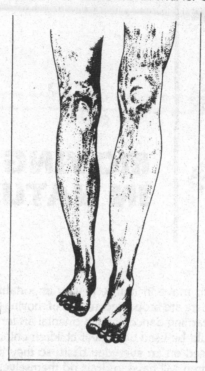

**Fox walk: come down on the outside of the foot and roll to the inside.**

flowing, and natural that he looked more like he was floating than walking. Two causes of today's poor walking habits are civilized roadways and heavy footwear. With the technologization of walking surfaces, humankind's walk has become sloppy, damaging, and weak. Our shoes are heavy, usually with heels of some sort, thick soles, and sometimes even ankle supports. If the Great Spirit wanted us to walk heavily on our heels, he would have given us extra-thick heel pads. This of course, has not been the case.

I believe the development of heels is directly a result of technologized walking surfaces. On these new hard surfaces walking became sloppy and to protect the foot, thick heels were added to shoes. These heavy shoes further destroyed humans' walk, to a point where modern walking is loud, fast, damaging, abrupt, and dangerous to the body and the landscape. We further perpetuate this walking problem by teaching our toddlers to walk in shoes that resemble little combat boots. From the time children can walk, their walk is already destroyed. Further complication comes from the way people hold themselves physically while walking. Our center of gravity is usually relocated in the head, thus a wider straddle and pitch are needed to balance the weight.

The next problem attributable to modernized surfaces is that the weight and forward motion of the movement are committed before the foot is placed on the ground. Thus, when walking, people tend to throw their head and body weight forward and attempt to catch up with their feet. By committing the weight before they feel the ground, people become easily injured when they move to the terrain of natural areas. This type of step is also very loud and harsh. Because the step hits hard with the heel, there is a jarring of the body, back, and neck, which puts tremendous stress on the whole physiology. That is why humanity suffers so many shinsplints, back and neck problems, and headaches. Many of them originate from our walk. Finally, because the weight is committed, modern humans must constantly watch the ground to know where they are stepping. If you are watching the ground, you can't be watching nature.

The basic premise of the fox walk is that the foot is placed on the ground before the weight is committed. Once the problem of not having to look at the ground is solved, and the pace is slowed down, then everything else seems to fall into place. The center of gravity in the fox walk is located at the center of the hips. With this positioning, the feet can be pointed directly ahead, in the line of travel, and the insides of the feet can seek a common line. In other words, there will be a zero straddle, and zero pitch. The back is centered comfortably on the hips and the head is held high, no longer pitched forward to watch the ground. This not only alleviates back and neck strain, but enables the fox walker to observe the landscape fully.

The step is accomplished first with a short stride. There is a point in taking a stride where walkers can go too far, pulling the body forward, committing the step. A shorter stride solves this problem.

Next, the foot should lightly touch the ground, bringing into play the entire outside edge of the foot, simultaneously hitting the ground with the ball, heel, and edge of the foot. The foot is then rolled inward, until the whole surface area of the foot is on the ground. Now walkers can feel exactly what they are stepping on. Finally, the body weight is shifted to the step, in a flowing motion, the step being now quiet and safe, with no jarring of the body. Notice that when walking barefoot on sharp stones, that you will never hit the heel, but you will walk, quite naturally, in a manner similar to the way you do in the fox walk.

The rewards of the fox walk will immediately be felt by children. Awareness increases as children are able to look around, there is less fatigue, and the walk is quieter and more flowing. There is also less damage to the landscape and to themselves, and they will naturally slow down. Children will also increase their walking distance, as the fox walk demands the use of the larger, stronger muscles of the legs—much more so than the modern walk—and there is less fatigue from jarring. Ironically the fox walk is found in all primitive cultures throughout the world, can also be seen in the Ninja art form, and is identical to the meditation movement of certain Hindu sects. It should be noted here that when coupling fox walking with wide-angle vision, a dramatic, physically induced meditation is reached.

Teaching children to fox walk is the same as teaching children to dance. It is a discipline with very definite parts, movements, and techniques. First teach the children to feel each step before their weight is committed. This will easily lead to placing the feet on the ground the correct way. Once the children are comfortable with the step, teach them to straighten their backs and lift their eyes off the ground. It is no longer necessary to watch the ground that closely. Have the children practice this walk until it is done naturally and in a flowing manner without thinking. This way the children will probably use the walk all the time, in or out of nature, and their bodies will feel much better.

As a note, I do not like modern footwear at all. Heavy shoes are too confining, too heavy, and far too restrictive. Heavy footwear restricts blood flow, weakens the feet and ankles, and causes unnecessary damage to the body as well as the landscape. Problems with cold feet in the winter are the result of restricted blood flow and feet that are out of shape. The best thing you can do for yourself and your children is to go barefoot as much as possible. At other times, wear moccasins or light canvas shoes without heels. You will find that you and your children will have fewer leg cramps, warmer feet in the winter, and less damage to the body.

## STALKING

Stalking allows children to get close to animals . . . many times close enough to touch them. Stalking is not just the act of tiptoeing through the woods but a science and art form as disciplined as t'ai chi or dance. Stalking makes children nearly invisible to animals—people as well— and brings children directly into the world of animals. Again, stalking is the same for all primitive cultures throughout the world, for the peoples that live close to the earth use nature and animals as their teachers. Typically the heron family teaches the correct way to hold and move the upper body and legs, and the cat family teaches how to place the feet, without sound.

There are a number of elements, techniques, and mental disciplines required for stalking. First, the stalking step is slow, dead slow, usually about one complete step per minute. Second, the motion is flowing, with no abrupt movements or shakiness. Third, the motion must be frozen anytime an animal looks toward the stalker. Finally, each step is compressed, describing the way the step slowly and silently compresses

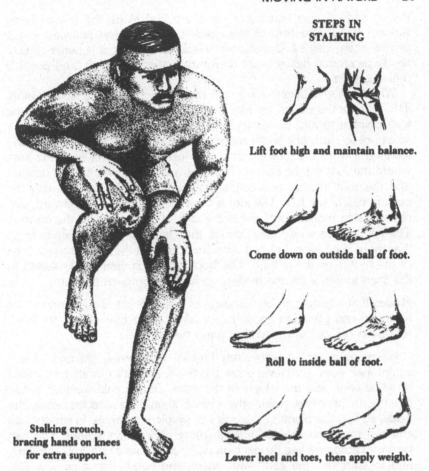

**STEPS IN
STALKING**

Lift foot high and maintain balance.

Come down on outside ball of foot.

Roll to inside ball of foot.

Stalking crouch,
bracing hands on knees
for extra support.

Lower heel and toes, then apply weight.

the earth. All of this minimizes movement and sound—the two things that most often give our presence away to animals. Ironically, when all these elements are brought together, children can stalk in a standing position, without aid of cover, and never be detected by an animal.

In stalking, the body is held in much the same way as for fox walking, and again there is zero straddle and zero pitch. Here the arms should be held close to the body, usually folded lightly in front, since animals can easily identify the human outline. The animal that is being stalked should always be directly in the center of vision, and at no time should the eyes be diverted from that animal. If the animal ever looks toward the child, the child should then freeze all motion and wait for the animal to go back to normal business or look the other way. Also, wide-angle vision should be used throughout the stalk. This will enable the stalker to watch the animal, while watching for movements of other animals in the immediate area that might see them and alarm the animal being stalked. It will also help children pick out the easiest pathway to the animal being stalked. Grandfather would always say it is better to take ten steps around heavy brush than three steps through it, and possibly make a noise.

When a step is taken, every movement is in very, very slow motion. The rear foot is picked up high, and slowly moved forward, with the toes pointed toward the ground. This action should be done with care so as not to catch any brush and make a sound. The foot is then slowly lowered toward the ground, until it is just a few inches from the area where the foot will be placed. The toes are then slowly turned upward and the foot inward, and contact is made with the ground with the outside ball of the foot. The foot is then rolled forward and inward, in a compressing motion, until the entire ball of the foot is on the ground. The heel is then slowly rolled down, then finally the toes. Keep in mind that there is no weight placed onto the foot until the entire surface area of the foot is on the ground. The body weight is then slowly shifted to the front foot in a flowing motion, to further compress the earth.

**Note:** If at any time an object, such as a stick is felt, the foot should be removed and placed in another area. Also at no time should the back foot push off, as this will tend to grind the earth.

When approaching within ten feet of an animal, children should squint their eyes, and never show the teeth. Animals quickly take notice of white teeth and the whites of the eyes. During cold weather, when the breath becomes visible, the breath should be directed along the body, so that the plumes of air are not visible to animals. In some cases children must crawl to get through more difficult landscapes. This can be easily accomplished by teaching children to move one limb at a time, and to compress the earth with knees and hands the same way feet compress the earth in the regular stalking position.

Begin teaching children to stalk by having them first sit in a chair and practice placing their foot correctly on the ground. Before moving on, make sure the children have memorized the step correctly and can do it in a slow and flowing motion. It helps to have the children practice freezing in the various stages of the foot position, so they don't feel uncomfortable when actually doing the step in the standing position. Then, have the children stand and go through several stalking steps. This will enable you to correct any position that is not done correctly. Keep in mind that it is best to start children stalking on the lawn, then move them to more and more difficult ground as their skill increases.

Once the children have thoroughly mastered the stalking step, you are ready to play the stalking game. The game can be played in a group or with one child. The parent or teacher plays the part of an animal, such as a feeding deer, and duplicates as closely as possible the actions of that deer. The child or children should then stalk the parent, freezing anytime the parent looks toward them. Anytime a sound is made or a motion detected, the parent should point it out so the child can correct it right away. When a group is playing, any child who makes a sound should sit down. The last child left standing is the winner of the game.

A variation of the same game is to have the parent, or even another child, sit on the ground blindfolded. In front of that person should be placed an object that the stalker will pick up and take back to the starting line. Now have the child or children line up and begin to stalk the blindfolded person. If that person hears a sound, he or she points, and the child must sit down. The child who stalks to the bait and brings it back to the starting line is the winner. As the child or children get better, increase the difficulty of the landscape, until they become proficient stalkers on all types of ground cover.

## CLOTHING AND FOOTWEAR

It is best to stalk barefoot. Barefoot, children are more sensitive to the ground and the objects that will make noise. In colder weather, moccasins are best, the lighter the better. No one can stalk in shoes or boots because there is no way to feel the ground, though children can stalk reasonably well in low, well-worn tennis shoes. I suggest that children make their own moccasins from a kit, which will also give them a sense of accomplishment.

The best type of clothing for stalking is a bathing suit. Children must be able to feel the landscape and brush with their bodies so they can get around it without crushing through. In cold weather, it is best to wear clothing that will not "whistle" when scraping against brush. Wool and napped cotton are great when it comes to being soundless in brush.

Another consideration is camouflage. Generally any type of soft camouflage clothing will work well, but darker-patterned clothing will also do just fine. It is important not to wear a solid color, but a check or a plaid, to break up the outline of the body. If children do not camouflage the scent of their bodies, then they will have to stalk animals only from the downwind side. To mildly camouflage body scent, children should wash with a natural soap, then crush up a fragrant, nontoxic plant and apply it to their arms, legs, feet, face, and chest. The same plant can be brewed like a tea, the liquid strained and put into an atomizing bottle, and sprayed on the body. (For better descenting refer to *Tom Brown's Field Guide to Wilderness Survival.*)

When learning to master stalking, children should strive to make it an unconscious action. It should become second nature, much like the unconsciousness of *natural* walking. To put it simply, if children have to think about the stalking movement, then they will probably make a mistake. Frequent practice commits stalking to the subsconscious.

**Caution:** Though stalking will often and easily allow children to get close enough to touch an animal, *under no circumstances* should children actually touch one. Even though an animal may seem relatively harmless or "cute," most animals can deliver a nasty bite or scratch if touched or cornered. Other animals, such as deer, can also deliver a damaging kick.

# 4

# TRACKING

Tracking is the ultimate extension of awareness. Without the ability to track, less would be seen, known, or understood about animals. The importance of tracking and of learning how to track cannot be stressed enough. It will open up a whole new dimension of understanding for children. With the ability to read tracks, children will be able to understand the secret lives of animals and each animal's relation to others and to the environment. Tracking is nothing less than an intricate art form and a science, complicated at times, yet easily understood by children.

Teaching children to track is like teaching children to read a book. The individual tracks are letters, and the trails form words, sentences, and paragraphs describing in detail a portion on each animal's life. Once children have learned to read the basics, the earth is no longer looked upon as just soil, but an open book or a journal. Thus each animal is an author whose words are printed by foot. Once children begin to read the ground, they will realize there is no bare ground, for each mark, each pock, crevasse, crack, dent, and disturbance is a track. In essence, each trail, each track, no matter how old, is like a window to the past, enabling one to understand a page, a part, or a chapter of an animal's life.

I will always remember the first time I became interested in a track. Rick and I were exploring an area we called Turtle Run. While searching mud flats, we came upon a huge track, one that was so big, we thought we had found that fearsome beast, the Jersey Devil. We ran to get Grandfather and told him what we had found. I guess we were so excited we babbled, and I doubt he understood anything except that we were asking about a track. We practically dragged him to the area, but had him approach the track alone. We were just too frightened to get too close to a track that could have been made by the Jersey Devil.

As he looked down at the track, he appeared to open a huge invisible book. He began to read, telling us the track had been made by a huge dog and that because the dog had turned and slid in the mud, the track appeared large. He said the dog had been interested in a rabbit that had a nest of babies in a nearby bush, but the rabbit, sensing danger, had bolted from the nest, leading the dog away from her young ones. We ran to the bush, to where he pointed, and magically there was a nest of baby rabbits, just as Grandfather had said. We were amazed, shocked, that he could read all this from such a distance, and we began to see how tracks could direct us to so many usually hidden treasures of nature. Grandfather read on, telling us of a mink that had hunted the waterways, raccoons that had searched the banks, muskrats that had dragged sticks, deer that had come to the water to drink, and of an owl that had killed a mouse near the shore. He read back day after day, animal after animal, making our heads reel with information we would have normally passed by. Then he read back tracks that were over two hundred years old, pointing to the depression of an ancient trail ending at a depression where a trapper's cabin once stood. I was hooked, and hooked for life.

But Grandfather didn't just follow the tracks, he read each track thoroughly. One track would reveal every movement, every turn of the head, every ear flick, tail flick, and muscle tremor. He could tell if the animal was nervous, or at peace. He could tell the sex of an animal, its size, weight, and general age, as well as the age of the track. He could close his eyes and actually see the animal moving through the tracks, with every movement, every emotion, and every purpose. We began to understand that tracking involved more than just following trails toward some end, for the true art of tracking gleans every nuance of information from each track.

From that day on, we saturated ourselves with tracks. We followed tracks, drew tracks, measured tracks, and learned new tracks each day. Everywhere we went, we stopped, fell to our knees, and read the ground. We progressed slowly, from easily read soils and mud, to areas of ground cover and beyond, always pushing our senses. From that first track, encountered at the age of eight, I swore that someday I would be able to do what Grandfather had done that day he read all the tracks at Turtle Run, and to this day, I am still building on that process started over thirty years ago.

When teaching children to track, it is not enough just to identify the track, but you must build a firm foundation of tracking basics. Once the basics are understood, the rest is easy, for children can then learn on their own. Children love to be detectives and solve mysteries, and trackers have to be detectives, for each trail is a series of never-ending mysteries. We cannot teach children the full science of tracking because it tends to get very complicated, but we can teach them enough to make them good trackers. The science will come later in life, as children mature, and if their interest in tracking becomes acute. What follows is the basic study of tracking, at a level any child can understand.

## MEASURING TRACKS

Measuring tracks is not only important for staying on the trail and identifying the animal from other similar tracks, but it gives a better understanding of how animals move. The first measurement that should be taken is the length and width of each foot. The length is taken at the longest part of the track, *not* including the claw marks, and the width is taken at the widest part of the track. It is important to note that no two feet on an animal, or human, have exactly the same measurements. The next measurement is the stride, which is measured from the animal's toes, to the toes of the opposite foot. In a human, the stride is measured from the heel of one foot to the heel of the opposite foot. In other words, the stride is taken from the left foot to the right foot, or vice versa. (*See illustration on following page.*)

The next measurement is the straddle, which is measured from the inside of the heel of one foot to the inside heel of the opposite foot. (*See illustration on following page.*) The final measurement is the trail width, which is taken from the outside of one foot to the outside of the other. (*See illustration on following page.*) At this point it is not necessary to teach the child to read the pitch or the true track, for it becomes too complicated. These basic measurements will help a child follow a trail easily, especially when other tracks are involved. However, the most important measurement is the animal's stride, which is the most basic measurement for following an animal.

**Note:** Though children should learn to use a ruler and tape measure, this is not required here. A simple measuring device can be substituted, called the "tracking stick," which will do away with having to remember a lot of numbers. (See the section, The Tracking Stick, in this chapter.)

## CLASSIFYING ANIMAL TRACKS

Certainly a field guide to animal tracks is helpful in teaching children to identify tracks, but there are easier methods. In the following section, children will learn how to identify and classify animal tracks just by looking at the track or track pattern. The *clear print classification* method

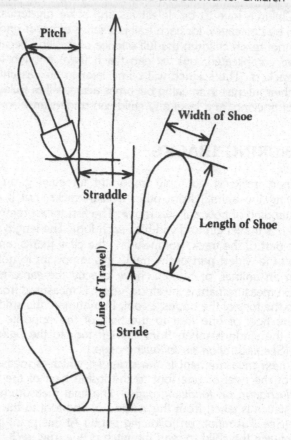

can be used when tracks are very clear, when children can see the toes, the heel pads, and the claw marks, if any. The *pattern classification* will be used by children when the track is unclear, just a depression in the ground. This method is used on the more difficult tracking soils and terrains.

Most tracks consist of several different elements. The toes, of course, are the front of the track, and are divided into two categories: the inner toes, which are at the center or middle of the track, and the outer toes, which are the outermost toes, on both sides of the track. (*See illustration.*) Next is the heel pad, the claw marks, and the toe ridges, which are the spaces between each toe and between the toes and the heel pad.

## CLEAR PRINT CLASSIFICATION

I believe that a very simple number method is the best way to teach children and adults alike how to classify clear animal tracks. All children have to do is remember the number of toes on one front foot and the number of toes on one hind foot to identify that animal. Most animal prints have the front and rear of one side of the body close to each other in the track, so it is best to do it in this way. The children will also have fewer large numbers to remember, which will make it easier for them to identify tracks.

## $4 \times 4 \times No\ Claws = The\ Cat\ Family$

### Feral House Cat

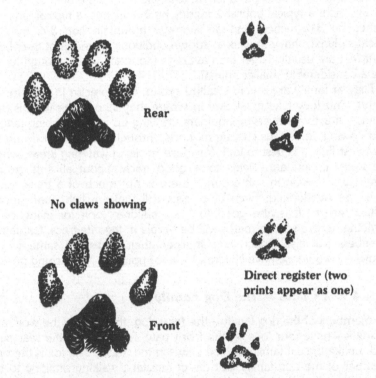

Rear

No claws showing

Direct register (two
prints appear as one)

Front

What the numbers mean is there are four toes on the front feet and four toes on the rear feet, and there are usually no claws visible in the front feet. The members of the cat family I will be dealing with in this book are the feral cat, the bobcat, the mountain lion, and the lynx. Generally all cats have zero pitch and zero straddle when walking, and they usually direct-register. In fact, cats are the only full family of animals that direct-register when walking. What this means is when the front foot is picked up off the ground, the rear foot on the same side of the body falls directly into that track. Of course, if the animal is in the process of turning, speeding up, or slowing down, it may not direct-register.

Also, the front feet of cat family members are considerably larger than the rear. If children look closely they may be able to see the smaller rear foot shadowing the inside of the front. All members of the cat family also have particularly round footprints. This will be of great help when tracking cats in a compression-and-pattern type of situation, which we will discuss later in the chapter. Generally the type of terrain, the area, and the cat's habits will distinguish the various cat family members. But children can also measure the tracks and accurately identify the animal. A typical feral cat track has a length and width measurement of 1½ inch by 1½ inch, a typical bobcat 2 inches by 1⅞ inches, a typical lynx 3¾ inches by 3¾ inches, and an average mountain lion 3¼ by 3½. Because lynxes have to walk in snow conditions for much of their lives, their feet are usually larger than average mountain lion's, though lynxes are a considerably smaller animal.

The cat family are a very stealthy group, very precise in their movements, and they take great care in where they step. Their walk is very quiet, but active, traversing boulders, moving up trees, climbing ledges, and flowing, in curious curving motions, through transition and hunting areas. At first, it is best to look for these tracks in watering areas, where the earth is soft and yields to a good track. Scout all soft ground carefully, for even in soft ground, there is not much of a track and it could be overlooked. Even large cats will make a light mark in the softest terrain. It is also good to have children look for evidence of climbing, where scratch marks will be visible in favorite trees. Cat family members will also stretch and sharpen their claws the same way a house cat would, so have children look for potential "scratching posts."

### 4 × 4 × 4 Claws = The Dog Family

All members of the dog family—the feral dog, the coyote, the wolf, and all foxes—have four toes on the front paw, four toes on the rear paw, and, unlike the cat family, exhibit claws in the tracks. The fox is the only member of the dog family that direct-registers, walking similarly to the cat, with zero pitch and zero straddle. All the other members of the dog family, and all other diagonally walking animals (see Diagonal Walkers, this chapter) indirect-register when they are walking. Indirect register means that when the front foot is lifted from the ground, the rear foot on the same side of the body falls slightly behind and to the right or left, when walking only.

As in the cat family, all members of the dog family have slightly larger front feet than rear feet. But unlike the cat family, the dog family have

### Dog

Claws showing

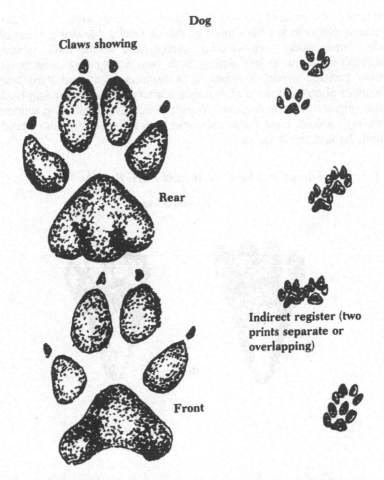

Rear

Front

Indirect register (two
prints separate or
overlapping)

very elliptic-shaped footprints when making compressions. Typically these prints are in the shape of an egg, with the wider end being the heel portion of the track. It is a little more difficult to tell the members of the dog family apart, mainly because feral dogs come in all shapes and sizes. But the feral dog print has the two inner toes larger than the two outer toes on every print. All other dog family members do not. The average length and width of a red fox track is 2⅜ inches by 2 inches, typical coyote 2⅝ inches by 2⅛ inches, and the average gray wolf 4¾ inches by 4¼ inches. Keep in mind that these are all front foot measurements and the rear foot will be slightly smaller.

Members of the dog family, though stealthy, are bold hunters and a little less careless in their walk. Though foxes will walk similarly to most cats, they tend also to follow the boldness of their other dog family relatives. Because of the way dog family members walk, their tracks are usually easier to see than those of the cat family. However, most of the dog family leave very winding, abrupt, and erratic trails, which are difficult to follow at first. Just as with your family dog, most dogs are very curious, especially when in a hunting area, and they tend to wander about, following their noses, sometimes even doubling back on the original trail. Have your children watch the family dog wandering through a field, or in the woods, and they will instantly understand the logic behind the dogs' trails.

## 4 × 4 × Claws = The Rabbit and Hare Family

Snowshoe hare

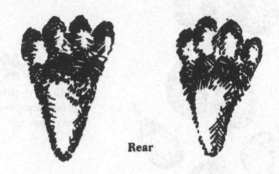

Rear

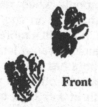

Front

Just like the cat and dog families, the rabbit and hare family have four toes on the front feet and four toes on the rear; however, the rear feet are usually two or more times larger than the front feet. The footprints also exhibit claw marks. The overall compression shape of the rabbits and hares looks like the top of a huge exclamation mark. This is because oftentimes rabbits or hares will bring down the entire foreleg and elbow with the foot, thus elongating the track. However, when moving quickly, only the foot and heel pad register, leaving a mushroom-cap–shaped compression mark.

There are many members of the rabbit and hare families, and the best way to differentiate among them is by habitat, habits, and area of the country. Many hares and rabbits are very close in size, and it is difficult to tell their tracks apart, especially because each individual can vary in size according to food availability. It would take the more advanced methods of indicator pressure releases to identify each individual at a glance, and pressure releases are just too complicated for a children's book. However, the length and width of the rear foot of a cottontail track is 2¾ inches by 1⅛ inches, a blacktail jackrabbit 2⅝ inches by 2 inches, with a whitetail jackrabbit track almost an inch larger. The snowshoe hare falls somewhere in between with the rear foot 3 inches by 2 inches.

Rabbits and hares are herbivores, living wherever there is adequate browse and good cover. They are hunted extensively by predators and tend to stick close to cover or in safe areas. In many cases, children will have to scout around and in brush for these tracks. Generally, however, these animals tend to come down hard, leaving a good solid print. If tracks of these animals are found in the open, then they were probably heading to a good feeding or cover area. Open trails are generally very straight and easy to follow.

### 5 × 5 × Claws = The Weasel Family

The weasels have five toes on the front foot, five toes on the rear foot, and claws found in the tracks. However, most weasels have very small heel pads compared with the size and surface areas of their toes. The weasel family comprises many individuals with varied habits, habitats, and sizes. Members of this group include the longtail, the shorttail, and the least weasel, all skunks, badgers, sea and river otters, the pine martin, the fisher, the wolverine, the minks, and the ferrets. Not only do the animal sizes and habits vary within this family, but so too do foot sizes. It is quite difficult to tell the weasel family members apart, and a good tracking field guide helps. I recommend *Field Guide to Animal Tracks*, by Olas Murie or *Tom Brown's Field Guide to Nature Observation and Tracking*. (For measurements of the weasel group, refer to track average chart in this chapter.)

Though weasels live a variety of life-styles, as a family they are tremendous hunters. Weasels are stealthy, silent, deadly, and fast, and their trails lace around the landscape with even more complication than that of the dogs. However, even though most of the weasel family

**Weasel**

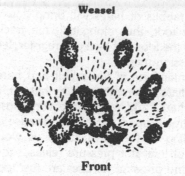

Front

Rear

is very secretive, they do leave good tracks. The best place to find weasel tracks is along waterways and in the soft ground around hunting areas. The compression shapes of the weasel family vary, but when viewing all four feet together in a pattern, the pattern appears boxy in shape and is easily distinguished from other patterns. (See Pattern Classification.)

## 5 × 5 × Claws = Raccoon, Opossum, and Bear

Though, like the weasel family, these animals have five toes on the front foot, five toes on the rear foot, and claw marks in the tracks, the tracks are easily distinguished from the weasel family. The raccoon, the opossum, and the bear tend to be very plentigrade, meaning flat-footed, and their prints appear very humanlike in character. The toes are not pads at all but very fingerlike, except for those of the bear. These animals have larger rear feet than front and tend to be very lumbering in appearance. Their tracks and trails are easy to find, especially along waterways, and most trails are relatively straight. However, when foraging, they can become erratic yet still easy to follow.

**Raccoon**

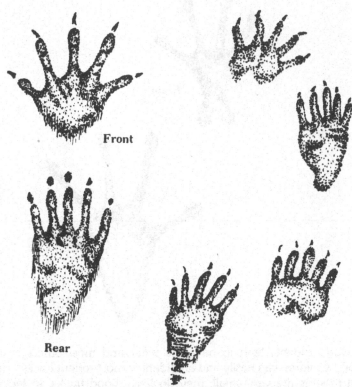

Front

Rear

## 4 × 5 × Claws = *The Rodent Family*

Most of the rodent family have four toes on the front foot, five toes on the rear foot, and claws found in the tracks. There are three exceptions to the rule of 4 × 5, however: the muskrat and beaver typically register 4 × 5, unless these animals get into deeper mud. When that happens, a little fingerlike appendage registers, and the animals then exhibit 5 × 5 registration. The other exception is the aplodontia of the Pacific Northwest, which registers 5 × 5 all the time.

The rodent family is a large, extensive, and varied group. Some members of the rodent family are all mice and rats, and tree squirrel, ground squirrel, muskrat, beaver, porcupine, and groundhog groups.

This family is so varied, there can be little else to use for identification of individuals besides measurements, combined with habits and habitat. (See track average chart.) The compression shapes of the rodents can vary from the cross shape, or ( + ) shape, to the shape of a fan. Typically

**Rodent**

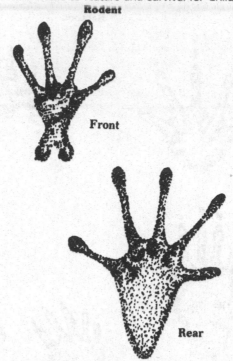

Front

Rear

the water rodents tend to have the latter and most others have the former. Children can easily find and identify most rodent tracks. Though most rodents are very small, they do leave good tracks. In fact, most people are startled to see what good tracks mice will leave, even in deep forest litter. Your children will have to gear their observations down to the minute, at times needing a magnifying glass to see the smaller tracks.

## 2 × 2 × Hooves = The Deer Family

The deer family have a two-part hoof on the front foot and a two-part hoof on the rear foot. It is a very extensive family and its members vary in size considerably, and include the whitetail, the blacktail, and the mule deer, moose, caribou, pronghorn antelope, bighorn sheep, mountain goat, colored piccari, and elk. Whitetail deer tracks can vary from under an inch long to 4 inches long, depending on the subspecies and on genetics and food; all other deer family members can vary considerably.

The front feet of all deer family members are slightly larger than the rear, and the typical compression shape of deer feet resembles an upside-down heart in shape. Deer family tracks are easy to find in all

**Deer**

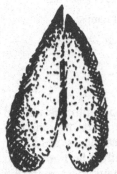

Dewclaws

Toes spread
when running

Front Foot: 3 (L) × 1⅞ (W) in.
Rear Foot: 2⅝ × 1½ in.
Trail Width: 6 in.
Slow Stride: 18-21 in.
Running: 6-9 ft.

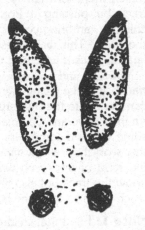

terrains, and children will have no difficulty locating them right away. Still, when the terrain is strewn with debris or develops a hard surface, the tracks may become obscured. I suggest you start off all children with tracking the deer. They are larger and easier than the other families and will give your children a solid foundation to build upon.

## Workshop

After you have explained the classification method for the various animal groups, then have the children make up a card containing all the information. A simple 3 × 5 file card will work well, and afterward you can put it in a plastic envelope to protect it from the weather. The card should look like this:

    4 × 4 × No Claws = The Cat Family

    4 × 4 × Claws = The Dog Family

$4 \times 4 \times$ Claws + huge rear feet = The Rabbit and Hare Family

$5 \times 5 \times$ Claws + small heel pads = The Weasel Family

$5 \times 5 \times$ Claws + flat-footed = Raccoon, Opossum, and Bear

$4 \times 5 \times$ Claws = The Rodent Family

$2 \times 2 \times$ Hooves = The Deer Family.

Once the card is completed, send the children out into the natural areas with the card, a drawing pad, and a pencil. Have the children search out soft areas, such as along waterways, on sandbars, mud flats, and any soft soil. Have them draw the clear tracks they find and try to match them to a family on the card. If you wish, have them mark the track by pushing a Popsicle stick in the ground nearby; that way children can bring you or the group back to the area where they found the track. This will be especially helpful if children are not sure what kind of track it was, or if their drawing is unclear.

You will find children will really enjoy going out and identifying the tracks. It is like giving them a key, or some secret code, with which they can penetrate the mystery of the tracks. Let them search out the tracks on their own, and you may be surprised how well they do. Undoubtedly some will find some very obscure tracks. Once the children have done this workshop a few times, take them into another area and specify the type of track you want them to find. Not only will they have to know the track but also the animal's habits and haunts as well; thus you teach them to track the landscape first, then the animal.

**Note 1:** I find that children will learn faster and remember more when they draw the tracks. This way the track is set in their minds, with more than just words.

**Note 2:** For younger children, or for children who have lived in a city for most of their lives, you may want to go out and show them several tracks before you turn them loose on their own. With very young children, it is also advisable to start with the larger tracks, such as deer, raccoon, or skunk.

## PATTERN CLASSIFICATION

This type of classification is used when there is no clear track, when there are no toe marks, claw marks, or heel marks, but just a vague depression in the ground. The first step is to identify the shape or outline of the track. This shape is called the compression shape, and will help the child find the family of animals to which it belongs. (Refer to the compression shapes in the Clear Print Classification section.) To further identify that track, children must learn to search around it, trying to find another similar depression. Children should then continue finding these depressions until they form a "pattern." It is from this pattern that we can fully determine the family. For an exact identification children will have to consider the habitat, overall trail, and actual measure of the pattern.

The following classification is for *walking* only. *Walking* is defined as when an animal is going somewhere with a purpose, toward a destination, and should not be mistaken for a *slow walk*, which will be discussed later in this chapter. Animals walk most of the time to conserve energy, and the only time they will ever change from a walk is when running from danger, in need of getting someplace fast. However, some animals do occasionally but rarely run for play.

### Diagonal Walkers

In this group are all members of the cat family, all members of the dog family, and all members of the deer family. What diagonal walkers do when they walk is to move opposite sides of the body at the same time. In other words, as the right front foot moves forward, so does the left rear. Most of the time the exact species of animal can be determined just by measuring the stride. There are a few animals that overlap one another in stride, but by taking into consideration the habitat, the geography, and what the trail teaches, we can generally determine the specific animal in question. It is also important to be aware that when diagonal walkers pick up in speed, their pattern changes. We will discuss these changes later on in the chapter.

**Note:** Remember, in reading patterns, it is difficult to tell if an animal is direct- or indirect-registering, for all we have is a depression and not a clear track.

### Bound Walkers

The weasel family are the primary members of this group, and fast or slow, the weasels will always try to maintain this pattern. This pattern is made when weasels push off with their back feet, landing on the front so the two feet are side by side, and bringing the rear feet up just behind the front. This pattern is continued, in clusters of four, with the stride measurements taken between each set of clusters. When one observes weasels' movement, one is reminded of a sewing machine needle, very elegant and very flowing, despite the up-and-down overall movement.

## Gallop Walkers

In this group are all members of the rodent family, and all members of the rabbit and hare family. This pattern is made when the animals push off with their rear feet, then hit with the front feet, either side by side or at a diagonal, depending on the species, then bring the rear feet around and past the front feet. Thus, in this pattern, the rear feet supersede the front feet. Explain to the children that when the front feet hit side by side, the track was made by a squirrel, but if the front feet hit diagonal to each other, then the track was made by either a ground-dwelling rodent, a rabbit, or a hare. Again, fast or slow, gallop walkers prefer to use this pattern most of the time. The patterns are set in clusters of four, like the bounding patterns, and stride measurements are taken between the clusters.

## Pace Walkers

These are the wide heavy animals, those that appear to be lumbering when they walk. The primary animals belonging to this group are the raccoon, the opossum, and the bear. Unlike the diagonal walk, which moves opposite sides of the body at the same time, the pacers move the same side of the body at the same time. In other words, as the right front foot moves forward, so does the right rear, and so on. Like the diagonal walkers, when moving faster, these animals will change their pattern. Stride measurements for the pace walkers are taken the same way as for the diagonal walkers.

## Workshop

The best way to teach children the various pattern classifications is to first describe a pattern and then draw it on the blackboard, or in the sand. Next the parent or instructor should slowly crawl through that pattern, so the children can see exactly what it looks like. Finally, have all the children crawl through each of the patterns. Now, children will intimately know what the pattern looks like, feels like, and exactly how an animal moves. You would be surprised how many people do not know how animals move and if you don't know the pattern, you can't track the animal.

**Note:** When children become more advanced and begin to follow trails, teach them to use the crawling, or "role playing," to help them figure out the animal trail. This crawling pattern method will also help out when tracks do not exactly fit the pattern and the children need to determine what the animal has done.

Please note that any animal is capable of doing any one of these patterns but an animal utilizing an uncharacteristic stride pattern is the exception and not the rule. However, it is best to make even the youngest children aware of this possibility so there is no confusion. Also, when diagonal walkers and pace walkers pick up in speed, they go to a trot, then to a bound, then to a lope, and finally to a gallop. In fact, between a pace and a gallop, there are nearly thirty-two different and identifiable pattern changes. That, however, is best left for the future and more advanced tracking science.

### The Slow Walk

There is a pattern many animals tend to use, besides their typical walking pattern, and this is called the slow walk. It is done when the animal is meandering, with no place in particular to go, and not in any hurry to get anywhere. The walk is executed as follows: The full body weight is pushed forward and the right rear leg starts forward. As the right rear foot touches the ground the right front foot starts forward, and as that foot touches the ground, then the left rear leg starts forward. Finally when the left rear foot touches the ground, the left front leg starts forward, and as soon as that touches the ground, the process begins again.

**Note:** It is a good idea to have children crawl through this one also.

### Sun Position

Learning to determine sun position is critical for beginning trackers. If the sun is high in the sky, there is going to be a shadowing of the tracks such that the tracks and the ground will look flat and lifeless. However, if the sun is at an angle to the ground, the tracks will have good shadowing; the ground will seem to come to life. It is best to have children track in the early morning, then again in the late afternoon or

Low-angle light is best. Keep the
tracks between you and the source of light.

early evening before sunset to take advantage of the best light conditions. Another important tracking rule for children to follow is to keep
the track between them and the source of light whenever possible. By
doing this, the tracks will literally pop off the landscape; even very
difficult, obscured tracks can be highlighted in this way.

### Workshop

One of the best workshops I know of for teaching the importance of sun
position also teaches children how to night-track at the same time. Have
the children gather around an open area of ground, so there is a wide
circle of earth in front of the parent or instructor. Now the parent or
instructor should hold a flashlight high overhead, pointed directly down
at the ground. This will wash out the ground, and there will appear to
be no tracks. Then the parent should move the light beam down toward
the earth, holding the flashlight and the beam parallel to the ground.
As the light is moved closer to the ground, the shadows will deepen
and the tracks will literally jump out at the kids. Their expressions
of awe and wonderment will long be remembered.

## *The Tracking Stick*

**Measuring length of foot**

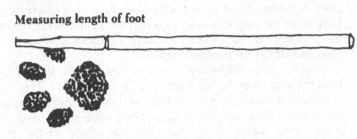

**Measuring length of stride (from toe to toe)**

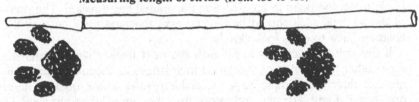

Probably one of the best devices for teaching children and adults how to follow tracks is the tracking stick. This stick enables the beginning tracker to follow a trail endlessly, even over the most difficult land-scapes. Essentially it is a measuring stick that allows children to know the measurements of a track without having to remember a lot of numbers. But more than that, the tracking stick helps the child find the next track by literally pointing right to it. (Though I believe in the use of the tracking stick for the first few years of tracking, I feel that it can become a crutch that slows the tracker down, and should be aban-doned as soon as a tracker's skill increases.)

The tracking stick is made from a long slender dowel that is pointed at one end. (Never use the tracking stick as a walking stick because it will dull the point and throw off the measurements.) Children can mark the measuring lines on the stick with a pencil or, better yet, use small rubber bands that are placed around the stick. This way the stick can be reused a number of times. (Primitive tracking sticks can be made quickly by finding a straight dead sapling, honing a point at one end, and using a sharp stone or knife to carve in a measuring line.

To mark the measurements of the track, hold the pointed end of the stick just above the tip of the track. Now move the rubber band, or make a mark, on the stick so that it is exactly over the heel of the track; from the point to the first mark is the length of the track. To determine the width of the track, hold the first mark over one side of the track and put another mark or rubber band directly over the opposite side. Now from the first mark to the second mark is the width measurement.

Finally, holding the tip, again, over the tip of the track, make a mark or place a rubber band on the stick directly above where the next track back is on the opposite side. In other words, the stride measurement of the stick will run from the tip, or point, of the stick to your third marker. (*See illustration on previous page.*)

Now, anytime children need to measure a track, all they have to do is hold the stick over the track and line up the markers. This measurement is not as accurate as a ruler, but it is accurate enough. As children follow the tracks, they will come to a point where the next track is not immediately visible. It is then the true magic of the tracking stick emerges. Holding the third marker over the center of the last visible track, direct the point in the direction the animal has traveled. The point of the tracking stick should be directly over the next track, and all the children have to do is look closely.

If the pointer ever fails to fall into the next track, then the animals have either lengthened or shortened their strides or they have turned in another direction. Simply have the children refer to the track at hand and see if there are any indicators that the animal has changed its walk. Also have the children use their own walks as indicators. If the children walk up a slight hill, the strides will shorten, and so too with animals. But if the children pay close attention to the track and the stick, it will be very rare that they cannot find the next track.

**Note:** One of the best ways to teach the use of the tracking stick is to have children track one another, or track the parent. This can be an exciting game for children.

### Plaster Casting

Probably one of the simplest activities used in track identification is the most delightful to children. Plaster casting of tracks helps a child to identify and preserve a track forever. Simply find a track, have the children mix up plaster by following the directions on the container, and slowly pour the plaster into the track, allowing it to overflow. Wait until the plaster hardens, then gently remove it from the ground. After an hour or more of thorough drying, the child can brush off the excess dirt and label the track. Anytime children wish to reconstruct the track, they can press the cast directly into damp sand, and the track is remade for further study. (Plaster casts used for this should be first coated in a liquid plastic to prevent water damage.) An assortment of plaster casts provides a good teaching aid, especially when teaching clear print classification, as well as being a fun and fascinating collection.

# SIGN TRACKING

I consider anything that is not compressed into the soil by a footprint to be a sign. Learning to read signs is the other half of tracking. They contain a wealth of clues that tell us so much about animals and their habits. Sign tracking is the ability to read landscapes, to pick up tiny shreds of evidence that build the overall picture of tracking into reality. Children take to sign tracking easily, and it is usually the first thing I teach children. With sign tracking children will not only be able to understand the secret life of animals but will be able to read the landscape at great distances. It will also enable them to pinpoint large concentrations of animals.

## *Landscape Tracking*

We must first start by teaching children to read the overall landscape. The landscape itself is a track, telling children where to find the most animals, and thus, leading children to good tracking areas. We will discuss here the landscapes that herbivores use, simply because where there are herbivores, there are also predators. Herbivores require three things in an area for survival. First, they need cover, thick vegetation that protects them from predation and the weather and allows them a safe place to raise their young. Second, they need a wide variety of vegetation, so that several sources of food are available to them throughout much of the year. It must also be in easy reach. Finally, they need a source of water, though this can be some distance away from their habitats. Some species can get their water from water-rich plants, or plants laden with dew, so the water source isn't always apparent at first investigation.

The depths of overgrown forests are poor areas for concentrations of animals. Certainly there will be animals there but not in large numbers. Deep forests have scanty underbrush and fewer reachable food plants. Fields, on the other hand, though rich in vegetation, have little cover and leave the animals unprotected. What children should look for are transition, or "fringe" areas. These areas are found between forest and field, or between field and stream, and along waterways. They have thick low tangles of vegetation that afford animals good protection and a good food source. It is in these areas the animals will be the most plentiful. Children should learn to spot these areas at considerable distances, and it would be a good idea to show these areas to the children from a distance, then take them into them to explore.

## PRIMARY SIGN

Remember this statement: Animals, like people, take the easiest route of travel unless pursued. Animals habitually seek the easiest routes of travel through the transition areas, to conserve energy and minimize injury. When many animals begin to take the same routes day after day, huge roadway systems are built into the transition areas, and many can be seen at a distance. It is on these roadway systems that children should begin to learn sign tracking, since it will teach the child how animals move through any given area, and these roadways are very easy to see and follow.

### Trails

By far, the largest pathways in the transition area are the trails. These trails are the super highways of the animal world and show heavy use. They are usually well worn, sometimes deep into the ground, where they form a troughlike route through the landscape. They are used by all animals, in all directions, and connect one end of the transition area to the other. Trails are rarely changed or abandoned. Most trails are devoid of vegetation and are easy for children to find. Building an animal blind by a trail will produce some of the best and most frequent animal sightings. (See The Blind, page 76.) Trails are one of the best places for survival hunting.

## *Runs*

Runs are less frequently used than trails and are specific both to what they are used for and the animal using them. They are also subject to change. Runs are less worn into the earth than trails and are usually characterized by broken, trampled, and matted vegetation. These are the backroads of the transition areas that carry animals to watering areas, feeding areas, and bedding areas. Generally these trails are the best for survival trapping, because children will know the specific animals that will come along. The size of the trail usually determines what animals are using them.

## *Beds*

Animal bedding areas are usually found in thick, heavy brush, which affords maximum protection from the elements and predation. Animal beds are well worn into the ground, showing continuous and long-term use. Bedding areas are typically hard to get to because they are placed

in ways that a predator will usually make noise when approaching and thus alert the sleeping animal. On the other hand, lays, or resting areas, are a one-time-use affair. Children will notice large depressions in the grasses and tangled brush. These depressions are the outline of an animal's resting body. During the course of the day or night, an animal may lie down to rest, creating these depressions. Again, they are usually used only once.

### Feeding Areas

There are several types of feeding areas, but two are the most prominent. They are recognized by the chewed and cut vegetation of the area, and are easily spotted from considerable distances. The first type of feeding area, comprising about twenty percent of the total is called a "patched" feeding area, and occurs where a run terminates at a rather large feeding area—a patch. The more prominent "varied run" feeding area is formed when animals are moving along a feeding run, nibbling here and there on their favorite plants along the way. The "varied run" feeding area usually constitutes about seventy percent of the total.

### Escape Routes

There are two types of escape routes: the "pushdowns" and the "established" escape routes. The pushdowns are one-time-use escape routes, recognized by their violently crushed and broken vegetation that leads off into thick vegetation in an erratic zigzag pattern. When pushdowns are used more than once, they are called established escape routes. These escape routes are made when animals are frightened or chased and forced to leave their trails, making it difficult for the usually larger predators to follow.

# SECONDARY SIGN

These are a wealth of smaller, more definitive signs that litter the trails and runs of the transition areas. Here children will have to learn to look closely and carefully, sometimes using a magnifying glass and tweezers to find many of the secondary signs. Children seem to love finding these secondary signs, for it entails unraveling some of the most exciting mysteries, and seems to capture their imaginations.

### Scratches

The landscape is littered with a wealth of scratch marks, ranging from those of a small mouse, to huge bear scratchings, and everything in between. Anytime animals cross debris they are bound to leave scratches. There are scratches left by animals climbing trees, digging for food, and excavating dens. Have children look for the scratch marks of squirrels climbing trees: these are the easiest to see. Then gradually introduce them to the more difficult scratch marks of the trails and runs.

### Chews and Gnawings

Gnawings are seen anytime animals attempt to gnaw through vegetation, wood, or even bone. The most classic examples of gnawing are the stumps left by beavers, but these are usually the largest and most dramatic. All gnawing animals will cut certain types of vegetation this way and often gnaw on bones or antlers to take in calcium. By measuring the size of the marks, children can learn to determine what has made the gnawing. Keep in mind that all predators and deer will also gnaw to some degree, and this measurement is taken from the size of the molar marks.

**Beaver gnawings,
showing evidence of sharp
chisel teeth**

Chews are seen anytime an animal bites off a twig, stalk of grass, or a bud. If the chew is sharp and angular, then it is caused by animals with incisors, such as rabbits, hares, or rodents. If the bite is squarish and a little frayed, then it is caused by a member of the deer family, and if the chew is ripped, punctured, and emaciated, then it is evidence of a predator chew. Predators do chew vegetation when they are ill, or when they have to supplement their diets. (*See illustration.*)

### Rubs

When animals are traveling along trails and runs, or when they are passing over, under, or around obstructions in the landscape, they will inadvertently rub themselves on that obstruction. Soon, with repeated

Incised
vegetation
(rodents)

Serrated
vegetation
(deer)

Chewed vegetation
(dogs & cats)

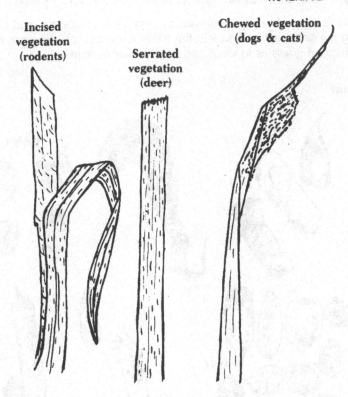

use, the areas will become slightly polished. Throughout the landscape these areas can be easily found, and are called "unintentional rubs."

"Intentional" rubs are made anyplace animals intentionally rub themselves, whether to scratch themselves or to remove velvet from antlers. Deer rubbing their antlers on a bush will produce a rub area. Raccoons scratching their backs on their favorite scratching post produce a rub area, and even birds taking dust baths will produce a rub area.

### Hair and Feathers

Animals are constantly losing hair and feathers. Looking closely at the landscape, children can easily find these signs and have one of the best clues to the exact animal. Learning to read this sign takes some practice, for it is a difficult one to learn through language description or visual depiction. Hands-on practice is really the only way to fully comprehend this aspect of tracking. The instructor must collect hair samples from dead animals, usually during hunting season, and tape them in a notebook. This way children can see and feel the various animal hairs and feathers. Usually, however, by deductive reasoning, and by knowing the animals that frequent the transition areas, children can make an educated guess as to what had left the hair or feather.

### Scat

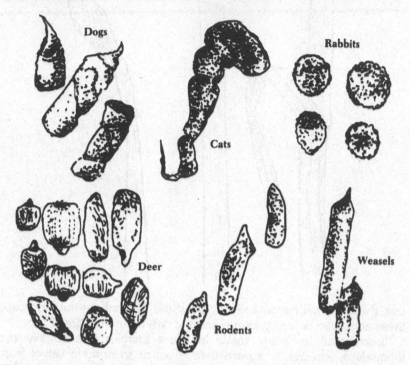

This is a very definitive area of sign tracking. By observing animal droppings not only can one tell what kind of animals deposited it but also exactly what those animals have been eating. I do not suggest that children handle or dissect scat, as is done in my advanced classes, since scat can carry disease. However, by simply observing scat—its shape and consistency—children can learn a great deal. (*See illustration.*)

### Broken Vegetation

As animals move through the landscape on their trails and runs, the plants are trying to grow back. As animals push through that evergrowing vegetation, they are bound to break or trample both new and old growth. Children should be made aware of these breaks, tears, and tramples, because they are of major importance to fully understanding the animals of a transition area. Broken vegetation can also aid children greatly when following a particular animal trail, or show children when animals have taken flight and created a pushdown.

## Workshop

Take the children into a good transition area and point out all the trails, runs, pushdowns, beds, lays, feeding areas, and chews, showing them how to read the landscape for sign. Teach them to look closely, to get down on their knees or bellies and scan the trails and runs. Whenever they find something of interest, have them call the parent over, and in some cases, the entire class should be shown the more interesting finds. You will be surprised how long children can lose themselves in transition areas discovering all the signs.

## Track Pack

One tracking aid children seem to love to put together and use is the track pack. The track pack contains all the equipment children need to help them with tracking. The pack should be small so it fits on the belt and is easily carried. The track pack should contain:

A SIX-INCH RULER, for measuring tracks.

TAPE MEASURE, for measuring strides.

TWEEZERS, for close work and removing small signs from the landscape.

MAGNIFYING GLASS, for close study of tracks or sign.

NOTEBOOK AND PENCIL.

SCOTCH TAPE, for taping hair samples in the notebook.

FLASHLIGHT, for night tracking.

POPSICLE STICKS, for marking tracks.

PLASTIC SANDWICH BAGS, for collecting sign.

More items can be added to the track pack as children's skill grows.

## The File Card Learning Method

One of the best ways to get children to learn the various tracks is the file card learning method. Over a period of time have the children draw an animal track on one side of a 3 × 5 file card, putting in the length and width of the track. On the reverse side have them write down helpful information about that animal such as habitat, food, and habits.

After the children have completed several of these cards, they can use them as flash cards to memorize the various animals. The children can also add them to the track pack and bring them into the field for quick reference.

Children's interest in tracking is quickly developed, but you as a parent and teacher must be ready to help them with their questions or to fire them up with new questions. I suggest the parent know most of this material before attempting to teach it to children. Familiar as you become with it, you will still be learning *with* your children each time you venture out. Tracking is not something that can be learned in a day, or even a year; each step of the learning process is a delightful adventure that children, indeed, all of us, can enjoy.

# TRACK CLASSIFICATIONS

| Group or Family | Toes Front | Toes Rear | Claws Showing? | Track Shape | Normal Gait | Gait Pattern, etc. |
|---|---|---|---|---|---|---|
| CAT | 4 | 4 | No | | Diagonal walkers | Direct Register |
| DOG | 4 | 4 | Yes | | Diagonal walkers | Indirect Register |
| RABBIT | 4 | 4 | Some | | Gallopers | |
| RODENT | 4 | 5 | Some | | Gallopers/ Pacers | Gallop |
| WEASEL | 5 | 5 | Some | | Bounders/ Pacers | Bound |
| RACCOON, OPOSSUM, BEAR | 5 | 5 | Yes | R   O   B | Pacers | |
| DEER | Hoof | Hoof | --- | | Diagonal walkers | |

# TRACK COMPARISONS AT A GLANCE*

| Animal | Page | Front Length | Front Width | Rear Length | Rear Width | Trail Width | Slow Stride | Running Stride |
|---|---|---|---|---|---|---|---|---|
| **CAT FAMILY** | | | | | | | | |
| House Cat (feral) | 137 | 1½ | 1½ | 1⅜ | 1⅜ | 3 | 7 | 12–40 |
| Bobcat | 138 | 2 | 1⅞ | 1⅞ | 1⅝ | 5 | 10–13 | 15–45 |
| Lynx | 139 | 3¾ | 3¾ | 3¾ | 3½ | 7 | 12–14 | 30–50 |
| Mt. Lion | 141 | 3¼ | 3½ | 3 | 3¼ | 8 | 14–17 | 36–72 |
| **DOG FAMILY** | | | | | | | | |
| Red Fox | 144 | 2⅜ | 2 | 2⅛ | 2 | 4½ | 10–14 | 18–36 |
| Gray Fox | 146 | 1⅝ | 1⅜ | 1½ | 1¼ | 3¾ | 8–12 | 18–36 |
| Coyote | 146 | 2⅝ | 2⅛ | 2⅜ | 2 | 5 | 13–16 | 16–50 |
| Gray Wolf | 149 | 4¾ | 4¼ | 4½ | 4⅛ | 7 | 16–18 | 25–54 |
| **RABBIT FAMILY** | | | | | | | | |
| Blacktail Jackrabbit | 151 | 1½ | 1⅛ | 2⅝ | 2 | 7½ | 9–12 | 48–144 |
| Whitetail Jackrabbit | 152 | 1½ | 1 | 3½ | 3 | 8 | 10–15 | 36–108 |
| Snowshoe Hare | 152 | 1½ | 1⅛ | 3 | 2 | 8 | 10–12 | 36–84 |
| Cottontail | 153 | ⅞ | ⅝ | 2¾ | 1⅛ | 6 | 7–2 | 15–36 |

*All measurements in inches.

# TRACK COMPARISONS (Cont.)*

| Animal | Page | Front Length | Front Width | Rear Length | Rear Width | Trail Width | Slow Stride | Running Stride |
|---|---|---|---|---|---|---|---|---|
| **RODENTS** | | | | | | | | |
| Meadow Vole | 156 | ³⁄₁₆ | ³⁄₁₆ | ¼ | ¼ | 1¼ | ½–1½ | 1½–4 |
| House Mouse | 156 | ¼ | ¼ | ⅝ | ⅜ | 1 | 2½ | 4–6 |
| White-footed Mouse | 156 | ¼ | ¼ | ⅝ | ⅜ | 1½ | 2½ | 4–6 |
| Norway Rat | 157 | ⅝ | ¾ | ⅞ | ⅞ | 3⅛ | 2½–5 | 5–8 |
| Bushytail Woodrat | 158 | ¾ | ½ | 1 | ⅝ | 2½ | 4½–7½ | 7½–10 |
| Chipmunk | 159 | ½ | ½ | 1⅛ | ¾ | 2 | 4–7 | 7–9 |
| Ground Squirrel | 160 | ⅝ | ⅜ | ⅞ | ⅝ | 2–3¼ | 2–7 | 7–15 |
| Red Squirrel | 161 | ½ | ⅜ | ⅞ | ⅝ | 4 | 5–9 | 9–30 |
| Gray Squirrel | 162 | 2 | 1⅜ | 2⅝ | 1¼ | 5 | 10–15 | 16–38 |
| Woodchuck, Marmot | 163 | 2⅛ | 1⅞ | 1⅝ | 1⅜ | 5 | 6–8 | 12–20 |
| Porcupine | 164 | 1¾ | 1¼ | 2¼ | 1½ | 8 | 6–10 | 10–24 |
| Muskrat | 165 | 1 | 1 | 2 | 2 | 3½ | 3–6 | 7–15 |
| Beaver | 166 | 2 | 2 | 5 | 5¼ | 8–11 | 4–6 | 7–24 |

*All measurements in inches.

# TRACK COMPARISONS (Cont.)*

| Animal | Page | Front Length | Front Width | Rear Length | Rear Width | Trail Width | Slow Stride | Running Stride |
|---|---|---|---|---|---|---|---|---|
| **WEASEL FAMILY** | | | | | | | | |
| Shorttail Weasel | 168 | ¾ | ⅜ | 1 | ½ | 2¾ | 7–12 | 12–16 |
| Longtail Weasel | 169 | 1⅛ | ½ | 1½ | ¾ | 2¾–3¼ | 10–13 | 14–18 |
| Least Weasel | 169 | ⅜ | ¼ | ⅝ | ⅜ | 1 | 6–8 | 8–12 |
| Mink | 170 | 1 | 1⅜ | 1⅛ | 1½ | 3 | 9–20 | 20–30 |
| Marten | 171 | 1¾ | 1¾ | 1⅜ | 1⅝ | 5–6 | 6–9 | 10–23 |
| Fisher | 172 | 3 | 3 | 2⅞ | 2⅝ | 4–8 | 12–18 | 19–30 |
| River Otter | 172 | 2⅝ | 3 | 2⅞ | 3⅛ | 6 | 15–18 | 18–30 |
| Wolverine | 173 | 4½ | 4½ | 3½ | 3⅜ | 10 | 16–18 | 19–36 |
| Spotted Skunk | 174 | ⅞ | 1 | 1⅛ | 1¼ | 6 | 4–6 | 8–12 |
| Striped Skunk | 175 | ⅞ | 1⅛ | 1½ | 1½ | 7–9 | 5–8 | 10–18 |
| Badger | 176 | 2⅛ | 2 | 2 | 2 | 9–11 | 9–12 | 12–24 |

*All measurements in inches.

# TRACK COMPARISONS (Cont.)*

| Animal | Page | Front Length | Front Width | Rear Length | Rear Width | Trail Width | Slow Stride | Running Stride |
|---|---|---|---|---|---|---|---|---|
| **RACCOONS, OPOSSUMS, BEARS** | | | | | | | | |
| Raccoon | 177 | 3 | 3 | 3¾ | 3⅜ | 8–10 | 12–16 | 16–28 |
| Opossum | 178 | 1⅞ | 2 | 2½ | 2¼ | 6 | 7–10 | 10–15 |
| Black Bear | 179 | 4½ | 4 | 6⅞ | 3½ | 14 | 18 | 24–60 |
| Grizzly Bear | 180 | 5½ | 5⅛ | 9⅞ | 5⅝ | 18 | 18–20 | 36–72 |
| **DEER FAMILY** | | | | | | | | |
| Whitetail Deer | 181 | 3 | 1⅞ | 2⅝ | 1½ | 6 | 18–21 | 72–108 |
| Mule Deer | 182 | 3¼ | 2⅝ | 3⅛ | 2½ | 6 | 21–24 | 72–180 |
| Elk | 183 | 4¾ | 3 | 4¼ | 2⅞ | 8 | 26–28 | 72–108 |
| Moose | 184 | 6 | 3½ | 5⅝ | 3½ | 9–10 | 30–33 | 96–120 |
| Mountain Goat | 185 | 3 | 1⅞ | 2⅝ | 1½ | 6½ | 15 | 48–72 |
| Bighorn Sheep | 186 | 3½ | 2½ | 3 | 2 | 7–8 | 18–23 | 72–108 |

*All measurements in inches.

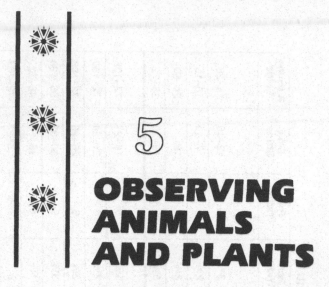

# 5

# OBSERVING ANIMALS AND PLANTS

The more children know about a plant or animal, the more they are likely to really *see* that plant or animal. Begin the animal and plant studies by consulting a good field guide, such as those in the Peterson Field Guide Series. Go out into the field with the children and help them learn to use the guides. Have them learn more than the animal or plant names; study the habitats and the life cycles. Teach them to know the spirit of the plants and animals more than the names. Once the children have mastered some basic identifications, it is then time to teach them how to fully observe the plants and animals. The following is a list of helpful workshops for knowing and observing various plants and animals.

## OBSERVING ANIMALS

### The Blind

A blind will allow children to sit, undetected by animals, in the landscape.

The first thing children should do when setting up a blind is pick the absolute best location. To do this, have them enter a transition area and study the trail network from afar, picking the most heavily used trails. The children should then choose an area near the trail affording the best natural cover yet giving a good view of the trail system and surrounding transition area. Better yet if the blind is also near the feeding areas, since the animals will be stationary for a while while feeding, affording the children a better and longer look. It is good to keep in mind that the children should never walk near the trails, for their presence there will certainly disturb the landscape, and subsequently the animals.

Building the blind is going to create some noise and activity, but the children should always build as quietly as possible. Using string and sticks, the children should build a loose frame toward the side facing the trail. In some areas, because animals may be all around the blind, it is best to put up four sides. Next the children should place natural vegetation all the way around the blind, anchoring it into position with the string. They should make the vegetation look as natural in the setting as possible, while making sure they can still get a good view of the trail. Sometimes the children may want to put a small stool inside the blind to make the stay more comfortable.

Once the blind is finished, it should be abandoned for a few days to allow the animals to return to their normal activity and to get used to the blind. Whenever approaching the blind, the children should always take the same route of travel, and move as silently as possible. With the concealing cover of the blind, the children are, to a certain degree, free to move, though all sound must be minimized. The best time for observing from a blind is in the early morning or in the late afternoon just before sundown. If the children are patient enough, they will be rewarded with a grand show of wildlife, and will begin to know the animals on an intimate level.

## The Cover Sit

The cover sit is similar to the blind, but it involves no building. The area is chosen the same way, only the children should seek out spots where the heaviest brush affords concealment yet good visibility. The children should stalk to the brush, moving into it as quietly as possible. Once inside the cover, they should position themselves in the most comfortable way, while also finding the best view of the trails or feeding areas. Unlike within the blind, the children have to take care with all movements. Though the brush will conceal much of the children, every movement must be done in a slow and fluid motion, much like stalking. Some children may want to bring along an old pillow or boat cushion to make sitting more comfortable.

## The Known Animal Blind or Cover Sit

The only difference in approach between the blind or cover sit and this is that the children know exactly what animal they are going to observe. Generally beaver dams, bird nests, deer bedding areas, dens, burrows, and the like are the most likely sites for a cover sit or blind. Building a blind in these areas, however, may permanently disturb animals. In these instances, it is best to build the blinds a good distance away and use binoculars to view the animals. Birds' nests should always be viewed from several yards away without building a blind. Whenever children deal with nesting birds or animals with young, greater care should be taken in approaching the area. Alarmed animals may abandon their young, or attack.

The children will have to determine the best time of day to observe these known animal locations. Animals in these areas usually live on some sort of schedule, and it is best for the children to get into these areas long before the animals come out since this will be the easiest time to approach the area without disrupting it. Children can also find a good cover sit position by observing the "sighted animal track time." This usually takes a little skill in the ability to age tracks, but it produces great results. Say children find deer tracks on a particular trail at the same time every morning. All the children need to do then is to get there before the deer do, and their wait will not be so long.

**Note:** A good way to determine the time animals use a particular trail is by using the "sweep method." The children select a trail and carefully sweep it of all tracks. Then, carefully returning at various times of the day, they can see when tracks are made. If the same tracks are made at the same time every day, then they have found a good cover sit area.

### The Observation Walk

The observation walk is a method of moving through a transition area and maximizing children's awareness and possible animal sightings. This walk is not a stalk, but it should be slow and deliberate, though it is not meant to be absolutely soundless. The purpose of the observation walk is simple enough—it breaks a bad habit. Children, and adults, usually walk through natural areas far too quickly, viewing phenomena from their usual height, hardly ever observing from different angles or with any plan. The object of the observation walk is to teach children to slowly and methodically search out a transition area, scanning the landscape with the utmost awareness.

To teach children the observation walk, have them first scan the landscape in semicircular fashion. Have them start by looking at the treetops, then slowly moving their heads back and forth, moving down the trees to the distant brush, then the near brush. As the children begin to scan closer to where they are standing, have them slowly squat down and follow the same sequence until they have thoroughly scanned the landscape up to a few feet in front of them. Teach them to bend back and forth, up and down, to look around bushes and tree trunks. Once this scanning is complete, have them take a few slow steps and then repeat the process. Within ten feet, they will see more animals than they would have if they had walked through at normal speed. In fact, because their speed and motion are dead slow, most animals will ignore their presence.

# OBSERVING PLANTS

## *From Birth to Death*

Children should observe the life of a plant from birth to death. This is quite easy to do with trees, and plants that come back every year. All the children have to do is look up the tree or shrub in a field guide, then watch the leaves emerge from the buds, grow strong, then change color in the autumn, and fall off. However, the baby shoots that burgeon in spring have to be observed carefully. Many plants are difficult to classify when they are young, so children may have to continue observing until the plant matures enough to identify. Children should then recognize the plant when it comes up the following year. The plant should be observed right through death, so that the children know what the plant looks like in the winter. You would be surprised how many good herbalists do not know what a plant looks like when it first comes out in spring.

Children should place a marker near the plant they are studying, so each time they return to the area, they know exactly which plant they have been observing. You would not believe how many plants grow up and around your children's plant, interfering with the plant, and sometimes even choking it off in competition. I would also suggest that the children go out to observe the plant several times a week, especially in the spring when growth and change are rapid. During the summer and fall, they would only have to go out once a week, for there is little change during those seasons.

## *Plant Habitat Study*

When observing and studying plants, children should learn to identify the areas the plants are found in. Do the plants like low levels of light? Damp soil? Dry soil? Sandy soil? Do they like growing in forests? In fields? Or along waterways? Teach your children to study how plants grow, what makes them grow faster or slower, what other plants are found around them, and especially what animals may feed upon them and live in, or under, them. Your children should also study the insects that seem to associate themselves with those plants, and what role the plants take in the balance of the overall landscape. Teach them to study all parts of the plants, from the stems to the leaves and seeds, so they will know them when they find them discarded in winter. Knowing plants in this way broadens children's knowledge of plants and how they are interconnected with all things around them.

## *Drawing Plants*

Probably one of the best ways for children to remember a plant is to have them draw it. Drawing plants forces children to look closely at the intricate detail that would go unnoticed by the casual observer. It is not important that the children be good artists, for the act of drawing in itself will bring the children close to the plant. The important point here is not the finished product but the process of getting the child to look closely and carefully. Make sure if a child misses something about the plant, like a hairy stem, you point it out. This encouragement can only help children look closer.

## Pressing Plants

One way many herbalists learn to identify plants is by using a plant press. Plant presses can get very sophisticated, but your children need not go to that much trouble. All that is needed are two pieces of plywood about 2 feet × 2 feet, with several holes drilled through to let moisture escape; some white construction paper; and some common blotter paper. When the plants are collected, they are placed on the blotter paper and covered with a sheet of white paper. The papers are then sandwiched between the plywood sheets, and pressed with the weight of a cinder block. This should be done in a cool, dry place, and left undisturbed for a few weeks. The plants can then be transferred to a notebook, or a spiral-bound photo album and labeled.

**Note:** Children can also dry plants and flowers by hanging them, upside down, in a cool, dry place for several weeks. Some flowers retain much of their original color and can be used for decorating purposes, or stored for future reference.

## Wildflower Garden

If children live in the suburbs or even in the city, they can bring a part of nature into the home with them. The wildflower garden is one of the better teachers, and it takes very little care. During outings, the children should collect wildflower seeds throughout late summer and fall, keeping them separate and labeled. The following spring the child can plant them in a garden plot that has been set aside. (This is their garden, and they should have the responsibility for its upkeep and watering.) Help children plant the seeds, creating the most natural garden landscape possible. Label the area in which the seeds are placed so the children can watch the plants grow from seedlings. The wildflower garden will not only teach your children, but bring nature home, and beautify your yard.

**Note:** Though I think it best for children to be able to collect seeds from their natural environments, sometimes it's simply not possible. If this is the case, keep in mind that many seed catalogs carry wildflower seeds.

# OBSERVING NATURE AT HOME

Children often feel they have to be in parks, national forests, or wilderness areas to practice their awareness skills. Actually nature is all around them and they do not have to go very far outside to discover its secrets or practice their skills. Reprinted here is a section from *Tom Brown's Field Guide to the Forgotten Wilderness*, which I think is pertinent and important to this book and your children. It will give your children a new outlook on their home and "backyard." Sometimes, it may even be helpful to read the following to your children.

As Rick and I sat and worked that second night in the Pine Barrens, we were engaged in conversations about the future. We each had visions of how we wanted to see and explore all this country's grand wonders, visions of the Grand Canyon, Yosemite, the Everglades, and the Black Hills. By comparison, the Pine Barrens seemed uninteresting and because we had spent so much time there, a bit boring. We felt that we knew the Pine Barrens quite well and that the prospect of new discovery was slight. Grandfather had been sitting nearby listening without comment to our conversation. We urged him to come over and tell us of the grand places he had lived and some of his adventures in the more awesome parts of the world. This was the beginning of one of the greatest lessons of my life, one I will never forget.

Grandfather told us that he had recently taken one of the most fascinating journeys of his life, one that rivaled anything we were talking about. We listened to his every word, imagining some wild and distant place as he described an exotic junglelike setting with huge herbaceous trees. In this jungle there were all manner of creatures, some docile, some very dangerous; boulders were of pure quartz; and the perils and adventures of this place were utterly fantastic. We listened for hours to the description of this place, yearning to go and visit it, for it was like no other place we had ever heard about before. When his story was finished, we asked him where this paradise was located. He said plainly, "Rick's front lawn."

We were floored. Never in my life had I ever heard anyone describe something as boring as a well-manicured lawn so enticingly. I scoffed at his words. "Go look at the lawn" was all he replied.

And so we would upon our return from the Pine Barrens, but all I could think of was how boring it would all be. I knew also that whenever Grandfather asked me to sit or look at something, it usually meant for quite a few hours. So I resigned myself to his instructions, and Rick and I went to his house. Grandfather placed us in the center of the lawn and told us to lie on our bellies. What unfolded before me was an adventure more intriguing, more vividly alive and wondrous even than what Grandfather had described.

Within moments I was hopelessly lost in this jungle of grass. I saw shapes, colors, textures, and things I could never have imagined. There was a whole world down there that I would not have believed could be so beautiful or intriguing. Tiny plants and fungi littered the grass forest floor. Miniature stones took on odd shapes, colors, and textures; some were dark brown, others black, some even crystal clear. The very earth itself was a marvelous blend of tiny jewellike boulders, minuscule tracks, bits of plants, and sundry other mysterious items. The earth was littered with bits and pieces of the animal world: insect parts, hair, claws, whiskers, tiny teeth, bits of skulls. There were seeds of all descriptions, flower parts—so many other things that a list would easily fill a notebook.

More intriguing still was the life-and-death struggle going on right under my nose. Wolf and jumping spiders stalked the grasses for unsuspecting insects, bringing them down as a mountain lion brings down a deer. Denizen fed on plants; some burrowed into the earth, and some laid eggs on the underside of plants. All this activity, beauty, intensity, and variation of life was found in barely a square foot of lawn. Never had I realized how much life I passed by every day without seeing. I understood fully from Grandfather's lesson that I could find a beauty and rapture of the senses anywhere I looked—if only I knew how. I will never again pass by even the most mundane landscape without knowing the myriad of things that are there, beyond man's conceitful eye.

I learned that I didn't have to go to distant, exotic places to find the grand vistas. By training myself to see, to break down some old prejudices, I found the splendor of nature in the "forgotten" wildernesses. The problem with most people today is that they seek the ultimate thrills and the grandiose entertainment even when they venture outdoors. We mistakenly admire the person who has toured the greater wonders of the world and ignore the people who seek out the little pockets of nature. And yet those who know how to look close possess a greater understanding of the oneness of nature. When they do finally face the grand and beautiful panoramas, they will know them in a much deeper way. They will fully understand the connection between the grandest mountain and the smallest blade of grass, and how each is dependent upon and a reflection of the other.

## LAWNS

The first rays of the morning sun dance across the lawns, causing them to glitter like some semitransparent, greenish glass. Droplets of dew sparkle and generate fiery rainbows. Small bejeweled spiderwebs look like tiny hammocks carelessly tossed across the blades. Because the tiny inhabitants are still chilled by last night's cold, there is no apparent movement in the grass. A robin alights momentarily on the shady lawn, then hops across to a sun splash. There, in the warm puddle of light, it pauses and cocks its head as if to listen or get a better view. Instinct tells it that the first insects or worms will begin to appear from this area as the sun stirs their inner fires and their cold blood warms to movement. Except for the robin, all seems frozen in time, dew, and sunshine.

The robin takes a few quick jumps forward, pauses for an instant, then pecks at the ground. There is a slight movement in the grass, and the robin pecks again, this time pulling a struggling worm from the earth. A few quick bounces and the robin is airborne, heading back to its nest, probably to feed its young. A good tracker knows that if a robin happens to eat the worm there on the ground, there are probably no young. Unless it suspects some predator is about, however, the robin will usually head straight back to the nest. By following the line of flight from a hidden position and repeatedly watching the robin collecting and feeding, the nest can easily be located and observed.

At this time I can either go back to the lawn for more study or get involved in the robin's activities. If I choose to stay with the robin for a while, I will make it a project that will last several days. For a long time, and at some distance, I watch the robin feeding her young. I do not want to alarm the mother, or interfere with the feeding schedule, but little by little, I move closer to the nest. This could take quite some time and a lot of patience, but it is well worth the effort. If the procedure moves into the second day, I will repeat the first day's efforts, only a little more quickly. With patience, and showing no threat to the robin, I will soon be accepted as part of the landscape, and the robin will go about its business as if I were not there.

I have had many intimate relationships with robins initiated in just this manner. On occasion, I have dug worms and fed the babies, apparently with the parent bird's approval. Sometimes the parent actually seemed relieved that someone else was helping with the task of feeding. One particular family of robins became my closest friends through a good deed I once did while feeding the babies. When I first arrived one morning, I noticed a snake was making its way to the nest and the parent robins were frantically screaming. I quickly came to the rescue and removed the snake, releasing it far from the area. Early one morning, a few days after I had removed the snake, the mother robin began pecking frantically at my bedroom window. I ran from the house, following her to her nest, where I found another snake on its way up the lower branches. Again I intervened and removed the snake.

Over the next few weeks, the parent robin and I became close friends. It would wait patiently on my shoulder until I finished feeding the babies, then swoop down and lend a hand when I had finished. When I dug worms, it would be waiting right beside me, plucking out worms I would otherwise have missed. The summer quickly passed, but we remained friends through it all and I even helped the young learn to fly. It was like raising my own children, and I was proud of them all. Surprisingly, the next spring there came a tapping at my window, and there was my robin friend and her mate. They were in the process of building another nest, and I would watch for hours the whole process. Of course, I helped by gathering twigs and grass stalks, which they readily accepted, but they didn't like the way I weaved the sticks into the nest. Every time I placed in a stick, it was rearranged. Despite my poor nest-building skills, the nest was finally completed, eggs laid, and I was a father again for another season.

Back at the lawn, the sun slowly dries the dew and the grasses warm and dull as the last of the lustrous dewy coat disappears. As the warmth begins to penetrate deeper, the inhabitants awake and begin to move. Lawns are like no other place on earth. They have an ambiance, a mood, and an appearance all their own. If, in fact, you could pretend that you were only an inch tall, the whole realm of the lawn would seem a beautiful but dangerous jungle. Long shoots of grass reach for the sun and form a canopy. Stems and blades intertwine into a thick mat to create darker and damper areas. Interspersed throughout all this greenery are the dead snags, those gray withered grasses that have fallen to the ravages of time, lawn mower, or insect and disease, and bits of tiny skeletons make a rich mattress of nutrients.

In the upper layer of seemingly endless grasses, there are other plants: crabgrass, broad-leafed plantain, dandelion, clover, and myriad smaller plants and baby grasses. Some are so tiny, succulent, and soft that you can hardly feel them when you touch them. In the damper areas, tiny mushrooms and bits of moss or fungi grow. All this intermingling of rich greenery produces an almost impenetrable jungle, or forest, that would rival any in the larger world.

Throughout this jungle are series of trails and runs created and used by all manner of beasts. The floor is littered with all sorts of treasures. Some can be seen with the naked eye, while others can be seen only with a magnifying glass. Looking closely, tiny stones and pebbles take on gorgeous, faceted shapes. Some are transparent, others are crystalline, splashed with rich pastel colors that are rarely seen in the larger rocks of our world. Strewn about the ground are bits of insect wings, carapaces, antennas, and other parts. Teeth, claws, whiskers, hair, scat, and innumerable other objects litter the mats of dead vegetation and earth. All around, also, are the scrapes, dents, pocks, and scratches left by animals. Tiny and delicate tracks, etched so finely in the soils, are barely visible even with a hand lens.

Gazing into this intricately tangled moss of life, one can't help but realize the wealth of life found within every cubic inch. All over this miniature landscape is the evidence of animals, their feeding habits, life-and-death struggles, and numerous other signs that absolutely boggle the imagination. So many questions come to mind as the eyes eagerly consume every fragment. What made that mark? What caused this insect to lose its leg? What kind of egg casing is this, or what kind of seed is that? There are so many questions and it would take years to answer even the most obvious.

Sometime during the night, a white-footed mouse had passed over the lawn. It had not hesitated, for it was in a dangerous area, and though the lawn did contain things it would normally have eaten, the owls and other predators that hunted these areas would find the mouse an easy mark. I discovered the mouse's right rear footprint firmly planted between two small tufts of grass. Its feet had hit in such a way, due to its speed and the classic gallop pattern, that it landed in bare soil. The motion had shoveled the foot underneath the dead grasses that covered the bare earth, thus creating a tiny cave. It was in this tiny cave that I noticed a small wolf spider, apparently resting after a long night's hunt. Though the wolf spider is not a nest builder, it will take refuge in small holes and under various other litter. This little mouse-foot cave seemed to do the trick and kept the spider out of the sun. Last night had been cold, so I suspect that hunting had not been good. Most of the spider's prey would have been made a bit sluggish by the cold night air; wolf spiders prefer to hunt at night when their prey are active but will hunt during the day when the opportunity arises.

I carefully watched this little spider for over an hour. Every time a small ant passed by, the spider would position itself as if to strike. It seemed, however, that nothing that passed met its fancy. Finally, a large housefly landed on a fresh rabbit dropping that lay nearby. Cautiously the spider slipped from its cave and disappeared around a tuft of grass. Sticking to the shadows, it edged closer to the fly, which appeared to be absorbed in tasting. Within a few inches of the fly, the spider sprinted, pounced, and bit the fly on the abdomen. The fly slowly died, and the spider began to drag it back to its little cave. For the longest time, the spider tried to get the remains of the fly into the little cave but to no avail. They were both just too big to fit into the cave at the same time.

Watching the spider was another predator, a mud dauber. Though the food for the adult wasp is nectar from plants, the food for its young are spiders, and this little spider was just what the wasp needed. The wasp had just completed another chamber of its nest, which was located under the eaves of an old garden shed. Using the mud from a small puddle at the edge of the lawn and mixing it with its saliva, the wasp had carefully constructed each chamber of the nest. Into one of these chambers, it will pack spiders that have been anesthetized by its sting—the wasp's answer to refrigeration—lay its egg on the spiders, and seal off the chamber. As the young grow, they will feed on the spiders that are still alive and fresh.

The wasp landed on a dried plantain leaf not far from the spider's mouse-foot cave and from there it watched the spider struggling with the carcass of the fly. Slowly, cautiously, the wasp stalked toward the spider, her antennas feeling out in front as if to test the air for possible danger. With one powerful leaping flight, she pounced on the spider and attempted to turn it over. The spider responded to the attack with an evasive lunge, then countered by trying to bite the wasp on the abdomen. The battle lasted for the better part of a half hour, both opponents avoiding the sting or bite of the other, but each showing signs of weakening. The struggle crashed through the grasses and disrupted the miniature landscape, the sounds falling faintly on the ears of a shrew.

The shrew was hidden in a small rocky tunnel near a rock garden close to the battle area. The shrew's hearing is acute but its eyesight poor, so it cautiously began stalking in the direction of the noise. With short bursts of speed, it narrowed the distance between itself and the battle by darting through the grass tufts. Attempting to get a better look at the disturbance, it approached nearer to the battle, concealing itself behind the thicker grasses and the tunnel network that wove through the area. With one pounce, it entered the area of the struggle but missed its mark. The spider quickly retreated to the grasses, and the wasp took flight. In a futile attempt, the shrew jumped at the wasp as it became airborne but missed again. Caution, probably from the memory of other wasp and spider bites, kept the shrew from pursuing its quarry any further, and it headed back to its little damp cave in the rock garden.

Nearing the mouth of its tiny enclosure, the shrew detected another sound coming from a nearby grass pile. This little pile lay next to the corner of the rock garden and was a natural catchall left by the lawn mower every time the lawn was cut. It was a damp area where all manner of worms and insects took refuge from the hot sun. It was also one of the shrew's favorite hunting areas. Again, the shrew cautiously approached the origin of the sound. It was a little more careful than it had been during the wasp and spider battle. This time there was no fight to cover up the sound of its approach, and sensing this brought on a certain physical cautiousness: nose twitching, ears cocked, and eyes squinting.

It entered the darkness of the grass pile, following its nose and ears to the sound. In a small room that had been a nest for a common vole, it sensed a salamander feeding on an insect. Without hesitation, the shrew pounced on the back of the salamander, biting the neck hard. Even though its bite is slightly poisonous, it seemed to take a long time for the salamander to die. When at last it did, the shrew did not remove its prey from the little chamber but decided to devour it there. Voraciously, it tore at the flesh until there was hardly anything left except parts of the viscera, the head, the spinal column, and parts of the legs and feet. While the shrew rested near the tunnel digesting the meal, a carrion beetle began to feed on the salamander carcass. Because the shrew has to eat almost three times its weight every day, it went back to the carcass for one last bite but ate the carrion beetle instead. With a quick run, it exited the tunnel and headed back to its little cave where it would take a short snooze before hunting again.

Hovering just above the grass pile was a female sparrow hawk. It had seen the shrew enter the pile and the movement that signaled its return for the beetle. Patiently, it waited on vibrating wings, watching carefully every sign that would indicate when the shrew was on its way home. Instinctively the sparrow hawk knew that it had only a moment in which to catch the running shrew, for its den was not far away and it was very fast. Also, the surrounding grass and rocks afforded many escape routes, so the dive had to be orchestrated perfectly. Suddenly the shrew scurried toward the den. Now, the hawk folded its wings slightly and dropped to a spot just in front of the opening. Instinct and experience told it that the strike would put the shrew right beneath its talons.

With a powerful pounce, it slammed the ground, grasping the shrew firmly in its talons. There was no struggle from the shrew, for the hawk's sharp talons and bone-crushing pounce killed instantly. It stopped, looked around for a moment, then was quickly airborne, heading back to its nest located in a hollow tree at the far edge of the lawn, its young ones eagerly awaiting the food it brought. Because the hawk's young were not yet old enough to eat by themselves, it tore at the flesh of the shrew. It would be only a matter of days before they would have the skill—and be of a size—to swallow such a catch whole. After a short rest, the hawk flew off again in search of another meal to feed its young.

At the far end of the lawn where the hedgerow met the grass and the lawn mower couldn't reach, a strip of lawn grew a little taller, making a good home for innumerable insects and animals. It was from this grass area that the mouse I met earlier had run, leaving in its wake the deep print used by the wolf spider for a temporary shelter. In fact, this grass fringe was the home of many of the larger creatures that hunted or foraged the lawn. And it was in this hedgerow that the robin had made her nest. Most of the other resident birds also used this hedgerow as a resting, roosting, and nesting area. On the edge of the grass fringe, a garden spider had spun its web, for it was here that the most insect activity takes place. The spider hung upside down on the zigzag center of the web, vibrating back and forth rapidly into a blur so as to become invisible anytime a bird or other danger came too close to the web.

The day before, a weasel had killed a young chipmunk near the grass strip but abandoned it before its meal was finished. Flies buzzed about, laying their eggs on the carcass, and maggots had begun to appear. One fat fly inadvertently flew into the corner of the spider's web and struggled violently to free itself. Sensing the struggling vibrations, the spider ran to its prey, stunned it with a bite, then wrapped it in silken web. The spider dragged it to the center of the nest, where it drained the fly of its life juices. This argiope spider had taken over this location from another of its kind when the original spider had been eaten by a local boattailed grackle. The new spider had built its web overnight, defending its territory from other smaller argiopes to insure its survival. A good nest location means greater chances of survival because of newer food sources.

After eating some of its meal, the argiope began repairing breaks in the nest caused by the small cottontail that had wandered through it the previous dawn. The work went quickly but the argiope rested frequently so as not to draw attention to itself. Any spider knows that any unduly drawn-out motion will only attract attention, making it vulnerable to predators. Many times I have adopted the local argiopes as pets, feeding them partially stunned flies and other insects that I have collected. There is no need to take them from their web and place them in a cage. As long as the food supply holds out, they will stay in the same location. They will even get used to your presence.

At my farm, on the outer corner of the lawn, there are many argiope nests. I have named many of the spiders, and they stay around all summer. Two spiders in particular know that when I show up, they are going to get a free meal, and they will actually run to the corner of their web and await my handout. One spider in particular takes the offering right from my hand; it happens to be the largest in the patch because of the amount of food I give to it. I have even gotten to a point where I can carefully stroke its abdomen, and it seems to love it. After a meal, it will raise its back legs and wait for me to pet it, never moving until I am done. Sometimes if I don't pet it enough, it will crawl up on my hand and refuse to leave until I pet it some more.

The cottontail that broke the spider's web is a usual inhabitant of the lawns and lives in a brushy corner of the hedgerow. It has a nest of four young cupped in some of the longer grasses near the hedgerow. From here it leaves the thicker grass cover and ventures out onto the lawns in the evening to feed. Except the occasional neighborhood dog, the cottontail has few natural enemies in this suburban lawn. Most larger hawks, owls, foxes, and other predators do not come this close to humans. The cottontail will, however, still use a great deal of caution when traveling or feeding, just as its wilderness counterparts do. It only comes out in darkness to feed but can be seen at dawn and dusk by any careful observer. If I take the time to look closely to the lawn, I will see the tiny roundish scat that litters the ground. Or if I look at the ends of some of the more succulent clover and grass stalks, I may find the sharp forty-five-degree cut that indicates the cottontail or another rodent has been feeding.

Other animals come to the lawns from the longer edge grasses and overgrown patches. At all times of the day or night, you can find voles, mice, and chipmunks foraging the grasses for succulent shoots or seeds. Snakes glide across this green sea in search of insects or other creatures of the night, and assorted toads do the same. In summer and winter squirrels will forage the lawns for stray nuts and seeds, while all manner of birds comb the lawns for insects, seeds, or succulent shoots.

The lawn is not a dead or uninteresting expanse of green there to decorously frame our homes, but a sea of life more complicated and intricate than any of our larger realms. Many—animals, birds, insects—*depend* on the lawn for survival. It is constantly awash in the motion of life, a grand provider of food, always a source of wonder and beauty.

Your children probably now understand the potential found in their own backyard. Yet the yard goes on to include the hedgerows, the gardens, the drainage ditches, the abandoned lots, and the ponds. Children could literally spend the rest of their days searching out the mysteries hidden around their yards.

## BRINGING NATURE HOME

It can be a family project to encourage nature into your yards, gardens, and hedgerows, a project that will also teach children the importance of creating and caring for nature. What must happen is to change the family's way of thinking and become wildlife-conscious. Get away from the sculpted gardens and lawns and allow a little wildness to prevail. There are ways of keeping this wildness unique and beautiful, even for those communities that have the most stringent rules. With just a little effort, the whole ambiance of your home can be changed and beautified for an abundance of wildlife.

### The Bird Feeder

The bird feeder is one of the classic attempts to encourage wildlife into the home turf. However, most people go about this the wrong way, failing to make the feeding station complete. Typically a family buys a bird feeder, or puts a slab of wood on a post, drops on some feed, and calls that a bird feeder. Certainly this will encourage some birds, but it will never reach its fullest potential. Other people begin to feed the birds in autumn, then grow tired of the procedure and terminate feeding by winter. Thus, many birds will probably die because they have become dependent on the feeder.

Any bird feeding station will work, but it is best to have several different types: some hanging, some free-standing, and some platforms. Along with the feeders, there should be close brush so that the birds can perch and feel secure when they are not feeding. Somehow brush tends to give birds a sense of security. What is also needed is a source of water, and the water should be changed and filled every day. This is important in the winter too. Ice should be broken away to allow the birds to drink. Food and seed should also be varied and you should provide suet and suet balls to satisfy the birds' overall needs. Feeding stations should look as natural as possible.

### Natural Gardens

Natural gardens attract many forms of wildlife, while they can still be kept attractive and obey community laws. Wildflowers and other wild plants can be planted in gardens, especially those gardens facing a larger natural area. Portions of the lawns can be let go, allowed to grow up naturally, especially in the fringe areas of the yards. Hedgerows can be left to go wild, with the outer parts cropped if need be, but with the fringe and inner sections of the row allowed to go back to wildness. Once a family becomes wildlife-conscious, they will come up with some unique ideas of how to bring wildlife home.

## Ponds

One major attraction of wildlife are ponds. In fact, in all of nature my most favorite areas are the ponds. Artificial ponds can be made anyplace without much work or expense. So many times I have just dug a hole, placed in an old baby pool, put on a water filtering device, landscaped around the edges with wild plants, and filled the water with pond lilies, fish, and frogs. Artificial ponds become havens for wildlife throughout the year. They also tend to become the centerpiece of the yard. If you have running water on your property or a lightly flowing drainage ditch, you may want to dam it, widen it, and landscape it wildly.

## Nesting Boxes

Birdhouses can be seen in every neighborhood, yet they are usually inadequate and placed in the wrong areas. First find out which birds will nest in your area, what they need as a nesting box, and where it should be located. Then set up several boxes at the edges of your yard, preferably by the fringe areas. This way when you go out into the yard, you will not disturb the nesting birds, and the birds will have a more natural look to the area. Nesting boxes should be cleaned at the end of the season and prepared for the following year. Do this in the early fall, in case other animals intend to use the box as a winter retreat.

Most of all get your children heavily involved in these projects. Allow them to make decisions on their own, and let it become their personal project. The more input they have, the more time they will spend with each project. When nature comes home, people gain a greater respect for it and are less apt to randomly destroy.

# 7

# AWARENESS GAMES

### The Stalking Game (Fort Apache)

This game is played much like the old game of "capture the flag," and it is best played at night. In this game, divide the children up into two equal groups. Each group should then go into separate areas of the landscape and build a fire, with supervision. Just outside the range of the fire, or lantern light, the group should hang a white cloth, or flag, barely visible from the camp. Four people are elected to stand watch at the fire. They cannot leave a fifteen-foot-diameter circle, but must stay within that circle and listen for oncoming stalkers.

The other members of the team then stalk away from their "fort," and head to the opposing team flag. The object of the game is to remove the flag without being seen or heard. If a stalker is "captured" by any of the watchers, then he or she is sent back to his or her fort, to be relieved by one of the watchers, that watcher now becoming a stalker. If, on the other hand, a watcher hears a noise, and there is no stalker there, then the watcher must then face the fire and discontinue watching. Parents or instructors should be at each fire to check the stalkers and watchers.

**Note:** A single child can play this game by using the main camp and his or her parent as watchers.

### Blindfolding

Blindfolding is a tremendous teacher and an exciting game for children to play. Blindfolding teaches children to reach out with the other senses, depending on these senses to "see." It also improves balance, for when the sight is cut off, the balance mechanism is completely transferred to the inner ear. Blindfolding will also improve children's ability to stalk and to feel the landscape with their bodies. When blindfolded, children must proceed slowly and feel, thus encouraging a marked improvement in stalking skill. Finally blindfolding teaches children to reach out with their inner senses; as time and distance become distorted, the mind turns to meditation. It should also be noted that this exercise improves children's ability to travel at night.

## The String Walk

Set up a long string across the landscape. The string should be about three feet off the ground and wind through all sorts of terrain. Without knowing where you've placed the string, the children are blindfolded and asked to follow the string, using their hands to guide them. Make sure the children do not put any weight on the string, or use it to help balance; it is just a guide. Make sure also that the string travels over many semidifficult areas, so the children have to crawl, pick their way through brush, and go up and down slight inclines. Adults should be placed all along the string to aid the children. At different points in their progress the children should be asked the direction back to the main camp, or whether they know exactly where they are in the woods. This will keep children actively checking position and direction.

## The Blind Drum Stalk

This game should be played by older children and is one of the most challenging and exciting awareness games. Take the children a good distance from camp and have them blindfold themselves. Now, back at camp, one of the parents should play a drum, beating it once every four seconds. The object of the game is to have the children stalk back to camp listening to the drum, which will serve as their only source of orientation. Simply because of the way sound carries over distance, the drum will seem to move about the area; the children will be forced to pay attention. They will also have to stalk without a sound, taking care not to run into brush or get tangled in ground debris. As the children's skills develop, the game areas can become more and more difficult, or spread out in great distances from the drum source.

**Caution:** There should be plenty of adults in the woods to supervise the children. Adults should also point out to children if they get off-course, near danger, or if they are making too much noise.

## Blindfold Tracking

Blindfold tracking improves children's ability to find tracks by touch. After finding a good, deep deer trail, blindfold the children and place their fingers lightly into the first track. Using what the children know about stride and pattern, have the children lightly feel for the next track, continuing along until the children finish that portion of a trail. As the children improve, move to more difficult terrain and tracks. This will greatly enhance children's ability to track at night without the aid of a flashlight.

**Note:** I suggest using the blindfold for perfecting many skills—especially survival skills that must sometimes be done in the dark. However, do not have children perform skills requiring knives or sharp rocks. This can be a very dangerous practice, and is only for advanced adults.

## Blindfold Identification

Lead the blindfolded children off into natural areas. Every so often, stop and have the children feel a track, a flower, a tree, a rock, or any other entity they are familiar with. Now, see if the children can identify that entity. Give them hints if they get stuck. This practice will add the dimension of touch to what they already know. Another variation of the game would be to have the children explain an entity to the group. The children cannot say what the entity is, but only describe it in terms of its texture or feel, its smell, and/or the sound it makes. This method will help to expand the children's use of all the senses.

**Note:** I have a great deal of success using these same methods with blind people, several of whom have come through my standard class. What their achievements have taught me is that there are no real handicaps when it comes to fully experiencing nature. I have had blind students build shelters, fires, gather food, and track animals with a relative stride. Their ability to stalk is also truly remarkable.

## The Night Sound Game

A great way to teach children night sounds is to have them sit quietly in the woods. A knowledgeable parent should pick out the various night sounds, explaining what each sound is and what it is made by. Not only should the instructor teach the obvious sounds such as frogs, crickets, whippoorwills, and cicadas, but also the sound of footfalls, running water, winds, and other light sounds. Then, see if the group can pick out more sounds, using their focused hearing. The child who picks the most sounds is the winner.

### The Swamp Crawl

One of my favorite exercises is the swamp crawl. This activity is done much like follow the leader. It takes children into a new, seldom explored realm and attempts to break down the many barriers they may have to getting dirty and immersing themselves in nature. I lead the children into the deepest parts of the swamp on their hands and knees. Along the way I point out and explain all the tremendous things they would normally miss if they were concentrating on trying to stay clean, which really means trying to remain untouched by the landscape. During the process the children must also take the animal trails and runs, traveling much as the animals do. If the going gets touchy and mucky, I simply wallow in the mud, and the children will willingly follow my example. The swamp crawl seems to awaken children's sense of wonder and adventure, and gives them permission to get dirty, real dirty.

### The Stream Float

A slow-moving stream near your camp can be a tremendous playground for children. On a warm day, take the children to the stream to float. If they are good swimmers, have them float without any help, but choose a fairly shallow stream and a short distance over which they should float. Encourage them to relax into the water, to open their minds, to explore the stream fully by feel, smell and sound, to immerse themselves in the lifeblood of the earth. If it is a long or deep stream, or if the children are not good swimmers, have them use an inner tube or life preserver for this exercise. Another good way to explore a stream is to have the children use a mask and snorkel. That way they see all the aquatic wildlife undisturbed, while quietly and effortlessly floating by. The stream float, like the swamp crawl, takes children into a seldom explored dimension.

**Caution:** Make sure the children are not exposed to the water for very long. Hypothermia can occur even in warm water. Be careful of deep water, hidden snags, submerged garbage, and fast-moving water. Do not push children into doing something they are not totally comfortable with.

## ENVIRONMENTAL WORKSHOPS

### Broken Soil

Have the children lie down on the ground, and pick out a square foot of ground in front of them. Next tell them you want them to carefully explore everything, starting from ground level, to several inches below the surface. Have them discuss each interesting thing they find, showing it to the entire group. As they dig, have them use their hands to work through the soils, to find stones, insects, and bits of debris. When the workshop ends, casually ask the children to put the earth back "exactly" as it was. After a while, undoubtedly, someone will say "This is impossible!" That is your opportunity to impress upon them how easily humans can destroy the earth, and only time, nature, and the creator can put the soil back the way it was. Nothing more needs to be said.

## The Broken Leaf

Along the same line as the broken soil workshop is the example of the broken leaf. Have the children tear a leaf in half. Next give them a Band-Aid and tell them to fix, or heal, the leaf by patching it up. Within a few days, the leaf will be dead. Explain to them again, that while humans can easily hurt nature, it is not so easy to heal it.

## The Oiled Water

Have the children take a small glass of stream water and look at it carefully. Now have them pour in a small amount of automotive oil and shake it up. Now ask them to remove the oil, using a small sponge and eyedropper. They will certainly make a good attempt at it but when they finally get what they think is all the oil out, have them feel and smell the water. Again the statement will be made "This is impossible." Then, of course, you can ask them to think about what really happens when there is a major oil spill.

## The Garbage Field Trip

Gather the children into a group and take them out on a hike. Go directly to the nearest pile of illegally dumped garbage and ask them to identify all the plants that are there. They will undoubtedly look at you in utter amazement, since there will most likely be few, if any. Ask them how long they think it will be before the plants will grow back, or how long it will take for the garbage to rot away. Pick up pieces of the garbage and show them how there are no plants growing underneath, and how barren the ground looks.

**Note:** It is important that during these environmental workshops you do not sermonize, overexplain, or hammer away at the point. Just doing the workshops is usually enough to provoke thought and plant the seeds of environmental consciousness.

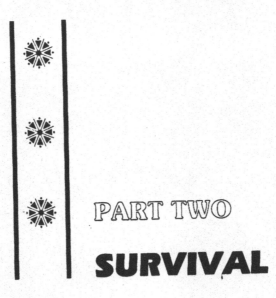

# PART TWO

# SURVIVAL

# INTRODUCTION

All too often, in adult and children's literature alike, the wilderness is looked upon as scary, mystical, threatening, harsh, and unknown or unknowable. Stories abound about the wilderness being a place of evil, where lurk ghosts and all manner of ferocious beasts. The wilderness, as has been taught for centuries, is something to be conquered and civilized, a place where none can live securely. From the story of Hansel and Gretel lost in the enchanted forest to more modern stories on the same theme, the fearful myth has been perpetuated. In history, we are taught of the plight of pioneers and their journeys to death. We are never taught that tragedy in wilderness is not the fault of nature but a result of the ignorance of humans and their inability to live with the earth. What humankind does not know, it fears, and what it fears, it destroys. Thus we have destroyed the earth, as much from fear as for profit. We have become a society of people who kill our grandchildren to feed our children.

One of the biggest challenges we have to deal with in educating our children about living with the earth is breaking the old habits and misguided beliefs about the wilderness. We have to teach our children they are not alien to that wilderness but a part of it, that going into nature is really going home. We have to reeducate our children, showing them the wilderness is a source of renewal, safety, and clarity. Here is the simple essence of reality. Our children must come to realize that the earth provides us with all sustenance, whether we are living in the purity of the wilderness or in the abstraction of society. We must teach our children, lovingly, that the earth will provide for them, even in a survival situation, but that the key to that survival is awareness and knowledge.

Ridding children of fear and prejudice toward wilderness is easy enough, accomplished by taking them "into" the wilderness frequently. In this way, we build an important familiarity, which in itself abolishes fear. (It is important too, that you, the parent, become familiar with the earth first, for any fear or hesitation on your part will be picked up by the children, if not by word, then through action and attitude. When learning survival techniques the aim is for these skills to become second nature. Practice the techniques one in conjunction with another. Only in this way will you and the children come to understand the inter-dependencies of survival actions. This method of approach also insures that the skills are most apt to be used in a real survival situation. Keep in mind that until children become familiar with their use, survival skills, like the wilderness, can hold frightening implications.

Survival living is not living a life characterized by debilitation, lack, discomfort, and pain. Instead, survival is very easy, relaxing, and en-lightening, provided the survivalist's skills are good. Whenever a sur-vival experience becomes debilitating, rest assured it is because the proper skills have not been mastered. Therefore, it is of utmost impor-tance for you to master each skill so the experience can prove uplifting.

Survival is more than just staying alive when one is lost, trapped, or injured; survival is a philosophy unto itself. For its serious practitioners, survival becomes a doorway to the philosophy of living as one with the earth, whereby survivalists live intimately the connection between them-selves and creation, where earth is "mother" and all entities of the earth brothers and sisters. This philosophy cannot be learned from hearing the words, but only through living close to the earth, removed from the umbilical cord of civilization. It is this oneness, this connection, we should teach our children above all else.

Survival is not detrimental to the earth, but rather a necessary part of its overall health. We are meant to be living close to the earth, not as a destructive, conquering force, but as an integral part of it. Children should not be taught to approach nature as something to be conquered, but with the attitude of caretaker. Only in developing this attitude will we be able to survive, to live in balanced harmony with the earth. We must learn to abide by the laws of creation, to become part of the natural system of checks and balances. The best way to achieve this goal is through that caretaker attitude. All we do should heal the earth; all we touch should benefit the earth: true survivalists always enter the wilderness with this attitude. We must show our children by example and teach them that everything we do in the wilderness has a reaction. Each action is all-encompassing; it affects everything else. For the action of "taking care," the reaction is positive and healing. Thus when children live survival, they live the laws of creation and become a healing force. "Healing impact" is the only way to teach survival.

## MENTAL ATTITUDE

If someone were to ask me what the most important skill for survival was, I would have to say mental attitude. Mental attitude, however, is one of the most difficult skills to teach to adults and children alike. It is the mental attitude that determines whether a survival situation is going to be a painful, debilitating, and uncomfortable experience, or a relaxing and invigorating one. Two people with the same knowledge of survival skills and physical makeup can view the same situation in two quite different ways and have two quite different experiences. If one views the survival situation with contempt, fear, and negativity then that is what one will live, but if a survivalist views a survival situation with a positive frame of mind, then the results and experience will be positive. What forms the basis for a positive mental attitude is the perfection of skills. When skills are perfected, the survivalist has an easier and more comfortable time. This in itself builds confidence and subsequently a positive mental attitude. Conversely haphazard and ineffective skills build negativity.

It is important to build children's mental attitude along with their skills. Each will reinforce the other and the children will no longer start from a place of negativity and lack, but come from a place of confidence and skill. There is, of course, much more that influences mental attitude than just skills and their perfection. First, children must realize they alone are in control of their environment. Certainly the weather, topography, and conditions are beyond our control, but ultimately we each have the ability—or responsibility—to control our own survival, comfort, and capacity to change. In a survival situation, we are in control of all things. Second, children must realize they have a choice—a choice to make things better or allow them to remain the same. It is up to each of us how we choose to view any given situation and what we choose to do about that same situation. Children must be taught that their attitude is itself a matter of choice—and that a bad attitude is a very poor choice.

I think teaching children they have choices is one of the most important lessons of survival. Not only does it fit into the survivalists' world but has application to children's everyday life. Children soon realize that in everything they do, think, say, or feel, the outcome is their own choice. It is their choice to be happy or sad, comfortable or uncomfortable, to pass or fail. They have the choice to take control. All life, all happiness, is a series of choices. The invaluable benefit gained is that with these choices, there soon comes a deep belief in the self. Children soon understand that all things are possible if they believe strongly enough in themselves and their choices. There are no greater basic lessons for a happy life than these basic mental attitudes, for once mastered, all else comes easily.

In essence, the best way to teach children that they have control and choice is to reword your everyday questions. When children make a statement that they are cold, instead of asking them why they are cold, ask why they choose to be cold and what they can choose to do about it. This way the responsibility becomes the children's, and they have to make the choice to do something about the cold. If they still choose to be cold and blame it on circumstances outside of the self, teach them they have the choice and show them what they can do about it. As you build a fire, or shelter, show that you are making a conscious choice—the choice to be warm—to do something about the problem. You are not blaming it on outside circumstances but are taking responsibility and choosing to change things for the better.

It is important also to teach your children that during a survival situation, they must learn to separate their wants from their needs. Show them that choosing to concentrate on wants will only make things worse, for we can never fulfill all our wants. Teach them to first take care of their needs, and to appreciate all those things that help them to take care of those needs. In essence, instruct them not to concentrate on what they don't have but to appreciate what they do have. In this same flow of thought, children can also be taught that comfort is relative. In other words, being comfortable all depends on what they think, believe, and choose.

## TEACHING CHILDREN

Survival is a very difficult skill to teach children, not because of the difficulty of the skill itself but because of the negativity that usually surrounds it and all the accompanying old fears and myths. Never teach survival skills through fear. In other words, never make a survival experience or skill filled with frightening stories, hardships, and pain. So often I have heard parents say, "You'd better learn to build this shelter if you don't want to die." This kind of approach will immediately frighten children and hinder any learning that might otherwise take place, for the skill becomes a command, rather than a game. Instead of accentuating the negative, concentrate on the positive, the play aspect and the confidence and sense of well-being that learning survival can bring. Use an approach that is relaxed, not demanding or pushy, but guiding and directing. Make each skill fun, filled with joy and wonder, with only passing comments about using it for survival purposes.

Your example and attitude are the most important teachers. Children will learn more from these than from all the words and workshops you can deliver. You must, however, first develop confidence in the skill, or at least show a confidence and patient persistence when learning a skill together with your children. You must develop a good mental attitude and realize you have choices too, before you can teach this to children. If you say one thing but do another, that will only confuse children, and the children will pay more attention to what you do rather than to what you say. If you accept failure in yourself, then you teach children to do the same. If you approach life from a position of lack and pessimism, then such is where your children will start, then fail.

Work with your children. Allow them to do much of the work, but you must get dirty also. You cannot be an effective teacher by standing back and ordering. Instead, *do*, and your children will also. Your participation is vital. If you don't work, sweat, play, and get dirty, then your holding back becomes an unspoken command to your children that you do not really approve. Most of all make each lesson fun, full of joy and laughter, where you become part of a team, not just a teacher. Take care that you do not spoon-feed your children as well. Instead, use coyote teaching, and allow your children to think out some of the problems. One of the best gifts we can give our children is to teach them to think, especially in a survival situation. It is children's ability to think out problems and modify skills that will make them good survivalists. Most of all, teach children self-reliance, so they don't *need* you in order to survive. In teaching children to think for themselves and to solve problems you teach them self-reliance. Remember, they won't necessarily have you near if they ever get stuck in a survival situation.

And finally it is important when teaching the following survival skills that you modify the skill to fit the age and interest of the children. You cannot teach three-year-olds to build a perfect debris hut, but you can teach them to cover themselves in leaves. You cannot easily teach five-year-olds to make a bow-drill fire, but you can teach some eight-year-olds. Each child and each situation is different. You, as the teacher, must learn the difference, what your children are capable of learning and doing. If children don't have an interest in learning something, don't insist. Instead, go on to something else and come back to the other skill when the children want to learn. As always, I believe children can and will learn anything if it is presented in the right way. And the right way always starts with love.

The survival section of this book is written for children from ages four through eleven. Some of the techniques can easily be taught to younger children, but do not expect too much from them. Generally you, as parent and teacher, must adapt the teaching to your children and their ability. I don't expect the younger children to complete some of the more complicated and advanced survival techniques at my school. But children from seven to eleven should be able to master all the techniques and skills in this book. Children younger than seven can probably master at least some of the simpler techniques in each chapter, which will serve to keep them safe in a survival situation. I suggest if you have children age twelve or older, they can use *Tom Brown's Field Guide to Wilderness Survival.*

# 8

# LOSTPROOFING

Perhaps the most important survival skill children can learn is how not to get lost in the first place. I call this skill "lostproofing." To me, before anything else is taught, this skill should be learned, practiced, and understood, not only by children, but by every member of the family. It is surprising how many people, even experienced outdoors people, do not know how to lostproof themselves. Every year backpackers, cross-country skiers, hunters, and outdoor enthusiasts of every age and gender get into serious trouble by losing their orientation and ending up lost, hurt, or worse.

I must say that I have never been lost. Turned around and disoriented certainly, but never lost. It was once said that "you are only lost when you have a place to go and a time to be there." I agree, but I must add that you must be at home in the wilderness and able to take care of yourself before you can say you can't get lost. There is hardly a wilderness you can't walk out of in a few days, provided you walk in a straight line, and avoid danger. There have been many times in my life that I did not know where I was, what day it was, or, for that matter, what week it was. For all intents and purposes, I would have been considered lost by general public standards, but for me, this "predicament" was exactly what I was trying to achieve—to free myself of the confines of society, free of time, and free of destination. Thus I was not lost. Bear in mind also that I am fully able to track myself back when I have to. The only other way to keep from being lost, other than what I do, is to learn to lostproof yourself.

First let me say that anyone, no matter how skilled, can become lost, even if only temporarily. Well-known terrain can become obscured and transformed into the unknown by darkness, heavy mists, or a severe snow whiteout. When the trails, landmarks, and lay of the land become obliterated, even the most skilled guides and outdoors people can get into serious trouble. The more skilled people are in wilderness, the more *likely* they will get through one of these situations. Most of the time skilled outdoors people will wait out a storm, or whatever is obscuring the terrain, while novices will blindly try to work their way home, getting more hopelessly lost and possibly injured by an unseen -hazard.

A myth that must be dispelled is one I call "a sense of direction." No one has a sense of direction, no matter how much time one spends in the woods. People who seem to have a sense of direction are just very aware of the landscape, sun position, and lay of the land, and thus seem to have an uncanny ability to navigate the wilderness. They do not have a "sense of direction." There is no way to learn to have a sense of direction, because even with training, a sense of direction does not exist. Those who may claim to have a sense of direction will reconsider when they try the following simple test. I suggest you have your children take this "direction test" as a way of teaching them they do not have a direction sense. Indeed, it would be a good idea to have your whole family take the test and record the results.

### The Direction Test

Go out onto a football field on an *overcast, windless* day, since sun position and air movement could subconsciously help you find direction. Make sure also that it is relatively quiet, where no continuous sound will give away your direction. Standing in the center of the field, on the fifty-yard line, face one of the goalposts and blindfold yourself. Have the other members of the family watch quietly from a distance, to make sure you don't blunder into anything. Once blindfolded, try to walk a straight line to the distant goalpost; have family members take note of what you are doing and the directions you are heading.

What happens will be utterly fascinating. Without the wind, the sun, or any noise to give away directions, you will find that it becomes almost impossible to even get near the goalpost. Essentially something quite astounding occurs: If you are right-handed—in other words, your right side is stronger than your left—you will begin to circle to the right. If you are left-handed, the opposite will occur. Most people will leave the field near the three-yard line. This should immediately teach all members of your family, and anyone who thinks he or she has a sense of direction, that they do not, not even close.

Being lost is like being blindfolded, for reasons we will discuss later on. When lost or blindfolded, an average adult can come full circle in

one square mile of wilderness. Children because of their size will circle
in less area. When I track lost people, it is important for me to establish
right away whether the people are right- or left-oriented, since their trail
will usually wander toward their orientation, making my job easier. It is
important for you as a parent to know which way each member of your
family tends to circle, including yourself. Knowing your own tendency
will help immensely when negotiating unknown terrain, or assist you
when you are lost.

Another good exercise to teach children that they do not have a
sense of direction is "the camp point." Take your family on a hike away
from your camp area, subtly, but frequently switching direction. If you
do not know the area well, I advise you to use a compass. Once you
have wandered for a while, stop and ask everyone to sit down. Now ask
them to point directly back to camp. Normally you will find a finger
pointing in every direction, even from the adults. Ironically no one will
be pointing directly back to camp. After you discuss what has happened, bring out your compass and show the family the true direction
back to camp.

### The Basics of Lostproofing

First, child or adult, you must be acquainted with the area where you
will be traveling. One of the best ways to do this is to look at a map.
Very young children can be made to understand maps better if you
draw it for them. Topographical and road maps are just too complicated
for most children. Study the map together, making sure your children
understand where they are and what the landscape looks like. Point out
roadways, trails, waterways, and nearby towns, as well as the general
lay of the landscape. Point out the directions these sites are in relation
to your location. Teach your children not to rely on sight alone for
bearings, but rather to pay attention to what they feel, smell, or hear.
Distant traffic, streams, and towns will make sounds, lowlands will feel
damp, and water can be smelled at considerable distances. Knowing
these things beforehand can prevent children from getting lost, or assist
them in finding their way out.

Yes, we all have heard it a hundred times, but make it a family law:
Tell someone responsible where you are going and when you will
return. That even goes for adults. Always stick to that plan. Children
should never venture into the wilderness or any woods alone. There is
too much that can happen to a lone child besides being lost or hurt, and
there is strength in numbers. Adults should also make a habit of not
going alone unless they are highly skilled and know the area well. I
have spent most of my life in the woods alone, and during the alone
times, despite my knowledge of survival skills, I am overly cautious. A

simple injury could cause a life-or-death situation in wilderness if a person is alone.

Make sure your very young children are always accompanied into the woods by an adult or, at least, an older child. It's a simple procedure to teach your young children where your camp is—do it. Very young children are easily sidetracked; they'll wander off and get lost. As a parent, the younger the child, the more you have to pay attention. A young child should never be left unattended, for even a moment, especially in the outdoors. I suggest for very young children just in case, put on a name tag and your campsite number. Some children know their name, address, and phone number, but many miles away from home children should have a backup address.

## Direction Awareness for Lostproofing

Direction awareness is the most important skill for lostproofing. It is children's lack of direction awareness or distractions from that awareness that usually get them into trouble. The typical scenario is this: A child is playing around camp while you are busy preparing lunch. Suddenly the child spots a colorful butterfly and tries to catch it. You do not notice that your child has left camp, following the butterfly until he or she is out of sight. Then the child spots a distant chipmunk or squirrel and tries to get closer. The child's mind is fully concentrating on the adventure and play, with no conscious thought of where he or she is. The child may then drift on to another adventure, then another, until suddenly he or she is a great distance from camp. Suddenly the child looks around and discovers in horror that this is a completely unknown place. Panic sets in as a desperate search for the trail begins. Screaming for help usually follows. Fortunately most little children will not usually wander out of calling distance from the camp, and the parents easily find them. Others are not so fortunate.

It is not easy to teach very young children to be directionally aware all the time. Young children are easily distracted by adventures, excitement, and exploration, even more so than older children and adults. It is quite difficult to keep young children's minds on their whereabouts, especially during adventures, but I feel that with a good teacher, and practice, children can learn to pay attention. It is straightforward enough to teach your children to tell you when they are going to chase that butterfly and to pay attention to their surroundings, but it will take a lot of awareness and effort on your part. You must constantly be aware of when your young children wander off, then chase them down and warn them. Sometimes it is a good idea to wander just behind them and await their realization they have strayed. They'll be frightened at first, until they turn and see you. This will punctuate your point, but that fear factor should only be used with hard-to-reach children, and then only conservatively.

One of the best ways to insure young children have the edge when wandering off is to give them whistles. Children love to play with whistles anyway, and the sound of a whistle carries considerably farther than the human voice. Instruct the children to blow the whistle loudly whenever they are frightened, lost, or in danger. Teach them, however, not to "cry wolf" since it could happen that no one will pay attention to the whistle if they do get lost, and need help. Above all, use a lot of love and patience with very young children, and don't expect too much of them as far as finding their way is concerned.

It is easier to teach older children the concepts of lostproofing, but distractions will still occur, though not for as long or as frequently, as with very young children. The greatest care should be taken in teaching lostproofing so it becomes second nature—something they do without thinking about it, something they do all the time, no matter what else they are involved in. It is this unconscious awareness of one's surroundings that creates the illusion of one's having a sense of direction. What follows is what all good outdoors people do when they are in the wilderness, at first consciously, then unconsciously.

## Fly Up Like an Eagle

It is important to teach children to take frequent overviews of the lay of the land and topography. Have your children imagine themselves flying high overhead like eagles and looking down on themselves. Have them imagine what they would look like, what the terrain would look like, from high above. Have them too imagine all the things passed over and where they are located, all as if from above. What the children should imagine is a living map. This way they will have a clear, overall understanding of where they are and what the general lay of the land would look like. This provides a sense of place, of distance, and the security of knowing exactly where things are on the imagined map. Mental imagery in this way keeps children thinking and paying attention to the changing overall landscape. Have them do this frequently as you teach them lostproofing.

## Prominent Features

One of the most important things you can teach your children about lostproofing is to constantly observe the prominent features of the landscape. Prominent features and landmarks are the street signs of the wilderness and will be of tremendous help when children have to find their way back to camp. Essentially I classify these "signposts" into two distinct categories for better understanding and recollection of children's position in the wilderness. *Prominent features* are large distant objects such as peaks, ridges, large ponds, hills, slopes, far-off groves of trees, or even the distinct shape of fields. *Landmarks* tend to be things up close such as strangely shaped trees, rocks, caves, flowers, hollows, streams, or anything else that will catch the eye and stand out.

When teaching children to find prominent features and landmarks, have them stop frequently and pick out some of each. Have them look at the landmarks and prominent features from many angles. It is a good idea to have them reference the landmarks as to how and where they lie in relation to the prominent features. It is also good to sit down before taking the return trip and have them recall the train of signposts in the order they will pass them on the way home. For instance, a trip home may sound like this: first we pass the large rock that looks like a turtle; then we go down a hill and see the big dead tree; from the area of the tree we can see the big hill. We go up the hill and find the long piles of rocks that look like a snake, and the snake will point to the trail leading down the hill and back to camp.

Using the prominent features and landmarks in this way also establishes familiar parts of the landscape where children will feel secure. Coupled with the map, created from flying up like eagles, a greater sense of place and direction are established. The Native American peoples used this method as their maps. Prominent features and landmarks were named, then handed down for generations as a way of teaching direction and routes to various hunting, fishing, and camping areas. These landmarks were passed along in parable fashion, so that all children needed to do was to recite a parable to find their way home. Many landmarks today still have their original Native American names, and it is fun to show those landmarks to your children. It is also interesting to note that pioneer ancestors used this same method. Little Bighorn is one of the more famous landmarks.

Children should also be taught to pay attention to the direction of the wind and the position of the sun. They should be made aware that wind direction can change during the day and that the sun is always moving in the sky. Conscious awareness that the sun moves in the sky is a key to an understanding of how shadows will change the face of many landmarks. A distant rock formation that looks like a huge weasel in the morning could change into an indistinct mass at noon as shadows become short. It's surprising that children are not consciously aware of the moving sun or wind at first, and these changes must be stressed. These guideposts should only be used for simple reference, however. Trying to teach children that the sun would be at their right when leaving camp and on their right returning to camp later on in the day can be very frustrating for the teacher and the children.

Sound, smell, and feel can also be thought of as landmarks. The sound of distant traffic, flowing water and waterfalls, and the noise of camp can be landmarks. Those sensory landmarks can vary with wind direction or the ebb and flow of people, and sound can be distorted or redirected by the landscape, but it is good to teach your children to pay close attention to the direction of sounds and sound in general as they travel. Smells are also a good landmark, but, as with sound, subject to change with wind and time. Feeling tends to be a subtle, though important, landmark; but again, it is changeable. The most important thing is to teach your child to use all the senses when traveling in the wilderness. The more all senses are put into establishing direction, the less likelihood there will be of becoming disoriented.

## Looking All Ways

Teach your children to look at prominent features and landmarks from *all* angles. That way if they encounter these features from any direction, they will know them intimately. The same holds true of the landscape in general, especially concerning trails. Trails will look different on the return trip because they are being viewed from a different direction. Children, and even adults, should stop frequently along trails and look behind them. That way on the return trip the trails and surrounding landscape will look familiar. I hear the same old story when I find lost people: They did not recognize the trails on the return trip. Remember too that trails will look different at various times of the day as shadows change or the sky becomes overcast. At nighttime trails are even more difficult to remember. Turning around and looking backward as well as all around is not only good lostproofing sense, but it teaches us to be aware of everything, of things we might have otherwise missed.

## Trail Markers

When you and your children get into a situation where the landscape and trails look virtually the same, then you must mark your own trails. I do not advise nor condone slashing trees or breaking branches as trail markers, nor do I suggest you use paint or cloth markers. These only mar and litter the landscape. Propping together a tripod of sticks or making a pile of rocks in a prominent place will suffice as trail markers. I suggest you create a few in each area, as other hikers may break them down, not realizing they are serving as your trail markers. Remember on your return trip to take them down and return the landscape to its natural state.

If you and your children still do not feel on sure footing with this natural way of lostproofing, make sure you carry a compass and possibly a map. This is especially important while you are learning to lostproof the natural way, as these items will back you up in case of mistakes. I very strongly suggest you master using both compass and map and pass this knowledge along to your older children. *The Boy Scout Fieldbook* contains a good how-to guide on orienteering and map reading. It is simple to learn, but a must, especially when you are honing your natural directional skills.

### Survival Pack

I always recommend that children and adults, especially when they are beginning, carry survival packs. A survival pack contains many of the items you will need if you are stranded, or will aid you in finding your way out of the woods. A survival pack should always be worn on the belt, not stored in a pack. Most people become lost when they are separated from camp and their packs, thus the survival pack should always be with them. Whether for adults or children, survival packs should contain the same items, and each child should know how to use them. It is up to you, as a parent or teacher, to teach your children to wear their survival packs. The best teacher is example. Wear yours, no matter how skilled you may be. Anyway children seem to love wearing that sort of gear and using it to create all sorts of real and imagined adventures.

The survival pack should contain the following: waterproof matches, compass, pocketknife, braided nylon fishing line, water purification tablets, small flashlight, small steel cup, two sheets of 6 foot × 6 foot clear plastic, 6-foot plastic tubing, fishhooks in a protective box, whistle, and some first-aid supplies. Other items can be added, but all should fit into a small 6 inch × 2 inch × 4 inch belt bag. The smaller and more compact the better. Keep it light so it is easy and comfortable to carry on the belt. Remember that children should be encouraged to carry survival packs when hiking; it will do them no good if it is left back at camp or in their pack. Allow children to play with and use the items in the survival pack, for this will familiarize them with their uses. Make sure, however, that it is stocked and ready to go for each camping trip. (The uses of the above items will be discussed in the following chapters.)

## LOST PSYCHOLOGY

If you have ever been turned around in the wilderness, or momentarily lost, you will undoubtedly remember the extreme panic you experienced. If the lost episode continued, the fear grew stronger and the sense of panic more profound. It wasn't long until that panic took over and you began to crash aimlessly through the landscape, putting your life in danger. Soon the panic would lead to shock, the mind no longer thinking rationally, and you would put yourself in a very dangerous situation. The shock would cause you to do things you would not otherwise do. You might walk into trees, run blindly through brush, forget to drink water or totally discard your canteen. You might remove clothing and wander in a daze. It is at this time of shock that people will tend to hurt themselves, or worse. Shock leads to exhaustion, then profound shock, then death.

It is this panic and shock that are the greatest killers in a survival situation. When the mind falters and panic takes over, we do not take care of our bodies, we do not prepare for a survival situation, instead, we get more confused, more panicky, and slip deeper into shock. When I track lost people, their confusion is evident in the erratic behavior, the accidents, and the flurry of random panics found etched in their trails. Many times, shock is so profound that people will not, or cannot, answer to their name. Hallucinations born of fear can run wild in the mind. Yet this kind of shock and panic can be prevented and overcome. Survival skills give you and your children an insurance policy against panic, irrational behavior, and the killer shock. When people know they can survive, that the wilderness is not a hostile and alien place, but one in which they can feel at home, shock and panic are alleviated.

It is during the time of panic that people begin to wander in circles. As mentioned earlier, right-oriented people will usually circle to the right, and left-oriented people will circle to the left. Many who are lost circle for days in a relatively small wilderness area, one they could have walked out of in less than a day. Children get so panic-stricken, they may not answer to their names, even if called out by parents, and they have been known to hide from searchers. Even when found, children, as well as some adults, may put up a fight or run away from searchers, even their own parents. In their panicked minds, everything and everyone become enemies, and rational thought is rare. Though these responses do not afflict everyone, this irrational panic is still evident in all lost people to some degree. Keep this in mind when teaching children. Panic kills, and being lost leads to shock. Teach them survival skills and rest assured they will then have an edge against panic and shock.

## What Children Should Do If Lost

Certainly survival skills are a good insurance policy against panic, but there are a few other things you should teach children to insure their safety. When children first realize they are lost, they should sit down and think. It is at this point children will either get out of trouble, or become hopelessly lost. Usually at the time children realize they are turned around, they are still relatively close to a known area and can find their way out. If, however, the children panic and desperately begin to find their way back, they will get even more disoriented and irrational. If children are trained to sit down and think clearly when an emergency arises, they can usually think their way back through landmarks and topography to safety. Sitting down calmly and looking carefully in all directions sets all the senses in motion, and with all the senses clearly working, the trail can usually be found.

If sitting down and rethinking the route fails to work, teach them to then help memory along by retracing the route a little at a time. Have them look in the direction from which they have just come. Teach them to recognize their own tracks and to use the tracks to seek confirmation of their trails. From where they are sitting, teach them to think of the direction they came from. Marking where they are now sitting, have them walk to the last area they remember. Once at the new location, have them sit down again, look around, and find things familiar. Once the direction is found again, have them mark the area, and continue, repeating the process until they work their way back to safety.

If, however, the children fail to find their original trails, they will have to use the *circling method*. This is easily accomplished by propping up a landmark right where they are sitting that can be seen at a distance. Long sticks propped in a big tripod, a tuft of grass hung in a branch, or even a natural landmark—an unusual tree or rock—will work well. Now the children should walk a straight line away from the landmark and begin to circle the area, keeping the landmark in sight at all times. The circles should grow out like a spiral, until the children find an area that seems familiar. Once an area of familiarity has been found, the children should set up another landmark and repeat the process, eventually working their way back to safety.

If the children are familiar with a map of the area and know there are trails and roadways around, then they can use the *straight line method*. This method should only be used if all else fails, for it can lead to dangers on the landscape. To avoid circling when the children are walking out of the wilderness, they must line up landmarks to insure that a straight line is being walked. This is accomplished in the same way a person would aim a rifle. The children look ahead to a distant landmark, then line that landmark up with another landmark of greater distance. They then walk to the first landmark and repeat the same process, now using the second distant landmark as the nearer sight. This process is repeated until the children walk out to a trail, road, campsite, or town.

Children should be taught to constantly observe the landscape during the process of trying to find their way out, listening, feeling, and looking so landmarks are remembered. Calling for help or blowing a whistle are also advised throughout the whole process, for there may be other people around. I find it necessary here to deliver this warning: With the number of children molested and kidnapped these days, children should hide when they get a response to their calls. The children should continue to call until they get a good view of the person, while not revealing where they are hiding. It is for this occasion that you must teach your children to make the decision whether the person is a potential threat or is going to help. Usually a group of two or more people are safe, but teach your children to be wary of a loner. When children finally get to a trail, roadway, campsite, or town, care should also be taken. It's hard to believe that some people would take advantage of lost and frightened children, but it does happen.

If all else fails, children should make a conscious decision to go into a survival situation. This is especially so if night is close or a storm is coming. It is at the point of exhausted options, however, that children have a tendency to blindly wander and can become panicky, even if they have survival skills. Children should try and return to the place where they first felt lost and begin their survival skills. In order, they should build a shelter, find water, build a fire, and then find food. Teach your children never to break that order. Just building a shelter will give your children all they need for a few days. Adding water, the children could safely stay for a long time. When teaching children to lostproof themselves, stress the point that they should stay put and await help. Wandering children make it very difficult for searchers. Assure your children that searchers will be on their way. It is also important to have the children mark their shelter so searchers can easily spot it at a distance.

### What You Should Do If Your Children Are Lost

The normal emotions and actions of parents when children are missing is blind panic. This panic only complicates the situation and wastes a lot of time and energy. Instead, when you realize your children have not returned in time, immediately contact authorities. Give them a description of your children, what they are wearing, where they are going, and the kind of shoes they had on. Also give a description of your children's favorite areas, the names and locations of playmates, and a detail of the circumstances surrounding the children's disappearance. The more accurate the description and the circumstances and the faster you go to the authorities the greater chance your children will be found immediately.

After contacting the authorities, get some help and begin your own circular search of the camp area, spiraling outward for quite a distance.

Have friends go to your children's favorite areas, or look on a map and see if there is anything interesting your children may have stumbled onto. Ironically many missing children are found near a source of water, probably because water is soothing to the human spirit. Have friends search out all waterways. It could be that your children have simply lost track of time, but in this day and age you can't take a chance. Make sure that anyone involved in the search looks deep into the brush areas, under logs and rocks and other potential natural shelter areas. Explain to them that your children know how to use the land, and tell them what to look for.

Work with authorities, not against them. Don't mess up tracks or evidence that trained professionals could use. Don't withhold evidence or get in the way; let them do the job for which they were trained. Generally sheriff departments, fire departments, or rangers are trained in search and rescue, but so are many police departments. Often a dog team will be brought in but rarely a tracker, as there are few good trackers and many authorities treat trackers with the same skepticism they offer psychics. Trackers, they believe, died out with the mountain men and ancient Native Americans. Too many times I've been called out too late or as a last resort: thus I find a body instead of a live child. Fortunately today I am training many law enforcement agencies and search groups to track, and we are now gaining wide acceptance. I now have tracker-trained people throughout the country and in several foreign countries, all with good records.

Most children are found the same day or within forty-eight hours after they were discovered missing. I never give up hope, and depending on the weather and conditions, I have found children alive and unhurt several days after they disappeared. Survival-trained children could stay safe even for several weeks. Don't ever give up. There is always hope no matter how hopeless you feel it may be. If you have done your job as a teacher, you insure your children's survival for a long period of time.

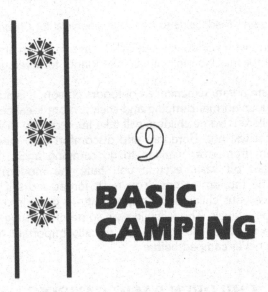

# 9

# BASIC CAMPING

There are many people who have never camped as a family. Baptizing children into camping for the first time can make or break their interest in camping. Most adults have had some experience, good or bad, with camping. Many adults have been in the Boy Scouts or Girl Scouts and at least have a taste of living in the outdoors. Adults, however, can usually get along with a lot less alone than when they are accompanied by children. Adults have learned to appreciate the finer things of nature as a whole. Children, on the other hand, especially if they have never camped before, present many more considerations and problems. Generally children camping for the first time will not be able to put up with the more primitive camps that seasoned adults are accustomed to. Many times children will become uncomfortable, bored, and upset at being away from home. It will be up to you to make their first outing comfortable and exciting, and then over time to lead them toward an appreciation of more primitive camping.

Granted, I was born and raised right next to the huge wilderness area of the Pine Barrens. As a child I was always interested in the woods, even before meeting Grandfather, yet Grandfather took great care and patience in building Rick and me up to the more advanced levels of survival living. At first we were encouraged to sleep in an old tent in the backyard, as most kids did. Then little by little as our confidence and knowledge grew, we were led deeper and deeper into the woods. With each subsequent step, we relinquished certain equipment until after eight months, we were camping in a full survival situation. Yet with each step, Grandfather kept the excitement and comfort level high, and we never experienced boredom or overpowering discomfort. Certainly I had an obsession with wilderness, but still the acclimatizing process took several months for me. Normally it will take longer for average children of today.

Even if you are a very experienced outdoors person, it is advisable to back off from your normal camping and seek a more ideal camp when dealing with children. Some children will take immediately to wilderness camps, but most will not. Boredom and discomfort may creep in and discourage them from ever wanting to go camping again. I strongly suggest you start off easy, even if you hate the modern camping methods and the modern camps. You must forget yourself and your desires, and give your children the opportunity to grow into the more advanced camping levels. The following are some of my suggestions for getting children to "love" to camp. It is equally important to parents who may have never camped before.

## TEACHING CHILDREN BASIC CAMPING

### Choosing a Camp Area

I suggest that instead of going into the far-off and isolated wilderness at first, you choose a public camp area with plenty of modern facilities. State and national parks, local parks and recreation areas, and even the more modern private camps afford a good first-time camp experience. I do not recommend you go to one of those trailer camps that has nothing more than block campsites in an open, uninteresting place. Instead choose a modern camp that is close to the wild areas, where each campsite is separated by some woodsy buffer to give a sense of privacy. Make sure the camp has comfortable facilities and possibly even showers or a swimming area; many children find it difficult to use the woods or primitive latrines as bathrooms. The campsite also should have many exciting activities geared for children, and possibly areas used by many families so your children can strike up new friendships.

### Equipment

The right equipment is important for children when they are camping for the first time. Much of the more costly equipment can be rented at a nominal fee from various outfitters. (Renting is advisable, since once your children gain confidence, you will no longer need such lavish equipment.) I suggest a large tent that is strong, waterproof, and allows free movement, even room for standing. The children will feel more secure, especially if a storm strikes the camp area. There is no reason to frighten children in a small, confining tent that threatens to blow away in the wind. Make sure the tent affords plenty of sleeping room for the whole family, as well as adequate equipment storage and some screened windows. It is also important to make sure the tent is impervious to biting insects. In essence, you want your beginning campers to feel safe, secure, and at home.

Make sure you have adequate sleeping bags for your children. Children tend to get cold easily, and it is better to bring a warm bag than to have them awaken several times during the night with chills. Sometimes it is even a good idea to bring along a pillow and a padded ground mat for children to make them more comfortable and insulate them from the chill and hardness of the ground. If your children even suggest they want to bring along a favorite stuffed animal or blanket, then by all means take it along. It is a good idea to overpack clothing for your children, including some warmer clothing, even in warm weather, as nights may get cold. Children tend to get themselves wet and dirty frequently while they play. I feel it's good to let children bring along a few toys or games if that makes them happy and secure. Yes, you will feel like a pack animal, but your children's happiness, comfort, and security are important.

Bring along a lot of food and other goodies. Modern camping facilities provide many places to cook. Bring many of your children's favorite foods, within reason, but the meals should be hearty, nutritious, and packed with energy. Familiar food and beverages will also make your children feel at home. I strongly suggest you do not bring along a TV, and a radio should only be used to check on the weather, out of your children's earshot, if brought at all. A good part of the purpose in camping is to get your children away from that kind of everyday garbage and into communication with the family. Unchecked, electronics will replace good conversation, adventures, and play.

Make your children's first camping trip comfortable, secure, and full of natural fun and adventure. Your whole family should gear its interest and activities to that of the children. If children would rather go swimming or play with other camping children than take a heavy plant identification hike with the adults, don't insist. These interests will be developed at a later date. Dedicate yourself fully to the children's needs and interests for the first few campouts and outings. Remember also that children will not be physically able to hike great distances, so keep adventures near to camp. Camp also in the warmer times of the year, and plan your campouts during good weather. There is nothing more boring to children than to be stuck in a tent with their parents for a day while it storms outside. It is better to change camping plans than to face bad weather. As your children's awareness grows, they will begin to love the adventure of storms and discomfort, but that will all come in time.

## Advancement

After accomplishing a few easygoing campouts, begin to wean your children from some of the unnecessary luxuries. As soon as your children grow more confident and savvy, get smaller tents, possibly even two—one for the parents and one for the children. If you only have one child, allow him or her to invite a friend along for the first few times sleeping away from parents. Leave home the toys and other unnecessary playthings. As time progresses, have the children camp a little farther out from the main camp. Take more adventurous walks, and seek more primitive camp areas. But take these adjustments slowly, allowing your children to grow and become more confident with less and less. Wean them lovingly from all but the necessities, over a long period of time, until the children are at home camping in a survival shelter, under very primitive conditions. Eventually they will find great pleasure in the finer things of nature.

As you slowly wean your children from all the frills and civilized camp areas, keep them busy with adventures fraught with excitement. Try to conjure up fabulous adventures as a family: keep the danger factor controlled and to a minimum, though. Visit unknown areas of the campgrounds and push farther out. Explore new areas—old towns, waterfalls—and observe all aspects of nature. Even use the opportunity to explore nearby towns and points of interest, mingling with the natives and learning how they live. Do crazy things you wouldn't do at home or in society, like having a mud fight, rolling down grassy hills, jumping into water from a rope swing, or eating without utensils. Have adventures of being the ancient Native Americans or mountain people. Stage mock battles, scouting missions, or sneak up on other camps. Anything and everything is possible; the only limit is the imagination. But let your children ultimately decide the adventure or the areas to be explored. Above all else let spontaneity be the ruler.

As the children grow in confidence and skills, let them help with the camp chores or take over certain chores as their sole responsibility. Allow them to help with the cooking, and when they improve make them responsible for the whole meal, allowing them to decide the menu. This also teaches children to become more self-reliant and also to cook. Put them in charge of the fire or of gathering firewood. But don't forget to allow them to do some of the sloppy chores, like cleaning up or packing up the garbage. This kind of responsibility creates tremendous self-confidence in children, which will carry over to their everyday life outside the woods. If your children balk at a chore or do a sloppy job, allow the chore to create the problem. If not enough firewood is gathered, let the fire go out until they collect more. Add excitement and importance to the chores. Take the page out of *The*

*Adventures of Tom Sawyer* where he convinced his friends to paint his fence.

As the children improve even more, begin to work on the survival skills outlined in the following chapters, along with awareness and nature observation. Become more primitive, taking along a tent for security, but building and sleeping in a debris hut. Make a fire with a hand drill and leave the matches in the pack. Catch some fish for dinner, or augment your lunch with wild edible plants. Lead children through the survival skills slowly, carefully, and lovingly, never pushing them beyond their limits. Make each skill an adventure filled with laughter and excitement. You create the atmosphere where your children will beg to learn.

Remember, take it easy, and take it slow. Make sure your children are comfortable and content. Tell stories around the campfire; play games; become a child again yourself. Never downgrade children for their lack of ability or stamina, for this will only give them a defeatist attitude. Watch for boredom and dispel it by devising some exciting game or adventure. The more fun your children have the more they will beg to return, time and time again. With older children you can go through this initiation quite quickly, though with younger children it can be a slow process. Make children of all ages aware of the dangers of the woods, and instruct them to respect the wilderness, but teach that wilderness is also a friend and a home.

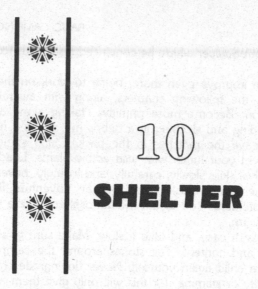

# 10

# SHELTER

In all my books and classes I stress the building of shelter as the first and most important physical survival skill students can master. Shelter is always built first in any survival situation, weather condition, or topography, for exposure is one of the greatest threats to the survivalist. Shelter also has great emotional and psychological benefits, for a shelter makes anyplace a home. Thus shelter is of the utmost importance for children, for it not only gives a safe refuge from the elements but also gives a certain sense of security and peace that is so important in calming frightened children.

As far as I am concerned there is only one shelter suitable for a survival situation—the debris hut shelter. In most survival situations survivalists are without any means of making fire, nor are they properly dressed, nor do they have any equipment other than what they are wearing. The shelter then must compensate for lack of clothing and sleeping bag and must work equally well without the use of fire. Thus, the debris hut is our only alternative, for all other shelters rely on some internal heating or warm blankets, robes, or sleeping bags. Even if older children become adept at making fires, the debris hut is a must, for there are conditions where adults would have problems building fires. The debris hut, because of its insulating properties, surpasses all other shelters in safety, ease of building, and protection. Therefore building a debris hut should be stressed and perfected more than any other skill.

It would be very difficult to teach your children to build a debris hut the same way I had to learn. Certainly each lesson Grandfather taught us was well planned, but because of his coyote teaching, there was some fear and discomfort involved. When we first learned how to build a debris hut, we were already familiar with semisurvival conditions, and though we were very young, we took the lessons and conditions in stride. I strongly suggest you do not teach your children the same way I learned to build this shelter, for it is much like teaching people to swim by throwing them into deep water. Instead use the way I was taught as a guide, then modify it to teach your children. Never force any teaching through fear or discomfort, unless your children are old enough and have enough wilderness time to overcome the discomfort, and the discomfort itself is part of the lessons.

## "GO ASK THE SQUIRRELS"

It was a bitter cold late November day when we left to go camping. Though we had known Grandfather for almost eight months, it was our first real cold-weather campout, and we were more than prepared and eager to meet the challenge. As usual, we packed up our old second-hand Boy Scout backpacks and stuffed them with old sleeping bags, thin blankets, an old ripped pup tent, and whatever canned food we could find. We had learned to build a fire with a bow drill that past summer, but we still carried matches. We were not yet competent in any of the skills we had learned, so we tended to pack as if we were going to be gone for six months in the Arctic. Carrying the backpacks was a tiring and labored process that made even short trips seem endless. The packs we carried were more for pack mules than for eight-year-old boys.

In the past, once the camp had been reached we would abandon the packs, then strike out in all directions to explore and learn. At night we would come back to the packs to set up camp and to eat. We didn't realize it, but the packs were our lifeline, our umbilical cord back to civilization. It was these lifelines to civilization that Grandfather wanted to sever us from, and as soon as possible. He saw them as a chain that would never allow us to travel free and wild in the wilderness. Depending on civilization, he believed, would never allow us to develop or realize our connection, our umbilical cord, to earth mother. It was on this campout that he finally cut that cord.

We reached our camp area by midmorning, set up our pup tent, cut wood, and set up camp, then followed Grandfather out into the woods. We started by tracking deer, then continued on to explore a cedar swamp, then to watch Grandfather make and set a fish trap, then to survey a thick part of the woods where we finally rested. It was then I noticed the weather was getting bad and it was nearing dusk. Cold icy winds were beginning to blow, and a few drops of rain were starting to fall when I told Grandfather we should be heading back to camp. I had no idea where I was or how far from camp I had come, for the day was an endless string of activity, and I knew we had walked far. Grandfather smiled at me for a moment with that smile I had come to know meant I was about to learn something, then said, "We camp here."

I could not speak, for my heart was in my throat and I was terrified. I was certain, especially with the oncoming weather, I was going to die. Trying to preserve the image of myself as a young warrior, an image of strength unshaken by the nearness of death or any discomfort, I said "No problem," which came out more like a squeak than a confident statement. Sensing now that we were in trouble, I ran to get Rick, who was just returning from the fish trap. With as much confidence and strength as I could muster, so as not to seem frightened to death in his eyes, I told him what Grandfather had said. I could see the pained fear in his eyes, nearing a controlled panic, for he too did not know how far we had wandered from our packs. With a shaking voice, he said "No problem" and pulled a Boy Scout handbook from his jacket pocket. "We'll probably find all we need in here," he said as he began to fumble through the pages nervously.

We huddled under a small pine tree and began to leaf through the book. In a section under survival we found a picture of a lean-to with a fire out front and several scouts sitting around laughing. We had never noticed before that the picture had been taken in the summertime and that the scouts had sleeping bags and cooking utensils all around them. Subsequently near the picture was a drawing of how the shelter should look after it was built. We talked a bit about building the shelter, where we would find the building materials, and how we could set it up without lashing, as we had no cordage. Just as we began to feel secure and confident, it began to rain and we cut short our discussion. Deep inside, though it was unspoken, we were both sure we would probably freeze to death, but the scouts looked warm and happy, so we decided to give it a try. Anything was better than sitting there and freezing to death. At least we would die as warriors. Grandfather, as usual, had disappeared.

We began to work feverishly, working up a sweat even in the cold weather. As we worked and the shelter took shape, we grew more excited and confident. We made a frame by using Y sticks with sturdy cross braces, and lashed them with some bull brier vines. We laid a framework of smaller sticks and limbs, finally covering the entire shelter with bark gathered from a huge dead pine tree we found nearby. The shelter looked almost identical to the one in the book, except it leaked in various places, but for the most part it was dry. Fortunately Rick also carried in some matches wrapped in waxed paper, and in no time we had a roaring fire just outside the big front door. Within minutes we were warm and comfortable and felt a certain sense of pride and relief.

Our first problem that night was that we had faced the opening of the shelter the wrong way—that is, into the wind. We constantly battled smoke and live sparks, or gusts of chilling wind laden with rain. The second problem was drainage. We had not taken into consideration the possibility of water runoff, and though the roof and sides of the shelter had only a few leaks, there was a river of cold water running under one side of the shelter. We had to huddle close together on the highest side, which was also the smokiest. We were also kept damp by the constant outside foraging trips for firewood. In our haste, we hadn't gathered much and most of the wood in the immediate area had been used for the shelter. By the time full dark had arrived it had become more and more difficult to locate any wood at all.

As we tried to sleep we discovered a few simple laws of fire, warmth, and sleep. First, because of the shape of the shelter, there was no way to lie down so both of us could face the fire. Second, because we did not have the proper clothing, the part of our bodies facing away from the fire was always cold, no matter how we lay. Third, as we fell asleep so did the fire, and we kept having to wake up and build the fire back up. It never occurred to us that we should have fire watches, where one of us would sleep while the other tended the fire. We hardly got more than fifteen minutes sleep at a time, and I doubt we had more than an hour of sleep the whole night. By dawn, with sleep and firewood scarce, we were left with just the two original sticks and the cross brace from the shelter. All else we had burned in our desperation to stay warm.

As Grandfather approached what was left of our shelter, we ran to him, telling him what had happened during the night. We then showed him the picture of the lean-to in the Boy Scout manual, the only page that hadn't been burned, and he began to laugh, almost out of control. At the time we could not see any humor in anything, but now looking back, I can see how funny it must have seemed to him. He looked at the picture again and said "That no shelter, that umbrella, nothing to keep you warm. Like house with no heater, lodge with no fire, or a tent with no sleeping bag." "But we have no sleeping bags, and we can't put a fire in such a small shelter," I said. "Then you must build a shelter for tonight that needs no fire or bedding," he said. "And how can I learn to build one of these shelters?" I asked, with a little disgust and fear in my voice. Knowing I now had to spend another miserable night in the cold, however, made me listen intently. He smiled and advised, "Go ask the squirrels."

I had known Grandfather long enough to recognize that this was his way. He would never teach us anything nature could teach better. Everything we wanted to know about anything could be found in "Nature's University," but we had to work for it. That was what was scaring both of us now, for the night was only a short day away, and the lessons learned from nature took a great deal of time, awareness, and patience, all of which were running thin. We had to learn what the squirrels had to teach quickly. We immediately started to study everything of their world. Most of the morning was spent just trying to find a squirrel, and a good part of the afternoon was used trying to find out what lessons about shelter they had to teach.

The squirrels taught us quite a bit about shelters in a short period of time. They also taught us about insulation and the way a shelter had to be built in order to repel rain. We found that the squirrels build huge leafy nests, high up in trees in branch clusters. They use these nests especially when no holes can be found, and even when they do find hollow trees, they always line them with soft materials. The squirrels taught us the value of insulation, consisting of tiny air spaces that trap and hold body heat, in weather wet or dry. They also showed us what materials to use and what shape to build the shelter so rain will not penetrate. Their nests were like huge fiber-filled sleeping bags where they would be out of the wind and weather, very warm and snug, even in a high, exposed tree.

Without hesitation, Rick and I began to gather all manner of forest litter and debris. We learned from the squirrels that it did not matter what type, only that there was a lot of it and that it created the all-important dead-air space when piled. We made a fascine of rakes from dead limbs and began to rake up piles of debris, piling it into an ever-growing domed pile in the center of our camp. We collected dead oak leaves, pine needles, dried ferns, dried sphagnum moss, even chips of old bark and sticks. Within a few hours we had a towering pile of debris. I was glad my dad would never see this, for I hated to rake leaves at home and this would only show him what I could do if I put my mind and energy to it. We finished at dusk, to ever-increasing winds, colder temperatures, and freezing drizzle.

Fatigue had now overtaken us and without hesitation we both burrowed inside the pile and fell almost immediately to sleep. I remember waking up periodically through the night, hot and sweaty, even though the debris was damp, then removing some article of clothing, only to immediately fall back to sleep. We did sleep soundly, until just a few hours before dawn. The night and activity had taken its toll on the shelter. With the removal of clothing, the constant tossing, and the relentless winds blowing debris from the shelter, we awoke almost at the same time, shivering. The debris had fallen down all around us, and we must have looked like two baby birds in a huge nest. The shelter had failed to stay up. We torched off what was one of the biggest bonfires I can ever remember lighting. We simply burned all the leaves, all at once, in our desperation to get warm. Morning found us huddled together next to a huge patch of charred and smoldering ground.

As Grandfather approached us, I glanced toward him and in a very disgusted voice declared, "Your squirrels are stupid." I suspect he had known everything that had happened, as he usually did, so no explanation was necessary. He said, "Do not blame the squirrels, for they are good teachers. It is you who did not listen to their lessons, nor did you look close enough into their shelters." I was so disgusted with myself and angry at the failure of our shelter that I climbed a tree and began to pull apart an old abandoned squirrels' nest. The reason our shelter had failed and the squirrels' shelter remained intact even during the most violent weather was the way they are constructed. First, there is an internal skeletal structure that houses the sleeping chamber and keeps the inner debris in place. Second, the outer part, or shell, of their shelter is held in place by a latticework of sticks that keep the debris from blowing away. I was so disgusted at what I had overlooked. It was a valuable lesson in observing and overlooking the little things.

Thus Rick and I learned the skill of making a debris hut. The debris hut has been used as a survival lodge since our ancestors were hunter-gatherers. I suspect they had learned to build these same shelters the way we had learned, by asking the squirrels. The last night in the camp was very warm and comfortable. Grandfather had helped us with the final lessons and modifications, and we slept soundly even though the rain and cold winds were stronger than they had been. From that lesson on, neither Rick nor I used a tent or sleeping bag again, and we traveled lighter and freer.

At this point I would like to leave the discussion of building the debris hut until later on in the text. Here I would like to discuss some basic knowledge necessary to building a good shelter and some basic alternatives. In the following sections, as we build the basic shelter knowledge, you will find knowledge that will be useful in teaching your children general survival techniques and know-how. It will also build a better understanding of the wilderness and its moods, which your children should be aware exist. The more children know of nature and various conditions and alternatives, the less frightened they will be.

## NATURAL SHELTER

I do not approve of any natural shelter as a place to sleep or for long-term use. At best, like the lean-to, natural shelters are simply umbrellas and will not keep survivalists, especially children, warm and comfortable in killing weather. Some natural shelters are dangerous, and children should be taught to spot these dangers quickly. Some natural shelters are fine in some weather conditions but of little protection in others, thus each natural shelter should be viewed as only a place to get out of the weather for a short period of time. In essence, a natural shelter should be viewed as a place for a short reprieve from bad weather when traveling or for a temporary comfort when in the process of building a debris hut. However, natural shelters are a very important aspect of survival, especially in escaping temporary bad weather. The following is a list of some of the different types of natural shelters and their uses.

## Windbreaks

Wind is one of the most dangerous conditions survivalists have to face. We constantly hear meteorologists speak of "windchill," especially during the winter months. Winds remove precious body heat; the faster the wind, the faster the heat loss. Generally windchill nowadays connotes the action of wind on bare flesh, but even fully dressed survivalists still suffer the ravages of windchill. In cold wind many garments tend to allow too much air in; thus the body gets chilled more easily. Where a light jacket may be very warm on a still winter day, a light wind on that same day could make the cold unbearable. Also, in high winds any exposed skin, such as ears, fingers, and face, are subject to frostbite. The same effect of cooling can be felt from a fan on a hot summer day. Though the temperature remains the same, the body is cooler.

Wind is a real and ever-present danger to anyone who is outdoors and unprepared. The reason wind is so dangerous is that many times its dangers go unnoticed and its warnings unheeded. A calm day can easily become blustery and cold within a few moments, leaving anyone in a real and dangerous situation. I constantly tell my students to always wear more than necessary when going out into the woods, even for a short trip. It's far easier to carry clothing when it becomes unnecessary than to suffer later on if the weather changes. Bringing more clothing or packing along a windbreaker is a good habit to get your children into. Blocking the winds also prevents dehydration no matter what the temperature. Remember, exposure to winds has the same consequence summer or winter; both are considered exposure, whether they are the drying winds of summer or the chilling winds of winter.

It is possible for people to freeze to death at 50°F. I know most people find that hard to believe, but it happens and happens frequently. The temperature can be 50°F, and if there is a strong wind and rain and the people are dressed lightly then they are in danger of hypothermia. Once on one of our basic courses just such a problem occurred. At our base survival camp the day seemed warm even though there was a light rain and a light wind. We left for a gathering trip and I told the people to wear warm clothing. Many of them looked at me as if I had become a mother hen, and my warning went unheeded. There were even a few people who just wore their T-shirts and shorts. By the time we got to our destination, the winds felt stronger because there were no windbreaks and the drizzle continued to fall. Within ten minutes more than half the class had to be sent back to camp. Some came close to the first stages of hypothermia, even though the temperatures remained the same as they had been back at the camp.

Winds can also dehydrate a body quickly, sapping it of moisture very fast. Even on a hot day it is a good idea to get out of strong winds, especially when water is scarce. On a hot and windy day it is possible to lose water so fast, you do not realize you are dehydrating, and you could essentially die of thirst. Certainly a gentle breeze on a hot day is very refreshing, but a strong wind on a hot day is downright dangerous. In all cases the best advice is to stay out of the wind and stay dry. If you can teach your children one thing only, then teach them that.

There are many types of windbreaks, ranging from thick brush to a fallen tree or a large rock. Windbreaks do just that—they break the wind and protect the survivalist. Half the battle of survival is getting out of the wind, and the dividends can be felt immediately. Children can be easily taught to find windbreaks with a game called Hide from the Wind. In the game each child is given a piece of string with a feather or piece of light paper hung on one end. After explaining to the children what a windbreak is and pointing out a few, tell them to quickly go and find a good windbreak, while you count to 100. When all the children have found windbreaks have them hold the feathers at various locations in the windbreak to see how much they move. The child whose feather moves the least is the winner. You can repeat the game several times, asking that the windbreaks get better. You will be surprised how easily children find good windbreaks, for it is part of their natural instinct.

It is important to work with your children. Experiment with the various kinds of windbreaks, finding out what kinds are better than others. It is also important to teach your children to look for potential danger in windbreaks. Have them look for windbreaks that could potentially blow over or collapse on them. Have them become aware of dead trees and limbs that could break off in the wind and injure them. Also teach them the commonsense dangers of landscapes and to avoid places that snakes, scorpions, or other potentially dangerous animals can hide. In landscapes where poisonous snakes and insects are prevalent, have them check potential windbreaks with a stick before seeking shelter there. This is also true of any other natural shelter, for a potential shelter for us is also a potential shelter for all manner of animals.

### Weather Breaks

Weather breaks are any natural shelter that partially or completely shelter survivalists from the weather. Generally these are not as easy to find as windbreaks, for they must also protect from above as well as on all sides, from all weather conditions. Much more care should be taken in locating a weather break and the area carefully scanned for dangerous conditions, since many weather breaks need to be crawled into or under to be used. Each weather break is different, depending on the location and size, and no two protect exactly in the same way in the same weather conditions. What may be a good natural weather break for hot sun and drying winds may not be a good shelter for driving rains.

### Brush Piles

In many wilderness areas there are brush piles left over from lumbering or general clearing of lands. Some of these brush piles make excellent temporary shelters from all kinds of weather. Some brush piles are packed too tight to get into or under, but some afford little crawl spaces. The tight lattice of brush tends to easily buffer against hot sun and high winds and can give good protection from snows and average rains. However, brush piles can become very dangerous for two reasons. First they may collapse and pin survivalists inside, immobilizing them in the brush tangles; however, that is rare and usually only common in huge piles of old brush. Second, brush piles are home for all manner of small animals, and where there are small animals, large and small predators, snakes, and all manner of insects can also be found. Great care should be taken when using brush piles in bear or poisonous snake country.

If children are strong enough, they can shore up and secure a brush pile with sticks. This way potential danger from collapse is minimized. By lifting part of the brush onto stronger poles and sticks the children can create a larger space to crawl into or create their own. This procedure also frightens away most of the animals that would be using the pile as a refuge. However, caution children about doing too much work, as it will only be used temporarily, and oftentimes a debris hut is easier to build. The crawl space inside a brush pile can also be upgraded by stuffing it with leaves and debris, thus creating dead-air space and adding warming capability to the shelter.

### Thick Bushes and Vine Tangles

Thick bushes and vine tangles can afford good protection from the wind, storms, and hot sun. They are only a temporary reprieve from the elements and are usually effective and safe. Though there is a limited supply of these natural shelters during the winter months, thick evergreens with low-hanging branches can be substitutes. Generally the thick bushes and vine tangles are similar in protection to the brush piles: they do not block out as much rain or winds, but they are safer. They also do not collapse, but the areas around these tangles should be scanned for tall dead trees that may blow down in a wind. Though these areas contain a wide assortment of wildlife, the animals are not as concentrated as in the brush piles.

## Fallen Trees

Fallen trees afford us potential protection in two ways. If the limbs and branches are thick and still hold their leaves after the fall, we can seek refuge in them. However the protection is minimal at best. If the trunk is still propped up on the stump, we can crawl beneath and get protection from the snows and rain. This can be very dangerous, especially because of the possibility of collapse. Have children check the trunk and stump thoroughly to make sure the hold is very secure. They can further secure the tree by propping several stout sticks beneath the trunk. If the tree is large enough and the surrounding brush thick enough, this makes one of the better natural shelters, but they are rare.

## Rock Piles, Small Crevasses, and Caves

These natural shelters can be found in various landscapes and make good shelter but can potentially be very dangerous. Anytime rocks, caves, or crevasses are found, they should be checked for sturdiness and confirmed to be solid. Also, all the rocks surrounding the potential shelter should be checked to make sure there is no potential for a cave-in or a rock slide. Again, animals will sometimes use these areas as we would; check first with a stick before entering. Teach children to be aware of bats, skunks, raccoons, and other larger animals.

Many times caves will afford all-around protection from storms, but again they are only temporary shelters. If good caves are found, they can be modified with debris for warmth and thus be made into long-term shelters. Be careful with fire in caves, as the heat may loosen rocks and cause them to fall or the entire cave to collapse. Like caves, little tunnels and hides can be found in rock outcroppings and piles as well as crevasses. They too can be used as temporary shelters but must be checked for potential danger.

### Traveling with Natural Shelter

When children are traveling home from an outing and they encounter survival conditions that threaten them, they can be taught to move with natural shelters. Teach your children to move from one shelter to another on their journey to safety. Teach them not to wait until they get cold or in pain before they seek the next shelter, but to take shelter as soon as they feel a little uncomfortable. That way they move from one sheltered area to the next. Certainly it will take more time to get home or to safety, but teach them to think and not to rush. Children are more vulnerable to exhaustion and hypothermia than adults are and can burn out quickly, which could result in a very dangerous situation. It is also a good idea to teach children to avoid old, dilapidated equipment, cars, and buildings found in some wilderness areas. They could easily get trapped, or the buildings could collapse. This same method of sheltered travel can be used in towns or cities when children are making their way home from school or play, especially during life-threatening weather.

### The Animal Home Game

The best way to teach children to find natural shelters is to have them play the animal home game. Tell them animals need protection from the weather as we do, then show them some natural shelters in the area. Explain to them that you are not interested in burrows or nests but natural homes for animals. Then turn the children loose on the landscape to find animal homes. The object of their game is not only to find their animal a good secure home but also the best home. After each child has selected a home, gather them all together and have each child lead the group to his or her animal home. All the children should then individually tell the group why they chose this area and what it would protect the animal from. Make the children aware of all the positives, then point out the negatives, then challenge the children to see if they can find better ones. As always, the children will astound you with their finds.


## CHOOSING SHELTER LOCATION

A good shelter in a bad location is a poor shelter. It is of the utmost importance to teach children how to select good shelter locations, for good locations will make even the most mediocre shelters better. When teaching children about location, make it a game. Walk in the wilderness with your children and pretend with them that you are looking for a good place to build a "clubhouse" or a "fort." I find that when I do not use the term "shelter" but add some adventurous word such as camp, fort, clubhouse, or hideaway, they easily become part of the adventure. This way when teaching children, it is no longer just teaching but an exciting adventure. As you walk and talk about the various locations, their good and bad points, help your children choose better and better areas, and see if they too can pick out the bad spots and tell you why. The following are points to remember when choosing a good shelter location.

### Never Close to Water

It is not a good idea to put a shelter any closer than fifty yards from any body of water, stream, swamp, or lowland. Where water is concerned there is always a mist and dampness that can saturate the clothing and shelter, chilling occupants. Certainly it is aesthetically pleasing to camp near water, and our literature abounds with pictures of camps along waterways, but it shows poor judgment and outdoor skills. Take your children to areas near waterways and have them feel the dampness of the earth and the damp atmosphere surrounding them. Teach them that the dampness can chill them in winter and summer alike. Explain to them how being damp or wet causes the body to lose heat, even on the warmest nights. Give them an example of how swimming in the summer cools the body, and how uncomfortable it would feel to be damp and cold in the winter.

### Well-drained Areas

One of the conditions frequently overlooked when choosing shelter areas is the way the land drains. Choose shelter locations in well-drained areas on high ground. Scan the surrounding landscape for tracks of water such as drainage marks or runoff channels worn into the earth. Also make sure the shelter areas are slightly higher than the surrounding landscape so water runs off away from the shelter. Not only should shelters shield from the storms above but also beneath. Teach your children by taking them out on a rainy day. Have them watch rain flooding various areas of the land, and where the rainwater collects and runs off, and have them imagine what a shelter would feel like with water running through it. In the summer have them play frog and lie in a puddle in the deep woods or stand still in the summer rain. Let them see how even on a summer day water can chill to the bone.

## Not in Thick Forest or Center of a Field

Never place your shelter in the center of a field. Certainly the shelter will get plenty of sun, but there are no natural windbreaks or buffers to bad weather. In the center of a field the shelter is ravaged by the elements and winds. Ironically a shelter should never be placed in a thick, tall forest. There are plenty of windbreaks and weather breaks there, but the forest is shielded from the sun and is perpetually damp. Instead good shelter areas are found in the transition areas, the fringe areas between forest and field. These areas have brushy plants, grasses, and vine tangles that block the storms and protect shelters, while allowing enough warming sunshine in to keep camps dry and comfortable. These are also the same areas animals choose to live and feed. Exploring them with your children can also serve to teach them to follow the example of animals.

Teach your children about the dangers of putting shelters in a deep forest by having them sense the dampness there, much as they did around water. Have them feel the forest litter, running their hands beneath the upper layer to feel how damp it is less than an inch below the surface. Do this even in the summer when the days are hot and dry, with the same results. Also have them feel the intensity of storms and winds while standing or sitting in the middle of an open area or field. Then teach them to watch the animals living in the fringe areas, how they are protected and dry.

## Never on Poisonous Plants or on Insect Nests

Children should be aware of the vegetation on the ground where they intend to put their shelter. Teach them the poisonous plants in their area, to a point where they can spot them at a distance. Teach them also to observe shelter areas closely for evidence of ant nests or wasp nests, or even the burrows of small rodents. There is no way to safely remove the plants or animals from these areas, and it is best to pick another area. Teach your children not to disturb the balance of nature by needlessly killing plants and animals. Even though they can be harmful to us, they have a right to live, for they were living there first.

## Danger Areas

Be aware, as always, of danger areas, and choose a shelter location free from dead trees, potential rock or mud slides, or other hazards that may cause damage during a storm or high winds. Choose areas that are secure, safe, and stable. Show your children a fallen tree and the damage it can do to other trees around it. Have them hold a small branch and have them imagine being it, with it, as it fell from a high tree. If you live in an area of rocks and mud banks, show them the damage rockfalls can cause by pointing out bruised and fractured trees and vegetation.

### Final Notes

Make sure the chosen shelter area has enough debris and material to build the shelter. A good shelter location without adequate debris means the children have to import materials and thus burn up time and energy. All fires should be kept far away from the shelter, as any shelter is easily ignited. When the children retire into the shelter, the fire should be put out completely. A debris hut will insulate from heat as well as cold, and by the time the survivalist realizes the shelter is ablaze, it is usually too late. Finally all shelter doors should face away from prevailing winds and storms. Usually this is toward the east, but if your children are unsure of direction then just have them feel the direction of the wind and adjust their door away from it. Wind and rain blowing in a shelter door will take the heat away from the inside of the shelter.

## THE DEBRIS HUT

As I have stated before, building the shelter is the most important physical skill for the survivalist to master and the first chore done in a survival situation; and the debris hut is the only shelter I approve of for a survival situation. The debris hut is the only shelter that will keep a survivalist warm and safe without fire or proper clothing despite the ravages of temperature and weather conditions. Building the debris hut properly is important, for an improperly constructed debris hut will not work well. Thus it is very important to teach your children the correct way to construct the hut, the best materials, the proper location, and the various modifications to fit each situation and topography.

After the shelter location has been chosen, it is time to build the debris hut. I would recommend that at this time the survivalist take an overview of the area, picturing the shelter, the door location, and where the building materials will be gathered. A sturdy sapling, rock, log, or prop is also selected and tested for strength. At this point a long and sturdy ridgepole is selected from the landscape. The length of the pole should be a little longer than the distance from the survivalist's feet to outstretched hand, held high over the head. At this point, one end of the pole is braced up on the prop and secured with other props, while the other end of the pole is resting on the ground. The height of the raised end of the ridgepole should be no taller than crotch-high from the ground.

Once the ridgepole is in place, ribbing is placed along both sides at an angle, with an opening left for the door. The ribbing is made from stout sticks placed close together. At this time the survivalist should crawl inside and check to see that the shelter is snug but still permits free movement. Remember, you are not building a palace but more a huge fiber-filled sleeping bag. Next a lavish assortment of fine brush is thrown over the entire shelter to create a netting effect. Thus the skeletal structure of the shelter is completed. This skeleton will support the outer debris and keep the inner debris in place.

Now it is time to collect the debris that will be placed on and in the shelter. Using forked sticks fused from broken branches to protect the hands, rake up piles of forest litter, dead leaves, dried ferns, grasses, mosses, anything that lofts high, creating dead-air space. When ground is covered with snow, green pine and evergreen branches can be used, but you will need much more of these to create enough dead-air spaces comparable to a normal hut. Green materials tend to flatten when piled, unlike dried vegetation, which maintains its general shape.

First the debris is piled on the shelter, creating a huge domed effect. Sticks are then woven around the door and more debris piled on so the door is near the ground and barely wide enough to snake through. From mid-spring through the summer and into mid-fall, two feet of debris all around the shelter is more than enough to shed all storms and keep the occupant warm. In the winter and in very cold weather three to four feet will be needed. This sounds like a lot, but an average adult can build an entire shelter in less than an hour. An average child usually takes an hour and a half. This may seem like a lot of effort and energy burned, but when you consider the alternatives, there is not much choice. If a shelter is not built by nightfall, one could succumb to hypothermia and eventually death. One way or the other energy will be burned.

Once the outside of the shelter has enough debris, a layer of light sticks should be thrown on top to hold the debris in place. A strong wind could easily strip the shelter. Do not use heavy branches and sticks to hold the debris, as these only tend to compress dead-air space and what we need to maintain is as much loft as possible. Once the outer shelter is complete, stuff the inside with the softest and driest debris you can find. Stuff the shelter from bottom to top, crawl inside to compress, then stuff it again. If the weather is rainy and all the debris is wet, then use it anyway. Certainly you will be wet, but you'll still be warm and alive. Debris huts work well, dry or wet.

When entering the debris hut for the night, enter feetfirst and work your way into the upper portion of the shelter. This way you have plenty of insulation between you and the ground. You should be totally surrounded by debris, warm, and relatively comfortable. At this time plug the door closed with a pile of leaves you have set aside just outside the door. Generally the door will not need to be fully plugged until the temperatures get well below freezing. During the day, when you are working, use the outside of the debris hut as a backrest to insulate and block the wind. If at any time you get cold, enter the hut and warm up. Stay put in the debris hut during severe weather, much like the animals do.

**Note:** Make sure the debris hut is marked well so it stands out from the landscape. Debris huts, by virtue of how they are built, blend in or disappear into the landscape. It is advisable to mark them so searchers can find the survivalist.

## TEACHING SHELTER TO CHILDREN

Children easily take to learning how to build debris huts, provided it is in the spirit of adventure, excitement, and play. There is a deep natural instinct in all of us to seek shelter, and we can capitalize on this instinct easily, especially in children. You too, as a teacher, must develop the sense of excitement, wonder, and adventure to add fuel to their fire. Play with them, but allow them to do most of the work, as the finished product will give them a sense of pride and accomplishment. Never call the debris hut a shelter but rather a squirrel nest, a hideout, a fort, or even a clubhouse. Build into your teaching a story line to add fantasy to your lessons. The more excited the children grow, the more they will put into building the shelter. Don't explain too much or get too technical, just do; then correct the problems while building the shelter or when the shelter is finished.

When I teach a group of children to build a shelter, I first teach them about natural shelters and to find a good shelter location. After I am sure they have understood the basic lessons, I take them out into the woods. There we begin to discuss the various animals, how they live, and where they live. I then ask the children to locate a squirrel nest, after explaining to them what they look like and where to find them. Usually within a few moments a nest is spotted, and that gives me a cue to ask some well-placed questions. First I ask them to see if they can guess how the nest is built and with what. As soon as they mention the leaves and debris, I ask them if that could be warm, and why.

Listen to all of them speak, for it will give you a tremendous insight into their perception. Learn to speak with them, not at them, and don't interrupt. Children can be some of our most profound teachers and can guide us back to our long-forgotten childhood purity and wonder.

Once the children have all spoken and the group has discussed the nest, that would be a good time to discuss insulation and how it works. Use something common to draw analogies to dead-air space, like fluffy blankets, the inside of a jacket, or the loft of a sleeping bag. It would also be a good time to discuss how birds fluff their feathers to create dead-air space to stay warm. Then draw their attention to the litter on the ground as you make a pile. Show them how the thick forest litter or grasses create piles replete with dead-air space. Ask each child to make his or her own pile, then bury his or her hands and feel the warmth. Go back to the squirrel nest and discuss how the squirrel uses the insulation. You will see the children begin to look at the squirrel as being "pretty smart."

It is here I like to sit the children down and tell them a story about how the animals taught the Native Americans about living with the earth. I draw their attention to the squirrels again, and tell them the squirrel shows us how to build good, strong shelters that can keep us warm and safe. And like the squirrels, we do not need sleeping bags, blankets, or even a fire to keep us warm. I also explain to children here in some way how important a shelter is and that it should always be built first if ever they get cold or stranded in the woods. I work in as much detail as possible as to the size and shape of the shelter, as well as how big the sleeping chamber should be. Later, when building a shelter, I correct any mistakes by carefully asking them questions about the cold, winds, and drafts, allowing them to work out the answers rather than by blatantly showing them. Then the fun begins.

Next I turn the entire group loose to build their own shelters or have the group build several shelters. This way they reinforce one another. I help them locate the ridgepole and set it up properly and do the same with the ribbing and the brush mesh.

Have the children stand on the ridgepole to make sure it is strong. It is important to keep the activity rolling along, accented with a sense of play and lots of laughter. Create situation fantasies like "a storm's coming and we gotta build this shelter to keep safe." Frequently allow the children to play in the skeleton; see if you both can fit, and marvel at the accomplishment. When it comes to gathering debris, there is nothing wrong with a leaf fight; laugh it up, and make the work play. Once the shelter is complete, stay around it for a while, build a fire, and make it home. Allow the children to play fort or clubhouse, to have leaf fights, and to crawl in and out at will. If you have older children, plan to stay overnight and have an adventure. But have your family tent and sleeping bags set up nearby if your children get upset or uncomfortable. This way they are not forced into staying there.

These debris hut exercises can be accomplished near family campgrounds, parks, or even in your backyard. If your children build a backyard shelter, encourage them to stay in it whenever they want. The more familiar they are with the debris hut and the more at home they feel, the more likely they will be to build one in a real survival situation. Eventually during the warmer times of the year, plan a shelter-building campout. Take all the usual supplies and gear with you to your camp, but promise one another you will not use the tent or sleeping bags unless you need to.

# MODIFICATIONS

Once the building of the debris hut has been mastered by your children, it is time to modify its use for different landscapes and building materials. In heavy grasslands, where poles and trees are scarce, trying building a freestanding domed shelter, using light brush and limbs as the skeleton. Stack the brush in a hollow dome, lavish on the grasses, and hold these in place with more brush. Stuff the inside with grasses and generally follow the procedure of the typical debris hut with plenty of dead-air space and a small but well-insulated sleeping chamber. Grass is hollow and tends to be an excellent insulator. Find a rock crevasse or small cave and stuff it with debris; you will not need poles and brush if the cave is small enough, for the rocks will support the structure.

When snow is deep on the ground, pines and evergreen boughs can be used to build the debris hut. Generally it takes much more material to build up the dead-air space, but it can easily be done. I strongly suggest this evergreen shelter only be done in times of emergency, not for practice, as too many trees are needlessly defoliated. When building shelters for practice, please make your children realize that this does throw the immediate landscape out of balance for a while. Small plants are killed, and precious ground debris is removed. Remember to break down the shelter and scatter it after use. Good survivalists always restore the area to its natural state.

## STUFFING

*Stuffing* is one of the best survival techniques to show children. Debris works well in any shape or form and can be used to keep children warm if they find their clothing is inadequate. Many times children will play far from home or camp only to be caught by bad weather. Sometimes they play so hard, they burn up much of their energy and succumb to the cold. In either case their clothing becomes inadequate and they have to warm fast or suffer frostbite and exposure. In this case I like to teach children to stuff their clothing with debris. If children do not want to build a debris hut in a survival situation, possibly they will remember to stuff themselves and they will stand a better chance. Certainly stuffing is a little uncomfortable and awkward, but it does warm you up quickly.

## THE SCARECROW GAME

One of the best ways to teach children to stuff is with the Scarecrow Game. Have the children remove their shoelaces and tie the cuffs of their pants securely to the legs. First have the children stuff the shoes, then standing, fill up the entire trouser area with soft debris. Tuck in the shirt and continue stuffing the shirt, down the arms, back, and neck. The hands can be protected by stuffing them inside the shirt, and if the shirt is long enough, it can be pulled up to protect the head. Once the stuffing process is complete, the children will look like huge overstuffed scarecrows. Have a scarecrow beauty contest and hand out prizes. Punctuate the point of how warm they feel while still making the whole process a game. Remember, children are very subject to peer pressure, so get the whole group to participate.

# PRECAUTIONS

Never scare or force the shelter building techniques onto your children. Play down the survival part and instead concentrate on the game. Lightly suggest this is done for survival as well as being a game, but don't hammer home the point. It's surprising how children will pick things up and use them in a survival situation anyway. You do not want the woods to appear as an enemy but an ally. Stress the friendship and positive forces between the earth and your children. Earth is the children's mother, and all the things of the earth are brothers and sisters. When you have to use a negative, modify that negative: for instance, call a strong and cold wind, the wind's "bad brother," where the wind in general keeps its good nature.

Have your children mark their shelters in some obvious way, as children hidden in landscapes are hard for searchers to find.

Teach your children to be aware of changing weather as well as dangerous shelter locations. The more your children are aware of the possibilities that could happen, the more they will be prepared. What you don't know can hurt you.

I must stress again the importance of shelter, and especially the debris hut. Out of all other survival skills this is the most important. Most people lost or in a survival situation ultimately die of exposure or as a result of the irrational fear of the wilderness. A shelter will make any-place home and a haven from fear and the elements.

# 11

# WATER

Obtaining water during a survival situation is the second most important task survivalists need to accomplish. The collecting of water is a little harder to learn and understand, because there is a certain degree of danger, and this possible danger, as well as the methods used to obtain water, are difficult but not impossible for children to learn. Many of the more advanced water-collecting techniques will need certain items found in the survival pack. Certainly adult survivalists can create many of these "tools" found in the survival pack from natural materials, but children have some limitations. The more advanced technique of the solar still, for example, would be difficult for young children to learn, but older children could easily master the technique. It is up to you to consider your children's age and ability, then decide what they are capable of learning.

When your children can build a good debris hut and find water, they can stay safe and healthy for a long period of time. These two elements, shelter and water, are of the utmost importance, and great care should be taken to have children master dealing with them both. Water is critical to anyone's health in a survival situation. Dehydration is a killer, and even a slight lack of water even for a short time can cause body and brain damage. Water is critical no matter what the time of year, summer or winter, for it is possible to die of dehydration at any time. It is not abnormal for people to suffer from some form of dehydration during the cold winter months, for drinking cold water tends to be something a cold person does not want to do. Lack of water will also cause a person to be more susceptible to the cold.

*Water Warning*

Today it is very difficult to find safe drinking water, even in wilderness areas. If the water isn't biologically polluted, it may be chemically polluted, or both. Unfortunately you can't see many of the pollutants in the smaller streams and waterways, but they can be present even in the clearest, most remote waters. Pure water tends to be the exception, not the rule. All water, no matter how clear, should be treated and purified in a survival situation. Getting sick on bad water can cause a simple survival situation to turn into a life-or-death struggle. When teaching your children how to collect water, stress that all water should be considered polluted until they purify or treat that water. Even streams and waterways that have been potable in the past can be polluted within a few days under the right conditions.

In essence, to be safe, all water must be purified or treated in some way. In most cases water purification is difficult, but your children can easily learn the methodology. Remember, however, that in a survival situation your purification abilities are very limited, though with a survival pack the purification can be done quite easily. Listed below are a few of the many methods of purifying water, though some are more effective and easier than others.

*Boiling Method*

The boiling method is quite easy. Simply bring water to a boil for at least five minutes. This can be done by placing a steel cup directly over hot coals or heating a rock until red hot, then placing it directly into a container of water. The hot rock will boil the water for a few minutes and kill all or most biological pollutants. Though the boiling method will rid the water of all the biological pollutants, it has little effect on chemical pollutants. I suggest at least a five-minute boil so that all the biological pollutants are destroyed. This will also help evaporate off any chemical pollutants that have a lower boiling point than the water.

*Filtering Method*

Though this method will not remove the biological or chemical pollutants from water, it will help clarify muddy or debris-laden water. The collected water should be allowed to stand for several hours, which will tend to settle the heavier particles to the bottom. Carefully pour the clearer water through a piece of white cotton cloth, or a corner of your cotton clothing, so the suspended particles are filtered out. Repeat the process several times if the first filtering does not clarify the water. In an emergency, when cloth is not carried in the survival pack, a bundle of fine grasses will make an excellent filter. I do not suggest children use any part of their clothing as a filter in cold weather, as this will render the clothing useless until it dries out. However, drinking slightly muddy water will do little harm.

There are several modern filtering devices that can be added to children's survival packs. These are filtering straws containing microporous filters, smaller than most toxic biological pollutants. The children can simply sip from a water source right through the straw or run the water through the filter. These filters are easy to carry and easy to use, but they do not remove chemical pollutants. Certainly to my hard-core and primitive survivalists, carrying anything manufactured or human-made is taboo, but we are dealing with children here, and they need the edge at first.

In a primitive situation I use a combination of dried grasses layered with sand to filter my water. But that creates a lot of work for children, and still some biological microbes work their way through. Remember that filtering, at best, clarifies the water but does not remove the pollutants. Only the modern micropore filters can accomplish this.

### Distillation Method

There are several primitive distillation methods for water, most of which are too complicated for children. However, the simple solar still is one of the easiest and best ways to accomplish distillation. Solar still distillation will usually remove most of the biological pollutants and many of the chemical pollutants, making it one of the most effective water purification systems. For children, the solar still will require them to carry the components of the still in their survival packs. The solar still distillation process is set up the same way as a typical solar still (to be described later), and the polluted water can be dumped into the pit, allowing the solar-stilling process to remove the impurities. The more advanced distillation processes require advanced survivalists to use apparatuses made from nature and are very difficult and time-consuming, especially for children.

### Chemical Method

There are many chemical water-purification compounds, liquids, and tablets found on the market. Most are very effective in removing most, if not all, biological pollutants. Some of the older-style tablets will not remove certain contaminants, as microbes have learned to resist these purification compounds. I tell my more advanced students to use a chlorine tablet, which does remove all biological pollutants, but these, and all other purification compounds, can be dangerous. I don't advise their use for very young children—only those children who know how to add the tablets and how much to use. A young child may tend to overdose the water and do more harm than good. Remember that many of these compounds are mild poisons, though harmless if used in the proper amounts.

I must stress again not to trust any water. Water sickness can cause severe health problems that can be deadly during a survival situation. Simple diarrhea or vomiting will dehydrate children quickly, putting them in greater danger than if they had stayed away from the bad water altogether. Stress the cautions of water collection with your children, and make sure they know exactly how to purify that water as well as where to find the water in the first place.

# FINDING SURVIVAL WATER SOURCES

## Natural Catches

"Natural catches" is an all-encompassing term denoting anything that holds or channels water. Lakes, rivers, ponds, streams, puddles, hollow logs, and even natural rock bowls are all considered natural catches. In a way even bogs, lowlands, and meadows could be considered natural catches. Fortunately throughout most of this country there is an abundance of natural catches; unfortunately these catches can be deadly polluted. When teaching children to find and utilize any natural catch, have them seek out the clearest water they can find. Quickly running water tends to be the best, but still the water should be filtered and purified, using any of the above methods.

Don't just tell your children how, but do it, going through the process of collecting and purifying. Children learn far better by doing than by just listening. Walk through various landscapes, from deep forests to dry lands, and help your children locate all the possible natural catches. When your children improve at finding these catches, have them look at the landscape, and then teach them to find these same catches at a distance, using the lay of the land. Help them to read the types of vegetation that love the damp areas, the gorges in rock outcroppings, or the lowland areas from greater and greater distances. Work these lessons into a general outing or exploration hike, even using the catches as a source of drinking water once purified.

## The Dew Wipe Method

When Grandfather first taught me to collect dew as a source of water, he told me a story of a young Indian boy stranded in a desert. The boy had been separated from his people and had traveled for days without

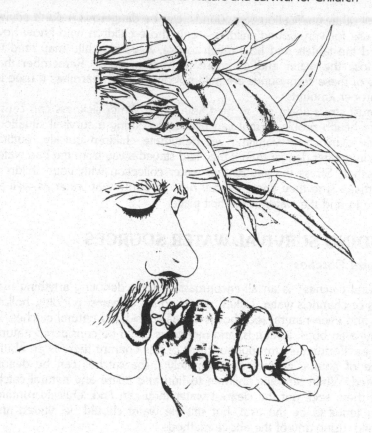

food, water, or shelter. Finally he found a cave and thanked the Great Spirit for giving him good shelter from the burning sun and drying winds. His thirst, however, was intense, and in the barren desert wilderness everything was dry and parched. He had been without water for so long, he began to feel very sick and his head pounded with pain. Certainly, he thought, the Great Spirit had given him this cave; now possibly it could help him find water. So the boy prayed and prayed, but he received no answer. He cursed the desert, and he knew he would soon die. But still no answer came.

At daybreak on the next day he ventured outside the cave to pray again. He prayed hard, but there was still no answer. Finally in utter frustration he broke down and cried, feeling that the creator had turned his back on him. Then suddenly he heard a squeak and, looking up, saw a mouse on a distant rock. The mouse appeared to be eating the rock, but the boy knew that couldn't be possible. His curiosity, now overcoming his thirst, caused him to stalk up to the mouse, and to his amazement, he saw that the mouse was licking the stone. Looking closely, the boy saw that the mouse was licking the dew from the rock and he began to do the same. Within an hour the boy was no longer thirsty. The Great Spirit had sent him a sign, answered his prayers, and saved his life.

The dew wipe method is one of my favorite methods of water collection, for it usually needs no purification process, and all children can learn to collect dew. To collect dew, simply have the children go out onto the landscape in the early morning or late evening and wipe the dew from the low vegetation, rocks, and grasses with a rag. The dew can be wrung directly into the mouth or collected in a container. It is surprising how much and how quickly dew can be collected, even in the driest parts of the country. The only hazards are wiping the dew from poisonous plants or chemically sprayed vegetation. Great care should be taken to teach your children poisonous plants, and the children should never wipe dew near a roadway or in farmlands when practicing. These areas could contain high concentrations of chemical pollutants. Children should also be careful in forested areas, as many timber companies spray the lands to retard undesirable plant growth. Generally, however, dew is one of the safest water sources.

## The Solar Still

Unless your children are older and accomplished survivalists, they will need to carry the apparatus for the solar still in their survival packs. The solar still is quite easy to make, with the only hard part being the digging of the hole in the proper location. The solar still will enable your children to obtain water in very dry areas and to purify any water obtained by other means. Again, in teaching the solar still, it is not enough just to describe it, but build it and drink the water. Build one every time you camp and gather some of your camp water from the still. Eventually allow your children to build a working solar still totally on their own. The more solar stills your children make, the better they will become at getting water in difficult situations.

Finding a good solar still location is half the battle. Solar stills should be located in damp areas, lowlands, at the base of hills, in dry streambeds, and in the bottom of dry gorges. They can even be set up next to a natural catch, where the soil is already saturated with moisture. In very dry areas green nonpoisonous plants, damp forest litter, and even urine can be added to the hole to allow the additives to enhance the moisture of the soil. Adding these things will give the solar still a better yield. Again, the best way to confirm that an area you have chosen for a still is good is to build a still and check the yield. This will avoid costly mistakes in a real survival situation.

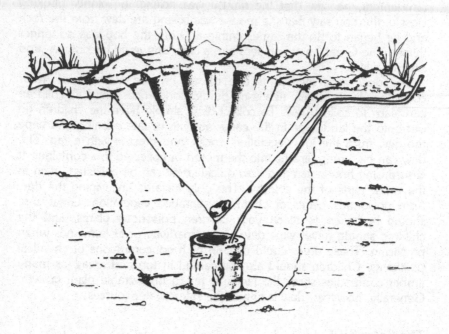

What you will need for a solar still is a sheet of clear, strong plastic 6 feet × 6 feet, six feet of plastic tubing, and a cup or container. Digging sticks and rocks are also necessary. To build a solar still, dig a large hole about two feet deep by three feet across, deeper and wider in drier areas. In some areas you must dig quite deep to reach damp soil. Place the cup or container in the bottom of the hole and insert one end of the plastic tubing into the cup and weight it in place. Now cover the hole with the sheet of plastic, and allow the other end of the plastic tubing to run out of the hole. Seal all around the edges of the plastic with dirt so no moisture escapes and no air gets into the still. Weight down the center of the plastic sheet, directly over the cup, with a rock or some other heavy object, creating a cone effect, with the point of the cone directly over the container or cup.

The solar still will work on a sunny or partly cloudy day. The sun bakes down through the plastic and begins to warm the earth in the hole. Moisture from the soil begins to evaporate, in what is called a greenhouse effect. The evaporating moisture then collects on the underside of the plastic, where it condenses and runs down the cone to the point, where it then drips into the cup. The solar still does not have to be taken apart to collect the water, but the water can be sucked right through the plastic tubing. Thus the seal does not have to be broken nor the solar still disturbed. In most soils a solar still will not have to be moved for several days. Remember that polluted water can be added to the hole for distillation purification.

A primitive modification of the solar still can be used to melt snow in a survival situation. It is dangerous for anyone to eat snow, for cold snow will only chill the body and possibly cause hypothermia. All snow must be melted before it is ingested, preferably warmed. A good way to melt snow is to first pack a depression into the snow, about two feet deep by three feet wide. Cover the hole over with a light layer of evergreen branches so they extend out beyond the sides of the hole. The sun will then warm the dark green evergreens and begin to melt the snow beneath, even on below-freezing days. Water is then taken from the hole and warmed in a cup over a fire.

When we are dealing with a survival situation and the possibility of dehydration, all we can hope for is to remove most of the biological pollutants. Most of the chemical pollutants cannot be removed, but we then must make a choice whether to drink or die of thirst. There are a few chemical pollutants that will kill immediately, but most have to be taken in large quantities. During a survival situation the survivalist will not reach the chemical poisoning point or experience any long-term effect with most very diluted chemicals. If you notice dead vegetation around and near the water with no visible life growing or living in the water, leave it alone. If, however, the water looks healthy and there are healthy plants and animals inside and out, purify for biological pollutants and drink the water. Teach your children to know healthy water, healthy water vegetation, and animals.

## An Environmental Message for Your Children

It is here, during the teaching of water, that your children will realize how polluted water can be. Certainly this will raise many questions in your children and will become a splendid opportunity to teach them a lesson with tremendous impact. Refer frequently to the water as earth mother's blood. Describe to them how many people look at the waterways and oceans as dumping grounds and how some people believe the water does not matter. Describe to them how factories, houses, and erosion destroy our waters and that many waterways may never be healthy again. Teach them what pollution will do to animals, fishes, and plants, as well as humans. Describe to them how it was possible not long ago to drink from all the streams and rivers of this country. You may find that your children get angry enough to get involved in cleaning up waterways or becoming part of youth groups against pollution.

# 12

# FIRE

Shelter and water are the most important survival skills children can learn. With them children can stay safe and healthy for a long period of time, with little else. However, the ability to make and use fire is an asset to any child. It is the third most important skill children need in a survival situation, even more important than food. Fire gives a child heat and light, signals for help, creates a definite security, and is a tremendous tool for cooking food, making other tools, and for purifying water. It is difficult to teach very young children to make a primitive fire from scratch, but every child should still be taught some basics of fire making. Very young children, from a mature five-year-old to age seven, should be able to use matches and maintain a fire, and children from the age of eight should be able to make a primitive fire.

Even though I was born on the edge of wilderness and fire was part of my life, Grandfather still led us to the making and using of fire slowly. At first he built the fires and added the wood, and we only collected the wood. Then, after a few weeks, we learned to maintain the fire, what wood burned better than others, and all the precautions necessary to safe fire building. We then learned how to use matches safely, and how to prepare the fire for the lighting. Then, after almost six months of building and maintaining fires, Rick and I learned to build fires using the primitive bow drill method. Thus, we learned to respect fire, through use. We also learned what a fire could do when it went out of control. Grandfather took us once to a blazing forest fire to see the destruction and feel the intensity of the heat, firsthand, which left a real and lasting impression on us forever.

I urge you to teach your children in much the same way Grandfather taught me. Teach them slowly, especially the younger children. Have them become part of the wood-collecting process at first. Then have them maintain the fire and, finally, build the fire from the start. Teach them to use matches safely. (The best matches to use in teaching children are stick matches.) Teach them the dangers of fire making and how to make a safe fire. Teach them to put out a fire properly before they leave a camp area. If you can, take your children to a site of a forest fire and show them the destruction. Show them that this is what could happen to a fire that is unattended, or a fire that is not properly extinguished.

Only you can be the judge of whether your children are old enough to understand, build, maintain, and use fire properly. Each child is different, and it is this difference that obviates hard or fast rules. The only rule is to take the teaching process slowly and carefully, making sure your children understand each part of the fire-building process and safety. Observe carefully how your children handle each process before deciding what they are capable of. Most children are very mature when given responsibility, especially the responsibility of fire. The trust given to your children during these teachings can be the lifelong bonding lesson of mutual trust.

## Safe Fire Locations

Before building a fire children must learn where to put the fire. The location of the fire is of the utmost importance not only for optimum warmth and light but also for safety. There are many dangers children will have to anticipate when searching for a good fire location, and the following are just a few of the more important ones. Certainly not every environment and topography can be covered fully: that is up to the teacher.

1.  Never build a fire closer than ten feet from any shelter. Natural shelters are like huge tinder bundles that could easily ignite from a tiny spark. Have your children make sure winds are not blowing from the fire to the shelter area, as some sparks can travel quite a distance.

2.  Never build a fire under a rock overhang or in a cave. The heat from the fire could cause the rock to expand, crack, and fall. Teach your children that even if a rock looks solid, it could contain small cracks filled with water. When the water heats up or boils, it could actually explode a rock, much like a bomb. Caution your children about using rocks around the fire. Teach them to collect rocks from high, well-drained places, never from streams, swamps, or damp bottomlands, as these rocks are the most likely to explode.

3. Never build a fire under an overhanging limb, even if the tree limb is green and quite high above the fire. The continuous heat could dry out the limb and eventually ignite it into flames. If snow is found on these limbs, it will eventually melt and fall on the fire, putting it out.

4. Do not build a fire too close to dried brush or grasslands. Like the debris from a shelter, these lands ignite easily. One spark could cause a severe grass- or brushfire that could eventually ignite the surrounding forests. In drier conditions of brush and grasses, great care must be taken in watching wind direction, as a small spark will easily ignite a distant fire.

5. Teach your children to select a fire area that is relatively free of ground debris and leaves. Have them also dig down and check the ground for any underground root systems, as fire can travel underground for quite a distance, sometimes many miles.

6. Finally teach your children to select an area with plenty of natural wind buffers. Natural buffers, such as rock outcroppings, fallen trees, and bushes, located at a safe distance from the fire, will prevent the full force of winds from blowing coals from the fire. It will also aid your children in taking the most advantage of the fire, free of the chilling winds.

I would also recommend that you mention to your children to choose several routes of escape if a fire does get beyond their control. Several routes are better than one, as forest fires are unpredictable at best and could cut off the only planned escape route. Children should also be made aware of the wind and how it can move a forest fire. Teach your children to get around a forest fire or to head for wetlands, lakes, or waterways. It should also be mentioned that the smoke from a forest fire is as bad as the flames themselves and to stay out of the smoke or crawl close to the ground.

### The Fire Pit and Reflector

Once a good, safe fire location is chosen, it is then time to prepare the area for the fire. First the children should clear the area of all debris, leaves, grasses, and forest litter, to about ten feet back from the proposed fire site. Usually the area has already been cleared by the collection of debris for the shelter. Using a sharp stick or rock to loosen the dirt, the children should dig the fire pit. (Caution your children against using their bare hands for the digging process, as they could get

cut from unseen buried debris and rocks.) Actually what is needed is more of a depression in the ground than a pit. The depression should be about one foot deep by two feet across and circular. Not only does this cradle the fire and coals for better concentration of heat, but it makes the fire safer and less likely to get out of control. Rocks can be placed all around the pit for further protection.

Children should then be taught to build a fire-reflecting wall. This is a high wall partially surrounding the fire, in the shape of a horseshoe. The wall is built to further protect the fire, reflect the heat, and conserve firewood. Use rocks gathered from a dry area, sod, dirt, or even damp firewood for building the wall. Teach your children to build the wall securely, with the opening toward where they will be sitting, but positioned so the wind is not blowing directly into them. With the fire wall the children will find they will be warm even with relatively smaller fires, as the wall reflects much of the heat that would have been lost. This greatly reduces the amount of wood that has to be collected.

Certainly children will gain tremendous warmth from a fire, but teach them also how to make their stay the most comfortable. Teach children never to sit on the bare ground, because the ground will deeply chill the body. Instead have your children gather a dry log to sit upon or a pile of debris to insulate themselves from the ground. Make sure you teach children not to put the debris too close to the fire or it may catch fire.

Children should also be taught to make a makeshift backrest of some sort, padded with debris, so the side facing away from the fire does not get chilled. A pile of brush and logs, padded with debris in the back area, will make an excellent backrest and block the wind at the same time.

The fire pit and reflector may seem like a huge effort, but it is necessary for a good and efficient fire. The amount of work put into it is far less than all the time and travel to collect firewood for an inefficient fire. The danger of not building a proper fire pit will put your children's lives in danger. Teach children the correct way from the start, so the fire pit and reflector become a necessity rather than a luxury.

### Gathering Firewood

The most important consideration in gathering any wood for a fire is that it must be dry. Wet wood should never be used to get a fire started. Feeding wet wood to an existing fire will cause it to burn poorly, resulting in too much smoke. This kind of fire will eventually die out. Wet wood is any wood that is damp throughout. The only place I collect any firewood, debris, or sticks for firewood is from standing dead trees and vegetation. I consider anything that is lying on the ground to be wet. No matter how dry you think the conditions are, always teach your children to gather firewood from a standing location. Teach them to break down small limbs and sticks from dead trees or gather dry herbaceous vegetation from standing brush only. Standing dead vegetation, even in the rain or damp environments, always produces dry inner wood.

One of the best ways to teach your children about wet and dry wood is to do this experiment. Take your children into the woods or fields and collect a small branch from a dead tree and a branch of equal size from the ground. Now carve into each branch and show your children the difference. The children will plainly feel and see that the branch from the ground is damp inside and the one from the tree is dry. Teach your children that the hands are very poor at checking for dampness in cool weather. Instead have your children lightly press the branch against their cheek or bottom lip. The cheek and lip area are much more sensitive in detecting dampness. It is also a good idea to teach your children how to distinguish poison ivy vines and other poisonous plants, since collecting or burning these could cause severe skin and eye irritation.

**Note:** During warmer weather, above freezing, a good way to teach your children to tell if wood is dry is to have them listen for a distinctively clear snap, when the stick or twig is broken. When any stick just crackles and frays, this is a good indicator the wood may be wet.

## The Tepee Fire

There are many different types of fires and designs: trappers' fires, trench fires, cabin fires, council fires, hunters' fires, and pit fires, to name just a few. For survivalists there is only one type of fire that should be used—the tepee fire. The tepee fire gets its name from the shape of the fire, not just because it was used inside a tepee. The tepee fire has a very efficient burn because the wood feeds itself and the air supply is direct. With that burn there is little smoke and few flying coals, and that configuration lifts the heat and light off the ground. Because of the hot and efficient burn, the fire stands up beautifully to weather, even a downpour. In fact, the burn is so efficient, it is a good practice to have your children keep some damp leaves near the fire. The leaves can be added to create smoke to signal searchers, for the tepee fire itself gives off little smoke.

It is best to build and light a tepee fire several times with your children before they do it by themselves, to help them understand the fire better. Begin with the smallest, finest, and driest kindling you can find. Frayed inner barks of trees, stalks of dried grasses, tiny pieces of twig, and other fibers are laid up against one another, creating a small tepee shape. Remember to leave a door, or opening, into which the tinder bundle or match will be inserted. From this light tepee base, begin adding layers of larger and larger twigs and sticks, working up to wood the diameter of the wrist. Building a fire in this manner makes it catch quickly and burn effectively, even in bad weather. A covering of grass stalks or slabs of bark can be used to protect the tepee fire from rain while your children are preparing to light the fire.

The tepee shape of the fire must always be maintained. When the fire burns down, add more firewood while still maintaining the tepee shape. This is a critical area for you and your children. Teach your children to be careful when adding firewood to any fire. Caution them about their clothing and about being careful not to burn their hands in the process. Firewood should never be thrown directly on a fire, but placed into position. Throwing firewood destroys the shape of the fire and throws ashes and coals out of the fire pit. It is also important to teach your children to clean the ashes out of the fire pit when it gets overloaded. Like with a wood stove, heavy ash buildup restricts the air and eventually the ash overflows the safety of the pit. The ashes are easily removed with a long stick just before the fire is restocked.

Teach your children to collect enough firewood during the day so they do not have to venture out in the dark. Looking for firewood at night puts children in danger of injury or of losing the location of the camp. Your children should be shown how to break up firewood—by smashing it against stumps or rocks or by laying it on the fire and allowing the flames to burn it in half. Firewood should be stacked away and to the wind side of the fire. This prevents any sparks from being blown onto the firewood and also helps break up the wind. I would also have children make a pile of dirt near the fire. The dirt will then be near at hand to throw on the fire if it gets out of control.

### Survival Tools

Up to this point in your children's survival skills, there has been no need for tools, but in building the bow-drill fire and with subsequent traps, tools will become necessary. There are two sources of tools your children use in a survival situation—a knife (if they have survival packs) and "primitive" tools. Your children should become proficient in the use of both, as well as in the precautions necessary to keep themselves safe and injury-free. Since the advanced skills are best learned at first by using a knife, I will discuss the knife first, then we will consider the more advanced primitive tool manufacturing and uses.

### The Knife

Only you can decide whether your children are old enough and mature enough to use a knife. I suggest for most children under ten years old that a good pocketknife be used. These are easy and safe to carry and also easily controlled by small hands. When purchasing a knife for your children, take them along. Make sure the pocketknife can be easily opened and closed. Buy a lock back blade, where the blade locks into place when it opens. This prevents the knife from accidentally closing on your children's fingers when in use. Let your children hold the knife, if possible, even use the knife, to make sure it fits their hands and they have control. Once a suitable knife is purchased, I would stress the following suggestions in teaching your children. Here, more than ever, great care and caution should be used.

1. First teach your children to safely open and close the knife. This should always be done in a sitting position. Make sure your children never walk around or stand with an open knife, no matter what the circumstances. Check to make sure your children open and close the knife away from the body, keeping the fingers well out of the way. Also teach children to open a knife away from other people, and to hold the blade pointed toward the ground when not in use. Now might be a good time to show older children how to sharpen and care for a knife. Younger children should not be expected to learn this, since it is very dangerous. However, you should allow the children to watch you when you sharpen their knife.

2. Once your children have learned to open, close, carry, and handle the new knife properly, it is time to teach them how to carve. Get a soft wood to start, such as yellow pine, basswood, cedar, or any wood that is easy to cut. Some parents start their children carving on a bar of soap. Select a piece of wood that is at least a foot long yet easy for children to hold and handle. Now it is time to teach your children how to carve. Make sure before your children begin to go through the carving motions that they never carve toward themselves or anyone else. Show them how to keep their fingers out of the way, along with any other part of the body. Never allow them to support the end of the stick on the leg but rather to hold the stick firmly in the hand. Any time support is needed for the wood, have them prop it against another sturdy piece of wood.

In teaching your children to carve, first teach them to remove a little at a time from what they are carving. Tell them it is much like peeling a carrot or potato. If they try to remove too much wood, the task becomes difficult. Show them how to carve with a slicing motion, explaining to them how a knife works. At dinner, if the family is eating chicken or meat, show the children how impossible it is to push a knife through the meat, but with a back-and-forth slicing motion the meat is easily cut. Explain to them this is also how a knife works on wood. Once the children have mastered simple carving, take them outside and teach them to cut the twigs and branches from a stick, how to carve notches, and cut small pieces of wood in half. The more children work with a knife, the better and safer they will be.

3. Finally explain to the children what not to use a knife for. Teach them not to put the knife in the dirt or run the blade into the ground. Explain that a knife should never be thrown, for it could dangerously ricochet, be damaged, or become lost. Teach the children never to run the blade along steel, rocks, or anything hard, for this will dull the blade. Teach the children the knife is a friend and a tool, never for play. Carelessness and inattention cause injury.

4. Never let children use a knife unsupervised, and after each use check the knife for sharpness or damage. Never allow the connection between knife and handle to loosen, or the knife could snap and cause injury. If the children don't like to carry the knife in their pocket, buy a pocketknife sheath and wear it on the belt or carry it in the survival pack. Teach your children never to leave the knife anywhere: it must either go in their pocket or be stored in a special place at home or in camp.

5. When you are watching children, never let your attention be diverted from helping them use the knife. There should always be more than enough supervision for each child. Teaching children to work with a knife is not a silent signal for a parent or teacher to begin doing some of their own work.

### Primitive Tools

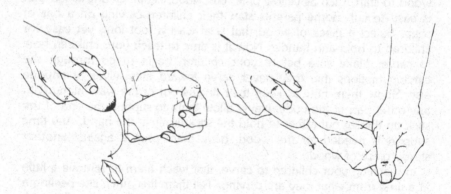

If your children have no knife, they should be taught to find, make, and utilize primitive tools. The best tools are made from rocks, and virtually all rocks can be used as tools in some way. Certainly the larger rock flakes are best for tools, but even pebbles can be used as tools if there is nothing else. Rocks carve wood more like files than like knives. I feel the first thing parents or teachers should do is have children work with a file on some wood. Have them file the wood to a point or file down a sharp edge or even make the wood into a certain shape. Have them use all sorts of files, from very coarse to very fine. Using files to work wood teaches children the rudiments of "rockworking." The next step would be to have your children learn to grind a point on an old broom handle by dragging it back and forth across rough concrete.

Once the children have mastered working with files and subsequently the concrete grinding method, it is time to move into working with rocks. Take your children to a place where there are plenty of rocks of all sizes—generally near the base of hills or along stream banks are good areas for rocks. Have them hunt for broken pieces of rock that fit the hand nicely, with sharp beveled edges. If none are available, show them how to take one large rock and smash it against another, breaking up the rocks. But have them stand back when they throw the rock to avoid injury. It is not important to teach children the names of rocks. Instead have them feel the "grit" of the rocks and experiment with them. Your children will soon know by feeling what rocks cut fast and what rocks cut slow and smooth.

Now let them use the sharp rock flakes the same way they used the files. For cutting have them saw back and forth with the bladelike edge of the rock. For smoothing they can either use the edge of the same rock for scraping or the flat part of a rock to sand, much as they did with the broom handle on the rough concrete. It makes little difference whether the rock is dragged across the wood or the wood is dragged across the rock. Many times, especially with the larger rocks, it is better to have children move the wood rather than the rock. It's surprising how fast your children will make and utilize the most primitive tools known to humankind. By learning to use rocks, the children will never be without a tool.

## The Bow-drill Fire

By far the easiest and most effective way for children to make a primitive fire is with the bow drill. The apparatus is not that difficult to make but will require a lot of practice in both making the apparatus and the fire. What I find best is to make the bow-drill parts for the children and allow them to practice making the fire first. Once they can make a fire repeatedly on your bow drill, then have them make their own. Many times children grow bored or tired making the bow-drill parts first, especially since the actual making of the fire is but a dream. This, by far, is one of the hardest and most involved skills children will learn, so be patient.

I will always remember the awe and excitement I felt when I watched Grandfather make a bow-drill fire. To me it was magic to create fire out of spinning wood. I remember asking Grandfather how the bow drill worked and he simply said, "Rub your hands together hard, and what do you feel?" That was the best explanation of the bow drill I have ever heard. I suggest that like Grandfather you first learn to build a bow-drill fire, then show your children. Once you have mastered the bow drill, you are better equipped to help your children when they have problems.

### The Best Wood

The proper selection of wood for the bow drill, especially the spindle and fireboard, is of the utmost importance. What you should teach children is to find the driest wood possible. The rule of thumb for bow-drill wood is never to use an extremely hard wood like oak, hickory, or walnut, and never a soft resinous wood such as pine, fir, or spruce. All other woods will work, though some are more difficult than others. The best and easiest woods for making fire are cottonwood, willow, larch, cedar, sassafras, alder, aspen, poplar, box alder, basswood, nonpoisonous sumacs, mulberry, sycamore, tulip tree, and sage are just a few of the better woods. Teach your children to identify the various trees found in your favorite camp area or along your most frequented hiking trails. Help your children to choose the absolute best woods when they first begin making the bow drill, as this allows for quick success.

**Note:** If children seem to have trouble telling the different woods apart, especially dead woods, teach them that if a wood is dry and easy to carve, then it is usually good wood for the bow drill. If the wood is hard and difficult to carve, or if it is sticky, then it is not a good bow-drill wood.

## PARTS OF THE BOW DRILL

**Note:** Children's bow-drill apparatus is typically smaller than adults'. The following dimensions given are for children's bow drills, not for adults'.

### The Bow

The bow for the bow drill is made from a light, sturdy sapling with a slight natural bend. The children should choose their own bow, with the bow measured from your children's reach and grip. The bow should be slightly longer than your children's arm from shoulder to outstretched fingers. Check to see that the fat end of the sapling is easily grasped by your children, typically the size diameter of a broom handle. All branches of the dead sapling should be cleaned off so it does not hang up the drill when spun on the cord. Make sure the bow is light enough

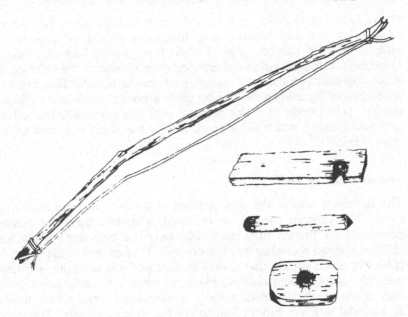

for your children to handle, so their form is not sloppy when making the fire.

The scope of this book does not deal with the more advanced survival techniques, for they are difficult for children to learn. The making of cordage is left out of this book for that reason. However, children have many other cordage sources. For the cordage of the bow children should use their shoelaces, the bottom hem of a shirt or T-shirt that has been twisted for strength, or a strip from their belt. I ask adults to put a piece of nylon cord into children's survival packs for just such a purpose. The cord should be about six to seven feet long by ⅛ inch thick. The excess length can be unraveled and used by the children for other survival skills. The cordage is then attached to both ends of the bow so there is no slack, but not tight enough to prevent the drill, or "spindle," from being wrapped on.

At this time your children should break down a branch from a dead sapling. The center portion of the branch should be about the same size diameter as a broom handle and slightly thicker at the base. Your children will use this for making the other parts of the bow-drill apparatus.

### The Handhold

The handhold of the bow-drill apparatus is typically made from the same type of wood being used for the spindle and fireboard. It is usually broken from the same branch at the thickest end. The handhold should fit snugly and comfortably in the hand but should not allow the fingers to wrap all the way around. Any roughness should be sanded or scraped away to prevent your children from getting blisters or cuts. Once the handhold is cut to size and feels comfortable to the children, a small depression is cut into one side of the handhold. This can be accomplished by using a rock or by using a pointed knife in a drill-like fashion. (The handhold is not finished until it is eventually burned in and then greased, which will take place after the whole bow-drill apparatus is made.)

### The Spindle, or Drill

The spindle is one of the easiest parts of the bow-drill apparatus to make. The children should cut or break a spindle from the center portion of the branch they have collected. The best size spindle for children is about six inches by no more than ¾ of an inch in diameter. It is best to pick a section that is very straight and free of knots, as these will only make carving difficult. Have the children slightly point both ends of the spindle with their knife or by dragging it along a rock, much as they did with the broom handle on the rough concrete. The bark should then be carved or scraped off the spindle. A good spindle diameter for the average child is about ½ inch.

### The Fireboard

The fireboard is made from the thickest end of the branch. To make the fireboard, have the children cut the branch to size with their knife or break it to size over a rock or log. The fireboard should be about six to ten inches long, almost twice as wide as the spindle, and about ½ inch thick. Scrape or carve the fireboard flat on both top and bottom so it slightly resembles a piece of lumber rather than a stick. A few inches from one end of the fireboard and directly in the middle of the board carve or rock-drill a depression, much like your children did for the handhold.

### Burning In

Now that the apparatus is completed the children must burn it in. This is accomplished in the same way a fire is made, only it is meant to set the sockets into the handhold and fireboard, not to start a fire quite yet. To "burn in" the apparatus, have the children first put the board firmly on the ground. The board should not lie directly against the ground but be placed upon some dried grassses, leaves, or bark to prevent any ground moisture from entering the dry wood. (Always keep the fireboard and

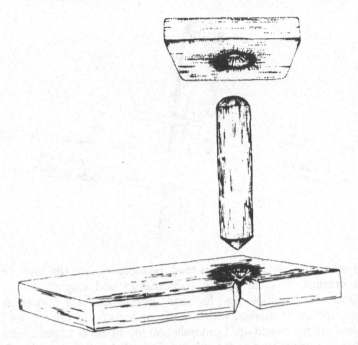

drill off the ground.) Now have the children put their left foot across the fireboard, slightly forward of the arch, so the cut hole is just an inch away from the instep. The shin of the left leg should be perpendicular to the ground, and the knee of the right leg should be slightly behind and a little to the right of the left heel. (Reverse the entire process for left-handed children.)

Now have your children wrap the drill onto the bow so the wrap is facing away from the bow. (*See illustration on following page.*) The children should then be able to hold the drill on the bow with their right hand and the handhold in their left. The bottom end of the spindle is placed in the cut depression of the fireboard and the top end is held in the cut depression of the handhold. The left hand and handhold are braced tight against the shin, so the drill is perpendicular to the fireboard. The bow should be on the outside of the spindle, away from the left shin, and the end of the bow should be grasped firmly in the right hand. (*See illustration on following page.*) Allow your children to hold this position, exactly as seen in the illustration, until they are comfortable and memorize the form.

Pressing down slightly with the left hand, the children draw the bow back and forth across the apparatus in a sawing motion, which also causes the spindle to spin back and forth. The speed and downward pressure are increased until the handhold and fireboard begin to smoke.

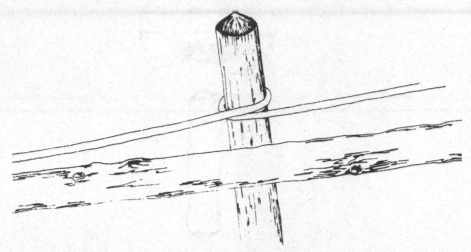

This may take your children several tries, possibly even a few days or weeks of practice, to build up the coordination and strength to get smoke. Once the handhold and fireboard depressions are burned in slightly, the spindle is marked with a knife or a rock, so the top and bottom ends are not mixed up. I generally get my students to put a light ring around the upper part of the spindle. Once the spindle and hand-hold are greased, you do not want your children to accidentally mix up

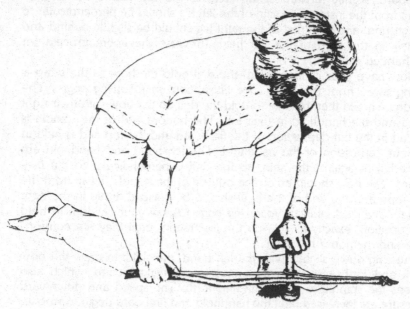

the ends, as this will get grease on the fireboard and prevent the children from getting a coal.

## Greasing and Notching

After the burning-in process, the children must then grease the hand-hold and the upper end of the spindle. This is to prevent friction and to allow the bow drill to work more smoothly. Greasing also prevents the handhold from getting hot or burning through. The children can easily learn to grease these areas with a number of grease sources. The oils around the sides of the nose and on the upper chin or the grease from the hair are sufficient. Pine pitch or any sticky sap can also be used. These are applied by rubbing the upper end of the drill and the handhold depression in the grease or oil. Make sure these areas are well greased. (Soap can be used if the children are practicing at home.) Never use water, for this will only bind up the apparatus as the wood swells.

A notch should be cut from the side of the fireboard to almost the center of the depression. (*See illustration on page 163.*) Have the children carefully cut this notch with their knife. At this point, children should be extra-careful not to get their fingers in the way or allow the board to slip. If the children do not have a knife, the wedge-shaped notch can be filed in with a sharp flake of abrasive rock. Typically the notch should cut out one-eighth of the depression in a pie shape. Have your children check the notch for jagged edges or rough spots, which could hang up the coal. The notch is one of the most important parts of the bow drill.

## Tinder Bundle

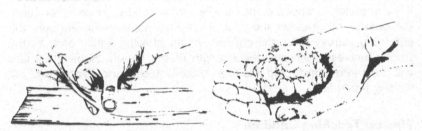

The last piece needed to make a bow-drill fire is a tinder bundle. There are thousands of plants that can be used to make tinder, and all children need to do is to experiment with the various dead trees and vegetation in any area to find tinder. Generally tinder is made from plant fibers that can be broken up and buffed into one fibrous ball. The inner bark of many trees, many herbaceous plants, and some grasses are all sources of tinder. The plants are buffed between the palms so the fibers fray. Any rough parts of bark or plant fiber are removed during the buffing process. Many plants will fiber up better when pounded lightly with a rock or stick, but most are easily buffed in the palms. Make sure you and your children experiment, sampling all manner of dead trees and plants for fiber. To make a fire, children will need a palmful of tinder.

### Making the Fire

The fire is made with the same technique the children used for "burning in" their apparatus. The setup is exactly the same, only the tinder bundle is placed directly under the notch, on the dried grasses or bark, to keep it dry. Again the spindle is spun in the fireboard, until there is plenty of smoke. As soon as the smoke begins to flow freely, the children should begin watching the notch. Eventually—usually after about ten more revolutions—dust will begin to pour from the notch. What has happened is that the friction between the spindle and fireboard have shaved off dust and produced a coal. The apparatus is then carefully taken away, with care not to disturb the coal, and the fireboard lifted free of the tinder bundle. If the coal and dust remain wedged in the notch, then the coal should be nudged onto the tinder bundle with a sliver of wood or a stalk of grass.

The tinder bundle is then lifted from the ground and gently closed around the coal, much like an egg is enclosed in a bird nest. Teach your children to be careful at this point, as the coal could break apart if handled roughly. The tinder bundle is held several inches from the mouth, not over the head, and the children should begin to blow air into the bundle. (The children should not be able to see the coal, since it is completely wrapped in the bundle.) If the children press in too hard, the bundle will smother the coal; if they do not press in enough, the coal may starve. Have the children begin blowing lightly and, as the smoke increases, increase the strength of the breath. Soon the tinder will burst into flames, and it is then placed quickly and directly into the waiting tepee fire.

### Tips on Teaching Children

Be a kind, gentle, and patient teacher. Many adults find it difficult to learn to make a bow-drill fire, and children may have more of a problem. Don't expect to teach children how to make a fire in just one day. Instead take several weeks or even months if necessary. Never pressure them, but as always, have fun, and enjoy learning the skill.

1. If your children seem sloppy using the bow, the bow may possibly be too heavy or long. Look for another.

2. If your children have trouble turning the drill and getting smoke, slim down the diameter of their drill; possibly it is too large for them to turn.

3. If the coal goes out before being wrapped into the tinder bundle, have the children take a few more strokes on the bow, beyond the point where they think they have a coal.

4. Allow your children to build up strength and coordination for the bow drill over a period of time much as for any athletic training.

5. Sometimes, to help your children get a feel for the pressure and stroke speed needed for a bow-drill fire, work in tandem with them. If the children are right-handed, put your left hand on their left hand, thus supporting the handhold and downward pressure. Grab the opposite end of the bow and help the children work through the proper techniques. I find this technique is one of the best silent teachers there is, for it teaches children just what must be done to get a fire.

# 13

# FOOD

Teaching children how to gather and prepare food in a survival situation is very difficult. In fact, teaching adults is difficult. So in this chapter I will attempt to simplify the food gathering and preparation techniques, covering only those I know most children can learn. Some of the techniques presented cannot be learned by very young children, and because of the complication and danger, they should not be pushed on them. For a more detailed description of survival food, refer to *Tom Brown's Field Guide to Wilderness Survival* but for the most part, what is discussed in the following chapter is more than enough information for most children.

I cannot stress enough the dangers and complicated techniques in gathering food, especially where children are concerned. There is the problem of proper plant identification, where many plants have poisonous look-alikes. There is the problem of animals having diseases, or the potential problem of children being bitten by animals injured during the hunt. There is the problem and difficulty in teaching children to hunt properly and to make and use the hunting tools. Finally there is the problem that most things must be thoroughly cooked. With this in mind, this chapter requires the greatest care in teaching children, for it can potentially be dangerous. Make sure the children thoroughly understand each part, and teach the information slowly and effectively over a long period of time.

Grandfather took years in teaching us how to gather food in a survival situation. He taught slowly, so each lesson was thoroughly understood, before venturing into a new lesson. We learned plants slowly, beginning with the easiest and then working to the more difficult. New plants were introduced into our diet every week, each of which we had to identify, collect, and prepare. We began our hunting exercises only during times of need, never for sport. We started with primitive fishing, learning to catch, gut, and cook the fish many different ways. We then moved on to more complicated hunting techniques, traps, and animals, until we understood all aspects of the hunt. This also included the reverence and thanksgiving for all life, and the gift of the animals' flesh for our use.

In Grandfather's teachings there was no separation or hierarchy among animal and plant spirits: they were all equal. "Just because we cannot hear a plant scream with pain [when pulled from the earth] does not mean it cannot feel pain," he would say. Thus, no matter what we used, what we took, there had to first be an extreme need. Nothing was done for sport, for an animal or plant giving up its spirit so that we could live was one of the most extreme and noble sacrifices. Everything too was a gift from the creator, so nothing was wasted. All parts were used for something, and any waste was considered bad medicine.

## SURVIVAL COOKING

Generally survival cooking procedures should be kept simple for children. When teaching children, these techniques should be tried one at a time during a normal campout. Select a meal that you wish to cook in a primitive fashion, and have your children help with the preparation and cooking. Each time the children go camping, try a new technique or a variation of the old. Allow your children to make the necessary equipment, prepare the fire, and cook the meal once they become familiar with a technique. I suggest you teach your children to cook at home or at least to help with the family food preparation. This will begin to build the children's confidence. (If your little boy states that only women are supposed to cook, then ask him who cooked the meals for the mountain men of old.)

### Spit Cooking

Spit cooking is probably one of the oldest and easiest methods of cooking that exists. I believe all children are capable of learning the spit cooking technique, and it is quite easy to teach. Begin on your next campout or during a family cookout by allowing your children to roast marshmallows on the end of a long stick. Let them then try roasting some stick bread. (Stick bread is made by mixing flour and water into a dough, then forming it onto the end of a stick, and roasting it until cooked.) When the family is on a campout, plan to roast something on the open fire, so the children will see firsthand how larger foods are cooked in this way. Your children will find that some sticks are better for roasting than others and will soon learn to use a longer stick to keep from being burned.

Your family should get primitive when spit-cooking something at camp. Cut and use Y sticks at either end of a low fire. Show the children how to "spit" the food on a stick, place it between the Y sticks, and turn it often so it cooks on both sides. Remember that spit cooking can be used to cook vegetables and grains in the form of bread. As the children advance, allow them to make their own shish kebab, even adding wild foods as they get more advanced. Always allow your children the freedom to experiment, and enjoy the foods with them. Children seem to love experimenting with cooking and pleasing adults and teachers with their culinary masterpieces. So play along, even if it tastes horrible; just help them improve the recipe next time.

### Bowl Burning and Rock Boiling

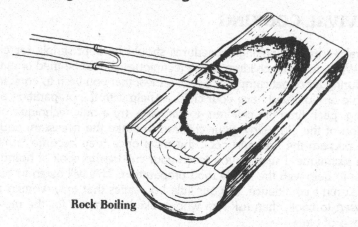

Rock Boiling

By far one of the best ways to prepare survival food is by rock boiling. Rock boiling allows us to make stew, which preserves more food value than any other type of survival cooking. Rock boiling is a little more complicated than spit cooking and requires a few more skills. Rock boiling also requires a few more refined survival tools and techniques than the simpler form of spit cooking. The first item needed is a suitable bowl or container to hold the food to be boiled. Making a bowl is easier than you would suspect, and children seem to enjoy making bowls in this way. Again, teaching them to make fire-burned bowls can be done during a campout or in the backyard. Once the entire rock-boiling process is learned, have the children make camp teas or soups to practice the techniques.

To make a bowl, have the children select a fallen branch or small log. Have the children break the branch to size—the larger the better. Make sure the wood is not rotted nor one of the poisonous species. Though the burning process and dead wood frees the wood of most poisons, it is good to stay away from yew, cascara, osage orange, and locust. Have your children slightly flatten one side of the log by removing some of the bark (they can also make a slight indent by pounding it with a sharp rock). Now have your children remove a hot coal from the fire with long sticks, and place it atop the flat side of the log, directly in the center. Allow the coal to begin burning the wood.

The children can speed up the burning process by placing the log and coal directly in the wind. Blowing on the coal lightly will increase the burning process even more, and the burn can also be directed. Once the coal goes out, have the children scrape the burn with a sharp rock to remove all the char. Repeat the process again and again, until the hole is deep and wide enough, creating a crater in the log, or a "bowl." After the bowl is scraped free of all ash, the children should lightly sand the inside of the bowl with a smooth rock. Typically a bowl will take a few hours to create, but it isn't that much work, especially since the coal is doing the cutting. (*See illustration.*)

Now the children are ready to rock-boil their meal. Rock boiling can be used for making tea, stew, soup, vegetables, and for purifying water. It is a very simple process, but great care should be taken, for the children will be handling hot stones. Have your children select several stones, each about the size of an egg or a little smaller. The stones should be placed in the hottest part of the fire. (Caution the children to stand back from the fire while doing this in case one of the stones explodes.) Again, collect all stones from a well-drained and dry area. Be wary of all rocks and stones containing silicates or quartz, because these shatter. Allow the stones to heat up for at least a half hour while the children prepare their meal.

Water and food can be added to the bowl the same way you would make soup, stew, or tea at home. Once the rocks are hot and the meal is in the bowl, the children are ready to rock-boil. At this point the children will need to manufacture a set of tongs or forked sticks to handle the rocks. Tongs are made by bending a sapling in half or by lashing together two sticks with a spreader brace. (*See illustration.*) Finally the first rock is carefully lifted from the fire and gently dropped into the bowl. (Some rocks may crack when hitting the water, so be sure to tell your children to check their meal for rock fragments.) The liquid around the rock will quickly boil for several moments and raise the heat level throughout the entire container. When the rock stops boiling the water, have the children remove the rock from the bowl with the tongs and drop in another hot rock. The process should be repeated several times until the food is cooked.

**Note:** Working with hot rocks and burning coals can cause a serious burn or forest fire. Make sure your children are very cautious with this cooking process.

### Fry Rock

The frying rock is one of the easier methods of cooking. Simply a flat rock is selected and suspended over a fire site with smaller rocks, much like a table. A fire is then built under the rock, and within an hour the rock is hot enough to fry on. The rock used for frying need only be slightly larger than a normal household frying pan to work, but it must be relatively thin. (*See illustration.*) Again, have your children practice cooking with a fry rock in camp. Allow them to fry up some potatoes or a fish. Remember to teach your children to treat the fry rock like a hot frying pan and to use long forked sticks when turning or removing food. Caution your children about the possibilities of grease fires. The grease can be channeled off any food by propping the rock down and slightly away from the children, so it drains directly into the fire, not toward the children.

### Rock Oven

Similar in ease to making a fry rock, a rock oven can also be fashioned by your children. Have the children build a rock box near the fire using thin rocks. An opening should be left in one side, away from the fire, like there is an oven door. Now carefully teach your children to rake coals toward the oven using a forked stick. Your children should then build up the fire all around and on top of the rock oven, leaving the doorway free of fire. The rock oven can be used as you would use your oven at home. Bread, vegetables, meats, fish, and cereals can be cooked in the oven. Once the food is carefully placed inside, with long sticks a few more rocks are used to seal up the door. The fire is then stoked until it envelops the entire oven in low, constant flames. It is a good idea to check the food periodically to keep it from burning. Again, have your children bake brownies or bread in camp using a rock oven.

# HUNTING

There is a lot to consider when teaching children to hunt. First there is the moral issue: whether they are psychologically mature enough to understand the meaning of taking an animal's life. Second is the question of whether children are mature enough to learn these techniques and to avoid the danger. Hunting is difficult to teach, for it is so complicated and dangerous. There is a lot that has to be taught, and it takes quite some time to teach it effectively and thoroughly enough to be understood by children. There is always the danger that an animal is contaminated by some disease, but that is rare. Another danger is that the children could be bitten by an animal that has been injured during the hunt. The biggest problem is that there is no way to practice these techniques, because primitive hunting is illegal in all states unless children are in a survival situation. In some states it is even illegal to trap a mouse in your own home.

With this in mind we must still find a way to teach children how to hunt, trap, and prepare game. I would suggest you begin with the proper gutting, preparation, and cooking of fish. Have your children assist with the process until they can do it all themselves. Then you may want to purchase a freshly killed chicken and go through the whole process as you did with the fish. If you are a hunter or you know any hunters, ask if you could watch them gut, skin, and butcher game during the hunting season. Most hunters will be glad to let your children watch or even help. However, watch the reaction of your children closely, and do not force them to do things that upset them. Remember that children today are not raised in a hunter-gatherer society. As far as the practice for hunting and trapping game is concerned, I will discuss legal alternatives in each section.

## What Is Edible

Virtually every land and freshwater animal is edible, with just a few exceptions. I like to teach people to stay clear of animal life that is too small and hard to collect. The spark of energy we get from eating a sparrow, for instance, hardly replaces the energy it took to hunt, prepare, cook, and eat that sparrow. Unless sparrows could be hunted in abundance, they are hardly worth the effort. I suggest children stick to larger game, such as larger birds; larger rodents, such as squirrels; and rabbits. Hunting very large game should never be attempted by a child, for the average child could not make a clean kill and the wounded animal could charge. I have effectively collected and eaten large numbers of crickets, cicadas, grasshoppers, grub worms, and found them delicious. Your children may decide otherwise. Never use a venomous animal, for the food is never worth the risk.

## Potentially Diseased Animals

It is important to teach your children to spot potentially diseased animals from a distance. Anytime animals look sick, injured, or generally disheveled, it is a sure sign those animals should be left alone. Also, if the animals are behaving totally out of context, out of the ordinary, like wandering as if in a daze, in circles, or if they appear bold toward danger, then this is another sign not to hunt these animals. The best way to teach children is to point out diseased animals anytime they are encountered on a nature walk. Like nature awareness, survival techniques should become part of everyday thinking. A simple rule to follow is When in doubt, don't hunt the animal. Teach children to use their gut feeling and intuition in the woods.

## Cleaning and Gutting

As I stated earlier, it is best to start children on the cleaning, gutting, and cooking of fish. Then if you are a hunter or know a hunter, ask if they will show your children how it's done. Your children should be very careful when gutting and skinning game, for the knife could slip and cause serious injury. It is also important not to let your children handle any game if the children have any cut, since disease could be transferred through the cut. In the same thought keep the hands away from the face during the gutting process. All game must be thoroughly gutted and skinned before cooking. I also remove the head and feet, as these could be considered disease centers, especially in areas where there are rabies. Don't let children take a chance by leaving the head and feet on the animal.

Teach your children what healthy internal organs look like. Any organ that looks atrophied or unhealthy is a sure indicator that the game may be contaminated. The animal should not be used in that case. Again, it is better to be a little overcautious in this regard. I now make a habit of not eating the internal organs of animals, such as the liver, kidneys, and heart. I feel that with the plethora of pollutants in the land, these "filtering organs" will contain high levels of contaminants even in a wilderness area. I used to eat them as a child, but now I use these organs for other survival skills and techniques. However, even without all the precautions, I have never gotten sick from eating wild game, and I have eaten wild game for most of my life.

## Cooking Animals

Animals can be boiled, baked, fried, and roasted on a spit. It is up to the children to decide which way to prepare the animals for eating. I suggest making a stew whenever possible, because stews preserve much of the food value. Make sure the meat is cooked until well done, treated much as you would in the cooking of pork. This insures that any disease will be cooked away. Don't overcook the meat so much that you denature the proteins, however. You will have to work closely with your children in the cooking of meats, so they will know when they are done.

## The Throwing Stick

I remember the first time I ever saw a throwing stick used. Grandfather had taken us on a long hike away from our main camp, and we had been gone for most of the day. It was midsummer, and we wore nothing more than our loincloths, nor were we carrying any supplies. Needless to say, Rick and I were starved by the evening and camp was still many miles away. As we sat back to rest, Grandfather hushed our talking and pointed to a squirrel in a tree, smiled, and said, "Dinner." For the life of me I could not figure out what he was talking about. If he did mean that this squirrel was going to be dinner, I couldn't see how, for he had none of his hunting equipment with him. Deftly he stood up and picked up a stick that was lying on the ground. In one smooth motion he knocked the squirrel from the tree, stone dead. I was shocked at the ease with which he was able to use that old stick, turning it instantly into a deadly hunting weapon. From that day on the throwing stick has become one of my primary hunting weapons for a survival situation.

One of the most primitive hunting weapons known to humankind, the throwing stick is also the easiest hunting technique for children to learn. Any child who can throw a ball well can easily learn to hunt with the throwing stick. The first thing children must do is choose a stick of proper size. Like everything else in survival, measurements are taken on the users' body, so the stick is custom-fit. The best stick for your children to use is one as long as their arm, strong, yet light. The children should be able to grasp the stick at the narrow end, where the fingers almost curl all the way around. This kind of stick will give the children good control and accuracy. Make sure the stick is relatively straight and free of jagged edges, especially in the handhold area. Rough-barked sticks tend to slow down when thrown.

There are two basic types of throw children can easily learn. The first throw is called an overhand and is used for animals that can only be hit when the stick is in a vertical position. The second throw, called the sidearm, is used the most and is universal for most hunting situations. The throwing stick is very effective and accurate for a primitive weapon. It combines the weight of the stick with a spin, so that the stick flies through the air like a helicopter blade. The spin on the stick gives it tremendous killing force, even with a light throw.

At first just let your children throw the stick freely in an open field to get a feel for how the stick is used. Set up some targets and create some sort of a game, allowing the children's accuracy to increase naturally. Allow the children to play with the stick for a few days, even setting up a throwing area in your backyard to encourage its use. I always allow children to throw the stick naturally at first, so they build up their throwing arm. Once the children are comfortable with the stick, I then modify their throws to increase accuracy, power, and control. It is at this point the children develop the overhand and sidearm throws.

The overhand throw is quite easy to teach children. The children's shoulders should be squared to the target (perpendicular), and the left foot should be out in front with the toe pointing directly at the target (reversed for left-handed throwers). The right foot is held back a com-

**Overhand Throw**

fortable stride length from the left foot. The form should appear as if the children were taking a normal step. The stick is held lightly in the throwing hand, down the back and perpendicular to the ground. (See illustration.) When the children throw, the stick should stay exactly perpendicular to the ground, with the motion not unlike throwing a baseball. This throw is effective for hitting an animal climbing up the side of a tree or for cutting through tall grasses.

The sidearm throw is similar to the overhand, except that it begins with the shoulders held diagonally to the target, and the throwing action is slightly different. Once again the feet should be comfortably spread, with the left foot again leading the right (reversed for left-handers). It is not important that the children point the leading foot toward the target; allow them to do what is most comfortable. The stick is held out behind the body, usually perpendicular to the ground. (*See illustration on the next page.*) The throw is delivered the same way one would crack a bullwhip.

**Sidearm Throw**

The body pivots at the waist and the arm follows, releasing the stick at the side with a snap. The stick should travel parallel to the ground. Keep in mind that this is an instinctive throw, and the sticks can run a little wild in the beginning. In a short period of time the children will become very accurate at this throw. Speed, power, control, and accuracy increase with practice.

Remember, the stick is effective only if it is spun like a helicopter blade as it flies through the air. It has a greater killing surface than a rock, so it is the preferred method over a slingshot. Children take to the throwing stick easily, with tremendous control and accuracy, even after just a little practice. The throwing stick is not a toy, however, and should be practiced only under adult supervision. The best place for practice is in an open field with some sort of backstop. All observers should stand behind the children who are throwing, as some shots may go to the sides. A throwing stick can cause serious injury, even thrown by children. Treat the stick with respect, as you would any hunting weapon.

## *Where to Hunt and Trap*

The best hunting and trapping areas are the transition areas (see Chapter 4). The transition areas, especially along the trails and runs, afford the best opportunity for hunting. Have the children make sure they are away from their general camp location, as their presence there will put the animals on edge. Caution the children, however, that they should know the way back to the shelter. Have the children walk slowly through the hunting area, paying close attention to sound and movement. When animals are spotted, the children should then stalk within killing range (generally twenty feet for children). The children should also be taught to get into the throwing position in a slow, stalking motion so the animals do not know they are being hunted. If the children find an area with heavy animal travel, they should conceal themselves in the brush and await the sought-after animal, just as they did when observing animals in the awareness chapter of this book.

When you and your children practice the throwing stick, create a game. Set up a row of targets—like small sticks with one end stuck in the ground—and challenge your children to a target shoot. Extra points can be given to the person who breaks a target stick in half, or even more points if more than one target is knocked down with one throw. To add even more accuracy to the game, use rubber army men or rubber animal toys as targets. Practice with targets on the ground, on a fence, and even in an old dead tree. This builds your children's accuracy for every hunting situation.

# TRAPS

Traps are as difficult to make as the bow drill, though not as complicated. Again, you will have to spend plenty of time with your children in this area to make sure they know how to make the trap, set it in the best location, and bait it properly. The first thing children must learn to do is camouflage the scent on their hands before making or handling a trap. This is easily accomplished by first having the children rub their hands with a fragrant nonpoisonous plant found in the immediate area. Then the children should rub their hands in the dirt to further remove any scent. This procedure should be completed anytime a trap is handled or set. At no time should the trap or bait touch the body, and I would suggest that the completed trap be descented in the same way before setting. It is important also that your children darken in any fresh cuts in the trap using soil, so as not to let the cut area stand out and give away the trap to the animals. Children should also know how to make a trap with both a knife and a rock.

## The Figure 4 Deadfall

Top View

Deadfalls are traps made with heavy logs or rocks; they are propped off the ground with a configuration of sticks creating a trigger mechanism. The trigger is baited in such a way that if an animal takes the bait, the trigger springs, dropping the deadfall and crushing the animal. Typically the deadfall is twice to three times the weight of the animal to insure a clean and fast kill. Deadfalls are placed in animal feeding areas, slightly out of the way, so the animals do not notice the trap. The deadfall must fall on hard ground for the trap to be effective; otherwise, soft ground could cushion the blow, and the animal could escape only to suffer a lingering and painful death.

To make a figure 4 deadfall, the children must collect three straight sticks. Two sticks should be of equal length, and the third stick about a third longer. A typical-size trap for a squirrel would be made from sticks about ⅜ inch in diameter, with two of the sticks being six inches long and the third stick being a little over eight inches long. Bigger animals will need slightly bigger traps, so teach your children to modify these measurements to fit the game being trapped. Once the sticks have been collected, have the children lay them flat on the ground and arrange them so they resemble a number 4. The stick perpendicular to your children is called the upright, the stick diagonal to your children is called the diagonal, and the stick running horizontally to your children is called the bait stick. Before you help your children make this trap, make sure you have made and set a few. This will help you to better understand the principle of the trap and subsequently to better assist your child.

The first stick to be carved is the upright. At the top end of the stick have your children carve a dovetail notch (see *illustration*), and on the side of the stick a right-angle edge is carved (see *illustration*). The right-angle edge should run about half the stick's length, centered in the middle of the stick. The right-angle edge should be in line with the peak of the dovetail. Have your children now carve a beveled edge into one end of the diagonal stick. This bevel will give the deadfall a flat place to rest upon, which stabilizes the trap. About an inch back from the bevel and on the opposite side of the stick is carved in a ninety-degree notch. (See *illustration*.) Finally at the opposite end of the diagonal is carved another dovetail, lying along the same plane as the ninety-degree notch.

Now your children should carve a point onto one end of the bait stick. At the opposite end of the stick have the children carve in a ninety-degree notch, about a half inch from the end and with the flat edge of the notch facing the blunt end of the stick. Now is the time the trap must be measured so the placement of the last notch can be determined. The stick is set up as seen in the illustration, but without the deadfall weight, and supported with the hands. Move the trap so it appears exactly as a perfect number 4, and mark the point of the bait stick that rests on the right-angle edge of the upright stick. At this point carve another ninety-degree notch on the side of the stick facing the upright, keeping the flat edge of the notch to the pointed end of the bait stick. Now the trap is ready to set.

**Note:** This description may seem complicated, but when looking closely at the illustration, you will see how easy it is. Some things are better illustrated than described. Keep that in mind especially when teaching children.

To set the deadfall, first bait the bait stick. This is accomplished by either skewering on a piece of bait or tying the bait directly onto the stick. Now place the upright and diagonal sticks together and hold them in place with one hand. Picking up the rock or log with the other hand, place the beveled end of the diagonal stick just under the raised edge of the deadfall. Make sure the upright stick is perpendicular to the ground and outside the lip of the deadfall. Carefully allow the deadfall to be suspended by the trap where you are holding it in place by pressing down on the far edge of the diagonal, much like a lever. Now hook the bait stick first to the diagonal stick and then catch it on the right-angle edge of the upright. Slowly and carefully remove the hands, and the trap is set.

To finish the trap, build a stick wall along the same side of the trap as the upright. This is accomplished by pushing sticks into the ground along the side of the deadfall, but not touching the deadfall. The object of the wall is to keep animals from coming into the upright side of the trap and taking the bait, as bait taken from this side would allow the trap to spin on its axis rather than be triggered. Animals must approach and take the bait from the bait stick side of the trap so the bait stick is pulled free of the upright. Again, the complication is simplified by the illustration. The trap area should always be approached as quietly as possible in order not to disturb the animals.

It is important to allow your children to make several of these traps until they can make the trap without consulting the illustration. It is also important to have your children practice setting the figure 4 until they can do it quickly. When you teach children how to set up the figure 4, impress on them three areas of concern. First, as always, teach children to be careful with their knife, especially during the close work necessary for making traps. Second, while setting deadfalls, the deadfalls could accidentally spring and collapse on the children's hands. It is important to teach the children to always keep the hands outside the fall of the deadfalls when the traps are being set. Finally never allow your children to leave practice traps set up, even if they are unbaited. Wild animals or pets could inadvertently wander under the deadfalls and kill themselves, or other children could get hurt playing with the traps. Be especially careful if there are babies or curious toddlers in the family.

### Baiting the Trap

Baiting the trap with the right bait is of the utmost importance. Fortunately it is one of the easier things to teach your children. Your children will need some knowledge of the animals, their habits, and generally what the animals like to eat. Then the children must become aware of the animals' feeding areas, and especially what the animals are eating in those areas. Children must observe what plants have been eaten first and are no longer available to the animals in abundance. Your children must then locate some of this "preferred" food and bait their traps with the best and freshest of it they can find. When in doubt, have your children put several different kinds of bait on the same stick, or set several traps with different bait. When at home or around camp, have your children lay out various plants, nuts, and berries in an open area, noting which are eaten and by what. This will give your children a better understanding of what bait would be needed if and when they get into a survival situation.

## *The Rolling Snare*

Snares are traps that typically kill animals by yanking them from the ground, breaking their necks, and virtually hanging them. Snares are usually of two types: baited snares and unbaited snares. Baited snares are placed in the same locations as the deadfalls—in animal feeding areas. Unbaited snares, such as rolling snares, are placed on animal runs. Unbaited snares are triggered when animals traveling along their run inadvertently slip their heads through the snares and trigger the traps as the snares tighten around their necks. Since I have already dealt with baited traps, I will discuss snares of the unbaited variety here. The rolling snare is one of the easiest traps to make, especially for children. Unfortunately all snares require some sort of cordage; otherwise children will have to use a deadfall.

Assuming the children have brought their survival packs and have some cordage, a snare can be made. The best manufactured cordage for a snare is a braided nylon fishing line of at least thirty-pound test. (Make sure your children carry some in their survival packs.) The first thing children must do is select a location for the snare. The only area in

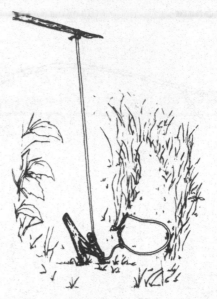

**Rolling Snare**

which a snare can be used is along an animal run, and the children must know exactly what kind of animals will use that run (see Chapter 4). Along that run too must be suitable saplings or branches that can be used for the traps. The branches, or "spring sticks," will be bent toward the trap triggers, which will hold the branches bent until the traps are triggered. It is the action of the bent branches straightening that lifts animals from the ground and breaks their necks. So the spring sticks chosen must be able to violently yank animals off the ground.

There are only two sticks that need to be cut and shaped for the rolling snare. Again, they should be handled and descented in the same way your children did the sticks of the figure 4 trap. The children should collect two sticks suitable to be made into angular hooks. The larger stick should have a long shaft on one leg of the hook, and the smaller stick should have one leg only slightly longer than the other (see illustration). These are cut from a dead sapling with very strong branches of about the same diameter as the trunk. The average size sticks needed for a snare to catch a rabbit are as follows. The small hook should have one leg 2½ inches long and the other leg 1½ inch long, both with an average diameter of ⅜ inch. The larger stick should have one leg about one foot long and the shorter leg about 2½ inches long, both with an average diameter of a half inch. All children need to do with the sticks once they are cut to size is to clean off any rough edges and cut a sharp point on the longer leg of the largest hook stick.

When the trap is being set, everything must be done in the trapping area, so great care must be taken to minimize the impact and noise on the site. Have the children push or hammer the long pointed end of the larger stick into the ground. This should be placed about a foot from the animal run. To one leg of the short stick, the children should securely tie the cordage, leaving enough length on that end to form the snare loop and leader and enough cordage on the other end to reach the tree when bent. Now have the children tie a slipknot on the short end of the string, making sure that when the loop is made there is enough cordage to reach from the hook stick to the animal run. The children should next bend down the spring stick and attach the longer end of the cordage to the tip of the spring stick (see illustration).

It is at this point, upon finishing setting up the trap, that your children are in the greatest danger of injury. The children should learn to keep their faces clear of the trigger hooks, for they could accidentally trigger off and possibly hook the children in the eyes, nostrils, or mouths. Stress this point to your children. By pulling on the small hook stick, the children should bend the sapling toward the hook stick that has been anchored in the ground, catching them together as shown in the illustration. Now the string is slipped through the slipknot, forming a noose that is a little larger than the animal's head. This noose is held open, across the animal trail, using tiny twigs, at the approximate height of the animal's head. Other twigs are placed on the animal run to funnel the animal into the suspended noose (see illustration).

All traps should be checked at least once a day—twice a day during warm weather—so the animal does not go bad. It is best to teach children to check the traps at a distance, for if the traps remain unsprung, the children will not have needlessly entered the area and possibly disturbed the animals again. The children should learn to carry their throwing stick or a club with them when checking traps. Your children should learn to approach all traps cautiously just in case a trap may only have injured an animal. It is a good practice to have children give the animals good blows to the head anyway, to make sure the animals were not just knocked out by the traps. Remember, the only time traps should be used is during an unplanned survival situation; at all other times they are illegal. Your children must never set traps for fun, because traps are nondiscriminating and will kill or hurt anything that blunders into them.

### The Pit Trap, or Mouse Bottle Trap

One of the easiest and most productive traps is the pit trap. This trap combines the elements of trapping, hunting, and a good knowledge of animal habits. However, the pit trap is very dangerous and produces

**Mouse Bottle Pit**

very small game. To teach your children to make the pit trap, first have them choose a good location for the trap. Since the trap is used for very small game, it is best located in the center of a field. Have the children dig with a sharp stick or stone a deep bottleneck hole in the center of the field. Once the hole is dug to arm's length and widened at the bottom, it must then be covered with a rock. A large flat rock is used, suspended from the ground by several smaller rocks, appearing much like a low table. The rock must be off the ground enough to allow small animals to easily pass beneath. The trap is now ready. (See illustration.)

There are two ways your children can work this trap. The first is just to leave it overnight, and the second is to force animals into the trap. The latter seems to work the best because it allows no time for the animals to dig their way out. The trap employs the principle that animals love to hide under things or to escape danger by getting under things like rocks, fallen trees, and crevasses. The children simply walk through the field making a huge circle around the trap, slowly spiraling closer and closer to the trap. The fleeing animals will instinctively seek cover under the rock and slip into the hole, where they will become trapped, unable to climb back out of the bottleneck.

There is a real danger here. Sometimes poisonous snakes are driven into the trap, and there are always animals that can deliver painful bites. Remember, every creature caught in the trap is alive and must be killed before the children stick their hands inside. This is done by poking violently into the hole with a sharp stick until the children are sure all animals are dead. I must admit there are very few children who can kill animals in this brutal way, myself included, and the children must be very hungry to go through with the process. This is one of the only traps that can be practiced, where in the end, the animals are simply let go by placing a branched stick in the hole, allowing the animals to climb out.

**Note:** All traps must be disassembled and filled in after practice.

# THE FISH SPEAR

Spearing fish for food in a survival situation seems like a very difficult hunting technique for children to use, yet on the contrary, it is quite easy, even for very young children. The only real skills required are the awareness to know where the fish are, the ability to stalk, and the making of a suitable fish spear. The fish spear will not work in deep, dark, or churning waters, for the children must see the fish and then get close to it for a shot. There are many other considerations and dangers connected to spearing fish, which will be discussed at the end of this section, and, as always, spearfishing is illegal in most states unless the children are in a real survival situation.

### Making the Spear

There are many ways to make a fish spear, but the easiest by far for children to learn is the Y stick method. The Y stick takes very little carving and is especially easy to make with primitive tools. First, have your children select a sturdy sapling, yet one they can get their hand around at the base. The sapling should be as straight as possible and much taller than your children can reach. Near the top of the sapling should be a place where the trunk splits into two equal branches. It is at this split, the Y, the children will make the gig end of the fish spear. The branches should be at least a quarter inch thick, to allow shaping and carving. Once the sapling is selected, it is then cut to size. The twin branches should be at least eight inches long, with the overall spear being a foot or more above your children's full height and reach.

   Have the children begin by cleaning the sapling of any other branches, rough edges, and sharp places. Next the children should keenly sharpen the ends of the twin branches to fine points. Just about a half inch behind the point the children should cut in a severe angular notch on both of the twin branches. Most spears should now be fire-hardened, unless the children are using an extremely hard wood. To fire-harden the spear, the children should hold the sharpened tips just above some hot coals, rotating the spear frequently, in order not to burn the tips. The points become fire-hardened when the wood turns to beige or dark brown, not black. To finish the fish spear (see illustration), the children should pull the twin branches together with a piece of cordage. Both tips will now be running parallel to each other and to the shaft.

## Using the Fish Spear

The fish spear combines the skill of stalking with the skills of hunting and awareness. Fish are usually located in shadows, on lee sides of boulders, and in deep pools. The water must be slow-moving, clear, and relatively shallow. The children should be taught to begin moving through the water, usually upstream, as they carefully look for fish. Once a fish is spotted, the children should try to get as close to the fish as possible, using the stalking method. Once they are near enough, the children must lower the end of the fish spear into the water so the sharp barbs are just above the fish. At this point the children should move the spear very slowly. Your children should look only at the barbs and not at the shaft, for the refraction of the water will make the fish look farther away than it really is. Watching the points of the spear, and not the shaft, directs the children to the exact location of the fish. Once the points are just a few inches above the fish, the children should thrust the spear into the fish and pin it to the ground. Then, using a combination of hands and barbs, they can lift the fish from the water.

### Teaching Methods and Cautions

One of the best ways to teach your children to use the fish spear is to actually make a spear and use it properly. Certainly it is illegal to fish this way, but there are plenty of other things the children can use for targets. Partially filled water balloons, pieces of waterlogged wood, and even an old sock stuffed with dried grasses and mud will do the trick. Once the children perfect hitting these stationary targets, attach strings to the targets and pull them through the water slowly. Jerk the pretend fish out of the way if the children move too fast or make mistakes. I taught my children by making a fishing spear with a blunt end. Over the end I tied on a piece of cloth stuffed with dried grasses. When practicing this method, they would use real fish and lightly bump them with the pole to show accuracy. I do not like to use this procedure very often because it disturbs the fish in their natural setting.

Never allow children to use the spearfishing method during the colder months. In late spring and early fall children should be taught to hunt from the banks and not enter the water. In the summer fishspearing should be done at the warmest part of the day, with clothing removed so the garments will remain dry. Hot days can still have very cold nights, and it is better to keep clothing dry at all times when possible. The children should not fish in fast-running water, near waterfalls, on slippery rocks, and in any water that is deeper than mid-thigh. There is no use putting children in more danger. Teach children to always be overcautious in any water, especially where they cannot see the bottom. It is a good practice to stay out of muddy areas, at least until the children check the depth with a stick.

# EDIBLE PLANTS

One of the greatest considerations in determining whether to instruct children about edible plants is to ascertain if the children are mature enough to identify edible plants. Ask yourself this question: "Would I stake my life on my ability to identify a plant species? Would I stake my children's lives?" Essentially when you teach children about wild edible plants, that is exactly what you are doing—staking your children's lives on their ability to identify those plants. Between the identification, collection, and preparation of plants, and so many poisonous look-alikes the task can become almost overwhelming at times. Above all other skills we teach children, this is the most time-consuming, and the most dangerous. I strongly urge you to take your time and make very sure your children know exactly what they are doing. Make sure you know what you are doing.

The best way to start with wild edible plants is to make it a family project. Wild edible plants are not learned overnight, but slowly, over a period of weeks, months, and sometimes years. I suggest you first build up your plant library, stocking it with books on plant identification guides. The Peterson Field Guide Series is one of the best overall field guide collections on the market. *A Field Guide to Edible Wild Plants of Eastern and Central North America* by Lee Peterson is an excellent guide to begin with. The book is well written and considers poisonous look-alikes. *Tom Brown's Field Guide to Wild Edible and Medicinal Plants* is written for the more advanced student, though it does give some good recipes, and background information.

Each time you take your children into the wild places make it a habit to identify plants—any plants, edible or not. This way your children begin to see the subtle differences in plant species, and to understand where certain plants grow, the various parts of the plants, and what they look like in different seasons. You will find that your children will enjoy identifying the various wildflowers at first, but then as their skill matures, all plants will become interesting. It is not enough to just have your children identify a plant, but have them spend some time observing it, where it is grown, how it changes with topography, and what it looks like when it is young or old. It sometimes helps to have your children try to draw the plant from memory, as this tends to set the image of the plant in the children's minds.

As the children improve at identifying plants, it is time to start teaching the wild edible varieties. Take one plant at a time, positively identify it, compare it to any look-alikes, harvest it, then take it home and prepare it along with your regular meal. The children must go through the whole process from start to finish, identifying, collecting, preparing, and eating. This way the children become familiar with the plant and its taste. Just eating a plant once is not enough; eat it every few weeks as a review. Augment the meals with teas made from various edible plants, and begin to season the family's regular menu with various wild herbal seasonings. Start off with easy plants that taste good to the children, ones that do not have poisonous look-alikes or need any complicated cooking methods.

**Note:** If you do not trust your ability to identify plants, then by all means, take one of the many courses offered through the National, State, or Local Parks Service. Many communities also have groups that meet to study all sorts of wildlife. Get involved with the group and learn all you can. You are dealing, ultimately, with your family's health and life.

In the scope of this book I will be covering just four species of wild, edible plants. (This plant section is not a field identification manual. For proper identification refer to any good plant identification guide.) Fortunately several representatives of any one of these species can be found throughout North America. These plants are relatively safe and easy for children to learn to recognize, with very few poisonous look-alikes or complicated cooking instructions. From these four your children can branch out and learn about more of the plants in their area. In most cases, however, these plants are usually enough to sustain children through most survival situations in most topographies. These plants I have come to know as the "Big Four."

**Note:** There is no way to predict whether children might have an allergic reaction to a wild edible plant or not until the children eat that plant. I recommend that the first time children eat any edible wild plant they only ingest a little. That way if there is a reaction, their system will not be saturated with the plant. Next time the children eat the plant, have them eat just a little more, then repeat the process again and again over a period of days, allowing at least thirty-six hours between eatings.

# GRASSES

Almost all leaved grasses native to North America are edible. (Check with a local field guide for proper identification.) Grasses are loaded with vitamins and minerals and are a good source of nutrition during a survival experience. The new shoots of grasses, up to six inches, can be eaten raw. When the grasses grow taller and older, they have a high concentration of cellulose, which is difficult for us to digest. I have always chewed these grasses and spit out the pulp, or I steep the grasses in hot water for a half hour and make a tea. This way I still get the nutrition, without the cellulose.

Grass seeds are also edible. They can be eaten raw, added to soups, and made into flour, by roasting and then grinding the seeds.

**Warning:** Even though almost all species of grasses in this country are edible, there are a few species of grasses whose seeds are toxic if eaten raw. I would strongly suggest you cook all seeds, just to be sure. Make sure the children eat only seeds that are green or brown, for purplish or blackish seeds could indicate the presence of a toxic fungus.

**Note:** After you teach your children about young grass shoots, make sure they can precisely identify them as grasses. Many plants in the young stage of their development can resemble grasses to children.

# PINES (PINUS)

Pines are a very important survival food for children. Any child can be taught to easily recognize pines from other evergreen plants, and pines are very widespread throughout North America. (See a good field guide for the identification of pines.) I cannot stress enough the importance of first teaching your children to positively identify the pine trees. There are several evergreens that are toxic, and your children's lives will rest on proper identification. Fortunately the identification principles are very basic and easily learned, and your children should have no trouble. I would, however, stick to those pines that are native to North America.

The pine tree is a highly edible tree and very nutritious. Pine needles can be broken or cut into tiny pieces and steeped in warm water for half an hour. The tea is very rich in vitamins A and C and is an especially healthful drink. Pine nuts, found within the mature cones, are edible raw, roasted, ground into flour and used as a soup thickener, or mixed with other natural flours and baked into breads. Pinecones are easily opened by placing them close to the fire. I have also made a delicious mush from the ground nuts. The male cones of the pine (the anthers) are usually rich with pollen in the spring and can be added to soups. The pollen and the seeds are high in plant proteins, which are so necessary to survival. Finally the inner bark and tiny rootlets of the pine are edible, best cooked in a stew or soup.

## CATTAILS (TYPHA)

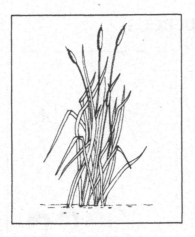

The cattail is one of the easiest plants for children to identify and one of the most delicious. Like the pine some part of the cattail is edible year-round, and it supplies us with tremendous food value. It is also very easy to collect and prepare. The cattail is found throughout North America, in damp lowlands, along waterways, and in swamps and bogs. Children should be very cautious in collecting cattails because of where they grow. In any damp area there is always the risk of getting wet, and during a survival situation children must stay as dry as possible. Another risk is that cattails may be located around areas of deep mud, which often looks deceptively safe and solid. The children could sink into the mud and become trapped. Though it is hard to confuse the cattail with any other plant, children should still be taught to know the plant well.

The cattail is literally edible from roots to top. The roots of a cattail are rich in flour. To obtain this flour usually involves quite a long process, but the easiest way for children to utilize it is to have them wash the root, cut it up, then add these cut roots directly to soups. The rinds are then removed before eating. This way the flourlike food is leached from the root and added directly to the soup. During the winter months the root is not the only edible part. Usually there are small shoots (corms) proliferating just above the surface of the ground. These can be broken off from the rootstock and eaten raw or cooked as a vegetable. In the spring the new shoots of cattail can also be eaten, cooked in stews, soups, or boiled as a vegetable. Finally in late spring the newly emerging cattail heads and pollen spikes can be eaten by cooking them like corn on the cob. The pollen can be collected and added to stews and soups.

**Note:** The cattail head is best eaten still wrapped in its papery sheath.

## ACORNS (QUERCUS)

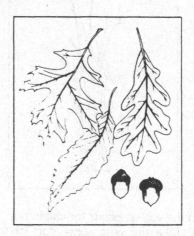

Children can easily learn to identify oak trees, but I find that very young children will mix up all hard-shelled nuts and call them acorns. It is best not to take a chance with your children's knowledge and show them exactly how to identify the acorn from all others. Oaks can be found in most areas, ranging from scrubby plants to huge trees. The inner bark of all oak is edible but slightly bitter . . . a taste your children will have to get used to. Despite the bitterness of the inner bark, it is still a rich emergency food source. The acorns of all oaks native to North America are also edible, though many are terribly bitter. Fortunately it is quite easy to remove this bitter taste by leaching the nuts. To leach out the tannic acid (the bitterness) from the nuts, first have the children shell the nuts and then crush the nut meats. The nuts should then be soaked in water for at least two hours, the water dumped, then the nuts soaked again and again. The children will know the nut is done when the nut meat has lost its bitter taste.

**Note:** Oaks from the white oak family are usually less bitter than those of the black or pin oak families.

I strongly recommend your children first know these four important survival plants before learning any others. I do not believe children really know a plant until they have collected, prepared, cooked, and eaten the plant several times. Again, the best way to accomplish this is to make it a family project, substituting wild edible plants for a dinner vegetable once a week. Make sure your children have no doubt about the identification of all new plants. Do not teach children plants that have posionous look-alikes. I might also suggest you do not teach your children plants that are difficult to prepare, rare to your area, or endangered. The following is a list of plants that can be easily learned by children after they have mastered the identification process.

Amaranth, Birch, Bulrush, Burdock, Catnip, Chicory, Chickweed, Dandelion, Greenbrier, Goldenrod, Hemlock Tree, Mint, Nettle, Plantain, Reed, Rose, Sassafras, Shepherd's Purse, Spicebush, Sumac, Sweet Fern, Thistle, Violet, Wintergreen, Wood Sorrel, and Yucca.

**Warning:** Plants should never be gathered near civilization. Do not gather plants near factories, roadways, houses, parking lots, parks, or polluted waterways. Those plants found near civilization will contain many pollutants, either in or on them. Gather plants only from wilderness areas that have not been sprayed with chemicals.

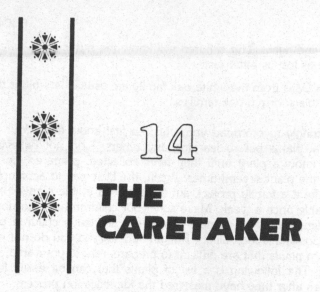

# 14

# THE CARETAKER

Teaching children to survive does more than give them an insurance policy for the wilderness. It is a vehicle to teach them so many other lessons. Whether your children ever use these survival techniques or not, they will gain a certain confidence and resourcefulness in everyday life. Through the survival lessons, children learn to think for themselves, depend on themselves, and excel, even in the most unforgiving circumstances. The children learn quickly that they have choices and are in control of their lives. This awareness of choice carries over into the children's daily lives and gives the children a sense of control. Yet there is far more in these survival lessons than just psychological dividends. We can use survival as a means of teaching more about the earth and the children's place in creation.

Through the techniques and skills of survival children can learn to live with the earth and to more fully understand its splendid complexities. Survival, like nothing else children can do in nature, brings them close to the earth in a real way. The dry concepts and philosophy of living with the earth leave the dusty confines of classroomlike teachings to become a real and vital force in children's lives. Conservation and reversing the destructive patterns and pollutants of humankind becomes a deeply rooted conviction in the children's hearts, not just a series of superficial facts and reasons. Survival can teach children to live through the heart, not just through the mind.

One of the most important lessons you can teach your children through survival training is to develop the caretaker attitude. The lessons of the caretaker are not learned overnight; children come to them slowly over a period of time as their awareness of the frailty of the earth and creation develops. At once nature seems to the children to be so strong and overpowering, but with time and knowledge, a paradox begins to develop. The children soon understand that nature is a strong survivalist against natural forces, but against humankind, nature can be very fragile. Humankind has the power to destroy or to protect nature, and children must learn that the protection of the earth is our sacred duty.

When Grandfather taught the lessons of the caretaker, they were strong and lasting, forever affecting our lives. Each skill was used effectively, not only to teach the obvious survival techniques, but to teach more valuable lessons, physical and spiritual. Thus each skill became sacred to us, for each was a philosophy in and of itself. Parents and teachers should be aware of every opportunity to use a skill or technique to teach lessons far deeper than mere physical survival. Children must learn of their impact on the earth and how each action has a reaction from the natural world, positive or negative. Thus children must learn to use survival as a tool that protects and helps nature, not a skill of destruction.

## Lessons of Shelter

When children build a shelter, they should understand what must be given up by nature to give them that shelter. When the children collect the debris from the ground, show them how this removes the protective blanket from the earth. Teach them that the unprotected soil erodes and that by removing the debris, they are also removing the food for future plants. Have them closely examine the debris they are using, noticing all the tiny insects, animals, and plants they will be disturbing or destroying in the building of the shelter. Then the children can begin to understand that dead organisms still do have life and fulfill a purpose, and that everything, dead or living, has an underlying purpose, even if it is beyond our frail human ken. Thus, when the debris hut is no longer needed, the children are then more likely to redistribute that debris hut back over the earth and return nature to its normal state.

Grandfather once taught us to respect the debris of the earth through a very simple yet profound lesson. We lay sleeping one cold and rainy night in our debris huts. Sometime during the middle of the night Grandfather removed all the debris from our huts, and we awoke with a start, wet and cold. As I watched Grandfather removing the last handful of debris from my shelter I asked him what he was doing. He smiled and said, "Taking some debris for my shelter." "That's my debris," I complained. "I need it to stay warm!" Grandfather smiled again and replied, "Is that not what the earth says when you remove debris for your shelter?" I learned the lesson well.

## Lessons of Fire

The making of fire contains far more lessons than are immediately apparent. First, it is important to teach children the potential destructiveness of fire, and how a campfire could soon turn thousands of acres, plants, and animals into a wasteland. The children should also see that the site of a campfire will scar the earth for a considerable period of time. Show the children some old campfire areas, how nothing grows from them, and how they leave a blackened scar on the earth. Teach them also that the wood for the campfire is also stolen from the earth's processes. When we burn firewood, we are burning food for so many animals and plants. Again, everything has a purpose, living or in death, and the children should be made aware that even firewood has a purpose. Obviously too fire pollutes the air with smoke and kills any plants or insects near its flames.

## Lessons of Trees

Grandfather taught us through some very profound lessons of the sacrifice plants and trees must bear when we use their flesh for survival. Grandfather once asked us to pretend we were trees: "By becoming trees," he said, "we should understand so much about the forest." Needless to say how excited we were, being faced with this grand lesson of understanding. We buried our legs in the ground, up to our knees, spread our arms, closed our eyes, and in our minds became trees. As we were holding the thought of being trees, Grandfather silently approached me, took out his knife, and began to cut my shirt-sleeve from my arm. I opened my eyes in shock, wondering what he was doing. As he picked up my arm and began to make a motion to cut my hand I pulled away, frightened, asking him what he was doing, but he didn't answer.

He grabbed my arm again and went to slice my hand, but I yelled again, pulled away, and freed myself from the ground. Still Grandfather remained silent as he began to approach Rick. Rick never gave Grandfather a chance to get near for, seeing what had happened, he pulled free of the ground before Grandfather approached. It was then Grandfather spoke, declaring, "I thought you wanted to play trees." We said we did, but that we didn't want to be cut, or not listened to. Grandfather then said, "But that is what real trees must bear. They scream, but you cannot hear them. They get cut, and they cannot run away. They must stand there and not move or speak. That is what happens each time a tree or plant is taken, and we must learn to treat them with the same respect and love we give one another. Because they do not move, because you do not hear them, does not mean they do not feel pain and sacrifice."

From that day on our understanding of trees grew tremendously. We could see how vulnerable they were, rooted in the earth, so they could not run from danger. We felt a certain kinship with the trees, as if we were their protectors. The same lessons can be used to teach your children, but I would suggest you do not use the knife as Grandfather did, for this may scare the children too much. Instead pretend you want to break off their arms, or dig them up, or even cut their hair. I even root kids in the ground, then push them over gently or try to climb on them. Once the children feel the sense of helplessness the trees feel, they will never look at trees the same way again.

Grandfather taught us so many more lessons in just the same way about our effect on the earth and creation. He asked us to think about what it would be like for a giant to steal us from our shelters and attempt to eat us or what it would be like to be hunted. Once while we were role-playing animals he chased us with a stick, pretending he was angry and wanted to beat us. We ran blindly, frightened, through the woods, until he began laughing. We were bewildered with his actions, for he never had shown us any aggression before. When we asked him what he was doing, he stopped laughing and advised, "Remember the fear you felt. That is the same fear the animals have when we hunt them."

It is so important to instruct your children to become caretakers of the land, to understand their impact on creation, and to feel what the plants, animals, and earth feel. Teach them how each thoughtless, destructive action has a far-reaching effect on the earth and how they must always think about what they are doing to the land, plants, and animals. It is important to show your children how the earth, scarred by humans, heals so slowly, and sometimes not at all. Teach them to take the responsibility of a caretaker and protector of the earth in a real way. Move your teaching from surrealistic classroom-type logic, and let nature touch your children in a real way. Use these lessons to reach children's hearts as well as their minds.

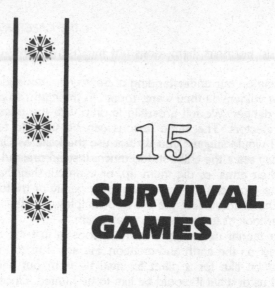

# 15

# SURVIVAL GAMES

I find the best way to teach children to become proficient in the skills of survival is through the excitement of games. Games tend to minimize the stress of learning the survival skills, making the learning fun and exciting rather than serious and frightening. Thus the skills are better remembered during a real survival ordeal. Presented here is a list of games I have used with great success. The games can be modified to fit a group or an individual child. This is in no way a complete list of all the games but simply an overview to give the teacher an idea of the possibilities. I am sure that with a little imagination you, as parents and teachers, can devise many others. Better yet, allow the children to come up with their own games, for they can be quite imaginative.

## The Survival Game

The survival game can be approached either as a discussion or as a workshop. The game teaches children to think quickly and hones their survival skills. To play the game, take the children on a hike through the woods. Tell them beforehand that at any given time you may stop and ask them to do or discuss a certain survival skill. At intervals throughout the hike have the children sit down, then ask them about a certain survival skill or have them accomplish that skill. Do not give them any hints about what skill they may have to do or explain. The object of the game is to teach children to think quickly and work efficiently. The children with the best answers to the survival question or the best and fastest accomplished skill is the winner of the game.

It is important to discuss each topic thoroughly with them, pointing out the pros and cons of each answer. Instead of immediately saying children are wrong, point out why or, better yet, have them figure out why some implement or technique would not be effective in that particular situation. Always encourage children, even if their answers are poor choices. It is better to find something positive about their answers first, then point out the mistakes. But, as always, keep the games light and fun; remove all fear with a sense of play and laughter. You can even play the clown, or a student yourself, reversing the tables and having the children do the teaching or asking the questions. It is important to somehow work the survival priorities into the game and ask the children what they should do first, second, third, and so on.

### The Fast Shelter Game

Fast shelter is a game that teaches children to react quickly while mastering the location and building of a debris hut. The object of the game is to see which child or group of children can build the best debris hut, in the best location, and in the shortest period of time. To play the game, divide the children up into groups or individually. Upon your signal the children then run from camp and build their debris huts. While they are building their huts, you should walk around observing their progress, offering helpful advice when needed. However, correct just the major mistakes and allow the minor ones to pass by. This way the children will learn later from their mistakes.

When the group or child completes a debris hut, the group or individual runs back to camp and tells you. Wait until each group finishes the shelter to end the game, noting who came in first, second, and so on. Next, once the group is back together, go out to each shelter as a group and have the children discuss the pros and cons of each shelter. Try to have them figure out what might be wrong with each shelter, rather than having you tell them. Don't be critical of the bad shelters, but rather approach the instruction with an emphasis on the positive. Find something to praise about each shelter, then casually mention its bad points. Allow the children to decide which is the best shelter, and why. It is the best shelter that is the winner, not the first shelter.

**Note:** Caution the children about rushing or getting sloppy with their gathering and building techniques. Children should pay attention while collecting so they do not injure themselves or other people. It is too easy to fall while running, or to poke the eyes with sharp sticks when collecting. Make strict rules about the game, concentrating on safety rather than speed. It is also important to ask the children to return the materials back to the earth in order to cause minimal disturbance.

### The Fast Fire Game

The fast fire game is similar to the fast shelter game, except there are a number of ways to play. The game can be played by teams or by individual children, and can employ matches or the bow-drill method of lighting the fire. To prepare for the game, have each group or child dig a fire pit and clear away a safe area around that pit. All the children should build their pits in one general location for safety reasons, and to better enable you to see all the fire locations at once. Once the fire pit has been dug, have the children hammer two stakes into the ground on either side of the fire. About two feet above the bottom of the pit have the children tie a string between the two stakes. The object of the game is to have the children quickly gather firewood, set up the tepee fire, and light it. The team or child burning through the string first wins the game.

Once the fire pits are dug, have all the children sit in front of them. As soon as they are all settled, start the game, and have the children go out over the landscape and bring back all the different types of wood and materials they will need to build the fire. They must have tinder, kindling, and firewood set up in a tepee fire before they can attempt to light it. During the building process correct any major problems or unsafe practices, but the less said the better. When the first group burns . through the string, proclaim that group the winner. There should also be a second and third place if the groups are big enough. Any group that mistakenly uses or collects living (green) woods should be disqualified.

**Caution:** Again, make sure the children are very careful when collecting and transporting the wood and materials for the fire. Make sure there is no running allowed, and make any necessary rule to keep the game safe. Do not allow the children to use knives during the game nor to build the bow drill. Running with a knife will cause serious injury. Make sure also that the fire-building area is safe, and keep some type of extinguisher or water nearby in case a fire gets out of control. Again, it is important to refill the fire pits to minimize any disturbance to the natural environment.

### The Fast Water Game

To play the fast water game, divide the children into small groups or individuals. Provide each group or child with a cup and a 4 feet × 4 feet piece of clear plastic, and have everyone sit down in one general location. At your signal, the children should go out onto the landscape, pick a good location for a solar still, and build the still. When the still is completed, have the children return to camp. Once all the children are assembled, go to each solar still as a group and discuss that still and its location. The winner of the game is the first child, or group, that gets a full cup of water from the solar still. Thus, it is not the fastest built solar still that wins here, but the fastest-working solar still. This will not only teach the children to build a good solar still but also to select the best location.

**Note:** Again, great care should be taken to insure the children do not get injured when rushing about. Each solar still must be clearly marked so no one accidentally steps into the hole, and all holes must be filled in after the game, with the landscape returned to normal.

## The Fast Trap Game

The fast trap game will teach children to quickly select the best trap location and to efficiently set that trap. Before the game begins, have all the children make the trap of their choice. Once all traps are made, have them sit down while you explain the rules. Once everyone understands the rules and the game, give the signal to start. Each child or group will go out onto the landscape, choose the trap location, and set the trap. When the children are finished, they should call out to you, and you will note who finishes first, second, and third. Once all the traps are completed, the whole group should go out and discuss each trap. Once again, it is not the first group to set the trap that wins, but the first group with the best trap.

**Note:** Never allow a set trap to be unattended, not even for a moment. Once you have inspected each of the traps, have them immediately dismantled.

## Hide-and-Seek Using Natural Shelter

Essentially this game is played much like the original game of hide-and-seek, but it stresses the use of natural shelter. You will find that the game teaches children to find natural shelter quickly as well as to choose the best shelter the area has to offer. The object of the game is to have the children run out onto the landscape and hide, not only from the parent or instructor, but from the weather. They should choose the deepest recesses of brush piles, rock outcroppings, and other natural shelters. The winner of the game is the last child found by the instructor. Usually the best hiding places are the best natural shelters.

**Note:** It is important to discuss each hiding place with the group or child after the game. The children should be able to play the game at a moment's notice as they walk through the landscape. This way the area is changed frequently, and all the natural shelters of any given area are not overused. It is also important for the parent or instructor to make boundaries for this game. You do not want the children wandering too far away from camp or their house, for they can easily get lost.

### The Blindfold Trap Game

The object of this game is to have children set up a simple deadfall trap blindfolded. The weight used for the deadfall should be very light, so if the children make a mistake, they will not get their fingers crushed. I find that Styrofoam blocks tend to work the best. Have all the children sit in one area with their trap sticks and deadfall weights directly in front of them. After the group blindfolds themselves, have them begin to set their traps, upon your signal. The winner of the game is the child who sets the first and best trap.

**Note:** You will find this game teaches children to work with their hands in the dark. Working in darkened conditions is sometimes a must in a real survival situation.

### The Rock Tool Game

The rock tool game is a fun game for children to play, and it teaches them to quickly find, make, and use rock tools. The game is simple enough and can be approached from many angles, but close supervision is necessary to eliminate injury. Have all the children go out onto the landscape and select a stick about two feet long with a one-inch diameter. Now, as they quietly sit around camp, pose a problem. Tell the children you want the stick cut (abraded) in half with a rock they either find or make. Give the command to start and have the children go out onto the landscape and select their tools. Once the tool is found, have them return to camp and begin to cut through the stick. The first child to cut the stick neatly in two pieces wins the game.

If, during the game, the children find their tool does not work, they will have to go out and find or make another. This way the children will quickly learn to select, make, and use the finest tools possible. You can then modify the game by asking the children to cut a notch, sharpen a point into the end of the stick, or even to build an entire trap. The game can be modified further by having the children manufacture their tools right in camp from a large stone. Once a tool is manufactured, they must demonstrate the tool works. Once again the fastest and best toolmaker is the winner.

**Note:** It is important to have the children work in one general area. This way the instructor can keep an eye on the children, help prevent injuries, and determine the winner.

## Survival Capture the Flag

This is a rather long and involved game, but the learning results are fantastic. The children should be gathered into two groups or teams that will be against each other. Make sure the teams are evenly divided so no team has a handicap. Upon your signal each group goes out onto the landscape and builds a survival village. The village should have shelters for each child, a fire area, and a flag located just outside the main compound yet within easy reach. Only when both villages are complete does the game begin.

The game should last at least overnight, but you should allow the children to use sleeping bags and provide water and food. The object of the game is to have the teams stalk each other and try to remove the opposing team's flag without being noticed. Thus there will be children stalking and children watching the flag. The game is continuous and goes on day or night until one team wins. If stalkers are spotted by the other team near their flag, they are sent back to camp to become flag watchers, while other children replace them. At night there must always be a guard, for no one knows when the opposing camp will send out the stalkers.

You will find that the concentration of the children is not on survival or on living in debris huts but on the game. Thus survival does not become a focal point, nor is it given too much weight. Not only do the children learn to stay in debris huts and run camp, but they also practice essential skills like fire watching, working with a group, and stalking. Allow the children to elect their own leader and to have democratic votes as to where the camp should be located, how it is built, and who will stalk or watch. Through the game the children learn survival easily. Because you have eliminated the emphasis on survival and focused the children's concentration on the game, many uncomfortable conditions are overlooked or ignored by them.

**Caution:** Safety must be stressed, especially since the children will be stalking at night. They must be aware of the landscape where they will be playing and avoid all possible dangers. Close supervision is necessary so the game does not get out of hand and turn into a free-for-all. I suggest you stay with each group while still becoming part of the landscape, and that you allow the children to make their own decisions. However, you may find that you may get caught up in the game as much as the children.

## The Throwing Stick Contest

The throwing stick contest can be set up in several ways—with child against child or group against group. The targets for the game can vary from large stationary targets to small moving targets, and everything in between. When one group plays against another group, set up the same number of sticks for each group. Have each member of the group walk to the throwing line and attempt to knock down the targets. The first group that knocks down all the targets wins the game. The same technique can be used with child against child, or you can set up a smaller target, such as a small piece of wood suspended on the end of a string from a high limb. The child who hits the target squarely wins the game. It is important to vary the targets in any game and to increase the difficulty as the children improve.

**Caution:** Make sure no more than two children throw at a time, and they are a good distance from each other. No children should retrieve their sticks until all sticks have been thrown and the game has stopped. All the children waiting to throw should stand well behind the throwers, never to the sides or too close.

**Note:** During the game you can correct any incorrect throwing methods. Stalking can also be added to the game so the children approach the throwing area silently. This way you not only build up the children's accuracy with the throwing stick but also hone their stalking skills.

### The Fish Spear Game

The fish spear game is a modification of the throwing stick game, and it teaches the children accuracy with the fish spear. Generally it is best to use just two spears—one for each group—to obviate spending a lot of time having each child make a spear. Generally the game is played in shallow, moving water. The children should be positioned in the water so they do not interfere with one another's spearing. Two targets are released simultaneously from upstream and all the children stalk to position, aim their spears, then try to spear the target. The children should only be allowed one thrust of the spear. The child, or team, that spears the most targets wins the game. I find the best targets for this game are old socks stuffed with leaves and a little mud to give them weight. You will find these targets float just beneath the surface and easily move with the current.

**Caution:** Make sure the children keep their feet away from the targets so they do not accidentally stab themselves. Also, choose an area with good footing, and as always, make sure the children carry the spears pointed down and away from them.

### The Survival Village

The survival village is not as much a game as it is an experience. Children are divided into two teams and placed in two locations on the landscape several hundred yards apart. Upon the signal, the children build the best single-person survival village they can. Some children should build the shelter, some children should build the fire, others should find the water, and others can set some fake traps or locate wild edible plants. The group that produces the first and best camp is the winner.

Again, this will teach the children to work as a team, and they will all be involved in making the camp. That way they watch one another and learn. At the end of the game each camp should be discussed for all its good and bad points. All the children should be gathered together during the discussion so each group gets to see the other's camp. The game can also be played child against child or even instructor or parent against the group. This will hone the instructors' skill and speed as well. Children love beating their instructors or parents at games, so let them win once in a while.

**Caution:** With all the activity of various skills each camp must be closely supervised. There is a greater risk of injury in this game than in any other.

# 16

# SAFETY AND FIRST AID

It is not my ambition to create a first-aid manual for children. The possibilities could easily fill a book by themselves. I urge parents and children to attend the many first-aid classes offered in most areas of the country. My concern here is with what can be done if someone is injured or sick in a survival situation and first-aid supplies are unavailable. I strongly advise that the primitive methods in this book be used only under severe survival conditions, where modern medical help is unavailable to children. What follows are a collection of some of the primitive first-aid techniques I have used for personal injury during a survival situation. All of the techniques have worked very well for me.

## SAFETY

If children learn to prevent injury through good safety practices, there will be no need for first aid. The most important point children should remember is that during a survival situation they must be more than careful, especially when alone. A simple injury during normal conditions will be of little consequence; however, that same injury in a survival situation can cost a life. Children should never take chances during a survival situation and should be cautious all the time. There is no room for daring, no matter how calculated the risk. The following are a list of common dangers, considerations, and precautions children should become aware of during general wilderness outings. Certainly there are many more, depending on the topography and special conditions.

## Loose Rocks

Children should be taught to avoid loose rocks, especially around rock slide areas. Loose rocks pose many dangers of injury and even the possibility of creating massive rock slides. Walking on loose rocks could cause children to slip and sprain an ankle, break a leg, or, with a good fall, cause full body or head injury. Rocks might also give way and cause children to tumble for considerable distances, possibly even being buried by the rocks. Injuries resulting from traveling across loose rocks are usually quite bad, and it is best to teach children to avoid all loose rock areas.

## Slopes, Hills, and Cliffs

Another area of concern is any incline, from slightly sloping hills to severe cliffs. Again, the trouble here is that children could lose their footing, slip, and fall down a hill or over a cliff. Teach children to walk along the most stable and flat areas when they have to cross these inclines. It is better to travel around them than to take a needless chance. If there is no way else around, have the children scrutinize the area carefully for the best and safest possible route. Sheer cliffs should be avoided altogether, unless they are older children with plenty of rock-climbing ability. Even then, climbing a cliff is taking a needless chance in a survival situation.

## Water and Mud

Water always poses problems, especially during the colder times of the year. A primary concern of survivalists is to stay dry, and falling into water will only make the situation more perilous. Deep and fast water also pose the possibility of drowning or being washed downstream, perhaps even of being battered by floating logs and submerged rocks along the way. Children should learn to stay clear of water, except the slow, shallow water that provides the best spearfishing opportunities. Anytime children approach water for any reason, they must be overly cautious. Waterways also pose the possibility of accidents from slipping in mud banks or on slippery rocks. It should also be a rule that under no circumstances do children walk across frozen lakes, streams, or waterways. There is no telling how thick the ice is or where a stream may enter and make the ice thinner in places.

Any muddy areas should also be approached cautiously. There is no way to tell how deep mud may be. In areas the mud may be only a few inches deep and a few feet away it may be several feet deep. Anytime children travel through mud flats or near mud holes, they are putting their lives in danger. Once children become lodged in deep mud, it is very difficult and exhausting to extricate them. When they do extract themselves from the mud, they are almost always wet, and the mud makes the drying process very slow. Frozen mud is also as treacherous as frozen water and should be avoided at all costs. I reiterate it should be a major rule that your children never walk across frozen waterways, especially in survival situations.

## Brush Piles

Brush piles give an advantage to survivalists when they are scouting out a temporary shelter, but they are dangerous. Children must be cautioned never to climb over brush piles, as support sticks could snap and the children could fall through. Falling into a brush pile could cause puncture wounds, gashes, and bruises. It might also trap the children and make escape painfully difficult or impossible. Sharp sticks could also impale children. If children are going to use a brush pile for temporary shelter, they must learn to check the pile for strength and security.

## Fallen Logs and Standing Dead Trees

Logs and limbs that have fallen and cover wooded areas can pose problems for children. Always caution your children about using fallen logs as a pathway or about crawling over or under them. Children could slip from the logs, or the logs could collapse on or under them, both causing serious injury. Fallen logs and limbs can also pose problems in travel, especially at night: children could trip over them or impale themselves on the broken branches. Children should learn to go around the larger fallen logs and step across the smaller ones, never stepping on them or crawling under. Children should always inspect and test any fallen log to be used as a possible temporary shelter.

Standing dead trees, or snags, also pose hazards, especially during storms. Children should always give standing dead trees a wide berth during windstorms, and they should never walk under their dead branches. Unless the trees are small, children should take care when pulling down branches for firewood. By pulling on lower branches, the children could shake loose higher branches or even cause the tree to fall. All snags should be treated as if they were about to fall and approached with the utmost caution.

## Trees

It is essential to instruct children not to climb trees either during a survival ordeal or when they are alone in the woods. Climbing trees puts the children at risk, and children must learn to minimize all risks during a survival situation. Edible nuts, fruits, and dead branches can be knocked out of the tree with a throwing stick; thus there is no need to climb a tree. Nothing in a tree is worth the risk of a bad fall. Even minor falls from trees can be fatal in a survival situation or when children are alone.

## Traveling in Brush

When children travel through any kind of brush, they should slow the pace and take the clearer routes. Traveling through heavy brush could cause children to trip, scratch themselves, and even damage their eyes. When children follow one another, teach them to walk several feet apart so any brush that snaps back will not hit the child behind. If the children must walk close together, it is important to teach the preceding child to hold the brush or branch, handing it to the child behind, then to continue on the walk or let the other child pass by. Branch snapback can cause serious injury to the neck, face, and eyes. Some larger branches could even knock a child down or unconscious.

## Snow

Snow always poses its own list of potential problems. Teach children to avoid all deep snow and to spot drifts from far off. Also teach them never to walk near snow-covered slopes, on snowy ravines, or on snowy riverbanks, for the snow could cave in or the children could slip and fall. Teach children to avoid snow-laden trees, ledges, or ice over-hangs, as these could easily give way and bury them. Chunks of falling ice could very seriously injure anyone. Most of all, if children fall into snow, have them brush it off immediately before it melts and soaks clothing. In snow conditions it is best to stay in the shelter and venture out only when absolutely necessary.

## Washouts, Holes, and Ditches

Washouts, holes, and ditches are all potential hazards to children. Washouts and ditches, especially in heavy erosion areas, can be well camouflaged, and the children may not see them until it is too late. The edges of washouts could easily give way and cause children to fall into them, and some can be quite deep. Remember that even a slight fall could cause a sprained ankle or deep cut, both of which are potentially deadly in a survival situation. Children should also be made aware of the dangers of mud slide areas, potential land-slides, or earth overhangs and ledges. When traveling over debris-covered landscapes, such as deep grassy fields or in leaf litter, children must be on the lookout for hidden seep holes, open dens, and pits. Large or small, these could cause serious injury to careless children.

### Poisonous Insects, Snakes, and Potentially Dangerous Animals

The two watchwords of advice I have for encounters with dangerous or poisonous animals are awareness and avoidance. Teaching children to be aware of potentially dangerous animals can be a tricky business. You certainly want to warn your children of the hazards, but you do not want to scare them out of the woods. I think that knowledge of animals tends to remove much of the fear, for most of the fear children will have is from the unknown. Teach your children the habits of all dangerous animals, where they live, what they eat, and where they might be encountered. Pertaining to dangerous animals, children should become aware of all warnings the wilderness has to offer.

As you teach your children about animals in general, also teach them how to avoid the dangerous ones. With poisonous insects and snakes, teach them to watch where they step. If they have to pass through areas that may harbor these animals, have them slow their pace and watch the trail carefully. The more they know about poisonous animals, the more they can avoid them. The same holds true for other animals. When in bear country, have your children do all their cooking far from where they will be sleeping. If they are approached by a potentially dangerous animal while eating, have them leave the food and vacate the area slowly and carefully, showing no threat to the animal. In most cases, though, aware children should rarely, if ever, be bothered by dangerous animals.

## FIRST AID

It is not my intention to create another first-aid manual for children or for the American Red Cross, as many other institutions have already done. Instead what I intend to set forth is an overview of first aid in a survival situation. I strongly suggest you use a good first-aid manual to teach your children and also employ the following suggestions to teach your children what they should do in a survival situation, where first-aid supplies, if any are available at all, are severely limited. Children should have a strong first-aid background before being taught survival alternatives. Survival first aid should only be used when all else has failed, and only in survival situations. These methods should never be used as an alternative when first-aid supplies or modern medicinal help are available.

## Survival First Aid for Children

It is important to teach children they are capable of accomplishing first aid during a survival experience. They must realize they are not helpless and even though there are no first-aid supplies available, there are still things that can be done for an injury. Practice is very important, for the more children know about first aid, the less likely they are to become upset. Staying calm in a situation requiring first aid is one of the most important things to do. In an emergency, taking action can have a calming effect on the sick or injured person and can prevent panic. Panic can lead to further injury or an even more perilous situation. Knowing the art of first aid, like knowing survival, prevents panic in an emergency situation. Panic is fed by the unknown, and by removing that unknown, you almost always remove the panic.

The value of teaching children first aid is almost limitless. First, it teaches self-help and gives children a certain confidence in their ability. This confidence is not only important for first aid, but for survival as well. Second, knowing first aid teaches children to help others and to take care of others during emergency situations. Third, knowing first aid gives children a sense of safety awareness. The most important skill in first aid is to know how to prevent illness or injury in the first place. First aid makes children consciously aware of dangerous situations and carelessness.

## General First Aid

There are several important basics to teach children about first aid before teaching them anything specific. First, get away from the situation or danger that caused the injury or illness. It is important either to remove the person from the situation or to take away the danger causing the injury.

Second, it is important to make sure the injured person is breathing comfortably.

Third, it is important to control any bleeding.

Fourth, once the person is breathing comfortably, and all bleeding is controlled, teach children to protect any wound or injuries from further damage and infection.

Fifth, children should then learn to keep the person comfortable and warm. Cover the injured person in cold weather or place the person in a debris hut. In warm weather place the person in the shade. All clothing should be loosened so the person is absolutely comfortable and there are no restrictions. Make sure the person is resting in a comfortable position and remains calm. It is important that children learn to talk to the person, keeping the person calm and reassured.

Sixth, make sure someone goes for help. If help is unavailable, keep the person quiet and comfortable until help does arrive.

## Specific First Aid

### Wounds

With wounds, it is important to stop the bleeding, protect the wound, and prevent infection. Children should learn to watch the person for shock and to treat for shock.

### First Aid for Wounds

Teach children to apply direct pressure directly to a wound. The children can use their bare hands if nothing else is available, but it is best to use a hand over a clean dressing. A clean piece of clothing or bandanna will work well in a survival situation if nothing else is available. Make sure the clothing used for a dressing is clean. It is important to teach children never to remove dressings once in place. If a dressing is removed, the bleeding may begin again. It is best to add more dressing to the wound. The children must then elevate the injured area above heart level. It is then important to keep the wound clean and the person resting. Finally the children must watch the person for shock, especially when the injury is severe. Then the children should get help.

### Prevention

1. Children should know how to use sharp objects safely and only for the intended purpose.

2. Children should never run with tools, sticks, rocks, or any breakable objects.

3. Children must learn never to take unnecessary chances in a survival situation.

## Shock

Shock may occur after an injury or near injury or as a result of an infection or illness. Some forms of shock are caused by a severe allergic reaction. Shock can even occur when someone witnesses an injury. The symptoms of shock are weakness, pale skin, and irregular and rapid breathing; additionally the person could become dizzy and pass out, and shivering may occur, even in hot weather. Shock can become very serious and life-threatening. Every person must be observed and treated for shock after an injury or accident. Remember, just being in a survival situation can lead some children into shock, then into profound shock. Sometimes it is good to view a survival situation as an injury. (Fortunately the chances of survival-related shock are diminished as children master the survival skills.)

First Aid for Shock

1.  The children must maintain the person's body temperature by wrapping the person in a blanket or by placing the person in a debris hut during cold weather. In warm weather the person should be kept cool and in the shade. Make sure the person is insulated from the ground as well as from the weather.

2.  The children should keep the person lying down, comfortably resting, calm, and elevate the feet.

3.  The children should talk to the person and reassure him or her constantly. Talking and reassurance are some of the most important survival skills children can have.

4.  The children should get help quickly, especially if a person is unconscious or not breathing.

## Animal Bites

First Aid

1.  The bite must be thoroughly washed with soap and water. If no soap is available or the children do not know how to identify a soap-bearing plant, they should rinse the area well in water.

2.  The children should cover the bitten area with a clean dressing.

3.  The children should keep the person resting and have the person avoid movement.

4.  The children should get medical help as soon as possible, then try to identify the type of animal that bit the person and remember whether the animal bite was caused by annoying or cornering the animal or if the attack was totally unprovoked. These details are important to the doctor.

5.  The person should be treated for shock.

Prevention of the bite is very simply summed up with one word: knowledge. The children should know the animals of the area, their behavior, habits, and habitats. They should develop a healthy respect for animals' space and the dangers of getting too close and violating that space. The children should be very careful when exploring various homes and hiding places.

## Snake Bite

First Aid

1. The children should immediately have the person lie down, remain calm, and remain immobile. Movement tends to pump the heart faster and thus circulate the poison.

2. Your children should next immobilize the part of the body bitten and keep the wound lower than the heart.

3. Your children then must go for medical attention. The children should note the markings on the snake to help identify the type of snake.

As in preventing animal bites, preventing snake bites comes from your children's awareness of that snake. The children should know the poisonous snakes of the area they are traveling, where snakes usually live, their habits and behavior, then avoid all those areas. Teach children never to put their hands or feet into dark places, cracks, crevices in rocks, under logs and rocks, or into holes. If they intend to use any of these areas as a possible natural shelter, the areas should be thoroughly checked with a stick before the children enter.

## Stings

Stings are usually only a life-threatening situation if an allergic reaction occurs. Then the person must be treated for shock and the children should seek immediate medical help. An allergic reaction can occur in persons who have no history of allergy. This is very true if there are multiple stings or if a person's condition is altered in some way (e.g. being hot and sweaty from strenuous exercise).

First Aid

1. The children should remove the stinger, if present, by scraping the surface of the skin or by pulling the stinger out. The sting area should never be squeezed.

2. The children should next put cold applications on the sting or soak the affected area in water. Ice will work best.

3. The children should keep the sting area lower than the heart and keep the person calm and comfortable.

4. If a bad reaction occurs or if the person has a history of allergy, the children should seek immediate medical help. It is important to always seek medical assistance for multiple stings and especially for spider and scorpion stings.

5. The children should treat for shock.

**Ticks:** It is important to have children remove all parts of a tick to prevent infection. Then they should cover the tick with heavy oil or grease and remove the tick with tweezers. Once removed, the bite area should be thoroughly scrubbed in soap and water.

The prevention of stings is the same as avoiding all potentially dangerous animals: awareness and knowledge.

## Burns

The children need to learn to relieve the pain of a burn by cooling the burnt area; next the burn area must be prevented from becoming infected.

First Aid

1. Have the children soak the burn in cool water or apply cool water directly to the burnt area. Severe and deep burns should just be covered and kept clean.

2. With severe burns the children should not break any blisters but should use first-aid ointment of any kind. Ice should not be used.

3. The burn should be patted dry once the burning has stopped, the area then covered and kept clean.

4. The person should be treated for shock, especially when the face, hands, or a large part of the body is affected, or when a deep burn occurs anywhere. Medical attention should be gotten as soon as possible.

Prevention

As always, teach fire building and its uses with the utmost caution. Teach children to be very safety-conscious around fire and with hot liquids and materials.

Teach your children that sunburn can be very dangerous in a survival situation, especially if blisters develop or if the person is sunburnt over a considerable portion of skin. The person should be cooled in cool water and treated for shock. Especially teach your children to be aware of dehydration in these situations and to allow the person to sip water slowly to replace fluids.

### Frostbite and Hypothermia

**Note:** Both are accelerated by wind and by humidity.

First Aid for Frostbite

1.  The children should immediately protect the frozen area from further exposure by covering it. Frostbitten skin will appear white to gray, pale and glossy, and will feel cold and numb.

2.  The children should immediately get the person into shelter—indoors if possible. If there is no shelter, they should get the person behind a good windbreak and use extra clothing or blankets to keep the affected area warm.

3.  The children should warm the area rapidly, using warm water, immersing the area. The frostbitten area should then be wrapped in a blanket. They should not use hot water, rub the frostbitten area, or warm the area by a fire or stove.

4.  The children then should elevate the affected area above the heart.

5.  Next fluids should be given to drink and the person treated for shock. It is best to seek medical attention as soon as possible.

First Aid for Hypothermia

1.  The person should be brought to a shelter or windbreak immediately.

2.  All clothing that is wet should be removed and any tight clothing loosened.

3.  Have the children put the person into a sleeping bag, wrapped in blankets or have extra clothing piled on. If a small shelter is available the person should be put into it immediately. Your children should get into the shelter with the person if he or she doesn't begin to warm up right away, or they should build a fire to warm the person.

4.  The person should be given warm liquids and medical help should be sought when available.

Hypothermia can be easily prevented by wearing proper protective clothing, such as wool, with rain- and windbreakers. Tight and restrictive clothing should not be worn, but rather loose layers. Layering of clothing helps to build up much-needed dead-air space. Exposure to the cold, high winds, and dampness should be limited. The children should learn to immediately recognize the early stages of hypothermia and to take immediate action to prevent its severity. Hypothermia kills. Eating well, especially in winter, is very important in keeping the body well fueled with energy.

## Heatstroke, Heat Cramps, and Heat Exhaustion

Children seem to take the heat and cold in stride when they are at play. The play seems to override any discomfort they would normally experience when not at play. With this in mind, you should instruct your children to be aware of extreme conditions, both of heat and cold. Heatstroke is a life-threatening condition caused by high temperatures, hot sun, and strenuous exercise. It involves high body temperatures where the person will not be sweating but rather has very hot, flushed, red, and dry skin. The person could become unconscious.

First Aid

1.  The children should immediately cool the person's body by providing shade, fanning, or with a cool body wash or sponge bath. The person can be submerged in cool water or cold packs can be used to lower the body temperature.

2.  The children should then treat the person for shock.

3.  The children should get help quickly, especially if the person is unconscious.

Heat Cramps

Heat cramps can be helped by seeking shade and rest, massaging the muscles, and by sipping water. The person should be watched for signs of shock. Heat cramps can be an early warning sign of heat exhaustion or heatstroke.

Heat Exhaustion

Heat exhaustion can be helped be seeking shade and rest, sipping water, lying down, fanning and cooling the body, and treating for shock if necessary. If left untreated, heat exhaustion can easily become the more life-threatening heatstroke.

### Prevention

The children should learn to take breaks from the heat and working on hot days. They should also drink plenty of water and slow down on hot days. It is a good practice to cool the body down periodically by splashing water or taking a cool swim.

## Poison Ivy, Poison Oak, and Poison Sumac

These poisonous plants cause an allergic reaction on the skin. They are itchy, red rashes, sometimes slightly blistered. Poison ivy, oak, and sumac are not contagious, nor do they spread. The skin will only break out where the plant has touched—some areas breaking out sooner than others, thus only appearing to spread. There is a danger that an infection could develop as a result of the scratching.

### First Aid

1.   The children should wash the affected area with cool water as soon as exposure is recognized.

2.   Clothing that may still be contaminated with the plant oils should be removed.

3.   The children should treat the rash with cool water or a soothing oil where available.

Prevention comes from the knowledge of what the plants look like, where they grow, and how they grow. In areas that could potentially contain these plants, the children should be cautious about where they step or what they touch. The children should learn to use protective clothing in heavy poison ivy, oak, and sumac areas, and the clothing should be carefully removed and washed after each outing.

## First-Aid Kit for Children

These items can be added directly to the children's survival pack if it is large enough. The pack should be carried with them at all times, for the children may never know when an accident will happen. Take a page from the Boy Scouts and "Be prepared."

Triangular bandages: used for holding dressings over wounds, for pressure bandages, and for immobilizing injury.

Gauze pads: sterile and absorbent, mixed sizes or large.

Roller gauze: for wrapping and holding gauze pads in place.

Thick, absorbent compresses.

Band-Aids, assorted sizes.

**Note:** The preceding first-aid skills are but a few of the many aspects children should know of first aid. Again, I recommend you first teach the children first aid from a first-aid manual, then discuss and teach the various survival alternatives.

# EPILOGUE

# YOU AND YOUR CHILD IN NATURE

This should not be the end, but the beginning. You and your children will write the pages beyond this book. Through it I hope you have drawn closer to your children, and both of you closer to the earth. However, no field guide will work unless you and your children create an adventure, an adventure you will both remember for the rest of your lives. You have a chance to give your children a gift, a gift of skills and awareness that are their birthright . . . the same birthright the blindness and hustle of modern society are trying to deny them every day. By teaching nature, tracking, survival, and awareness to your children, you are getting them back in touch with their roots and a forgotten reality. You are also leading them back to the earth, and to a life full of wonder.

Now we have created our children's summer camp program, and we hope these programs will fulfill the needs of those people and their children who want to return to the earth. I felt a need to create a summer camp program for children that differs from other typical summer camp programs and concentrates on the skills, techniques, and philosophies set forth in this book. The children's school at first will be an experimental program, which I hope will bring children closer to the earth through awareness, tracking, survival, and the Native American philosophy. I would enjoy hearing your comments, ideas, and any techniques that have worked for you and your children. Combined, our efforts could produce a program that would make children's dreams become their reality.

# INDEX

P.O. 0003671779